ABSOLUTELY POSITIVELY OVERNIGHT!

Wall Street's Darling Inside And Up Close

by Robert A. Sigafoos

St. Luke's Press
Memphis

HUB and SPOKES SYSTEM
(Federal Express Domestic Route Map)

Library of Congress Cataloging in Publication Data

Sigafoos, Robert Alan, 1923—
   Absolutely, positively overnight.

   Bibliography: p.
   1. Federal Express Corporation. 2. Express service—
United States. I. Title.
HE5903.F435S53 1983   380.5'24'06073   83-9482
ISBN 0-918518-27-X

FIRST PRINTING — OCTOBER 1983
SECOND PRINTING — OCTOBER 1983
THIRD PRINTING — NOVEMBER 1983

Acknowledgements

Many people gave freely of their time to make this book possible. To the following Federal Express employees, listed in alphabetical order, I wish to express my deep appreciation: Heinz J. Adam, Nancy L. Altenburg, David C. Anderson, James E. Bailey, James L. Barksdale, Harry G. Barrett, Terry S. Barron, Craig Bell, Philip G. Beckman, Wanda C. Benderman, Tina M. Boaz, Ralph Boen, Dennis N. Brandstetter, Kim Burien, James K. Burton, Bill Carroll, Bob Chaffee, David O. Chung, James E. Coleman, Daniel N. Copp, Alyce B. Craddock, Lisa T. Daniel, Brandon Davis, John A. Donald, Anne S. Duty, June Y. Fitzgerald, Dee Foster, Tim Fassinelli, and Sharon Frazier.

And also: Carolyn Gause, Charles C. Hartness, Vicki G. Hawkins, Robert D. Henning, Byron H. Hogue, Carol Jeselski, Dennis H. Jones, Dianne M. Julius, Edmund S. Kukulski, Connie L. Lampen, Barbara J. Lutz, Dennis M. Lynch, Patricia A. Lynch, Frank Maguire, Fred A. Manske, Jr., Thomas R. Martin, Kenneth R. Masterson, Robert P. May, Allen McArtor, Thomas C. McGarry, Karl S. McGarvey, Alan D. Miles and Gene Moore.

And also: Nancy T. Neil, Thomas R. Oliver, Jerry N. O'Roark, Brian E. Pecon, Robert C. Perez, James A. Perkins, Ronny J. Ponder, Danny W. Rhea, James R. Riedmeyer, Judith A. Rogala, Theodore E. Sartoian, Robert E. Schnaible, Armand Schneider, Clive A. Seal, Bhrugu Shah, Nancy H. Sheldon, Larry A. Shields, Frederick W. Smith, Karen J. Smith, Walter Soltan, William F. Speidel, Mary V. Stetler, Peggy St. John, Eric A. Vartanian, Theodore Weise, Carl Williams, Catherine A. Winterburn and Charles M. Woodward.

May I also thank the following persons, including several former Federal Express executives, who generously gave of their time: Carl Ally, William T. Arthur, Michael D. Basch, Arthur C. Bass, Charles H. Bishop, Jr., Joe Brady, Charles W. Brandon III, Nathaniel P. Breed, Jr., Gary Burhop, Leslie S. Burkett, Janet L. Clay, David Cotton, the late J. Vincent Fagan, David G. Feinberg, Michael J. Fitzgerald, Frances French, Roger J. Frock, Amil Gargano, Bob Gavin, Philip Greer, David M. Guthrie, Pallie Hamilton, William J. Hewitt, Sally W. Hook, Rose E. Jackson, Dr. James Johnson, William Lackey, Charles L. Lea, Jr., Leigh MacQueen, Douglas Marsh, David Mays, Henry W. Meers, the Honorable Wilbur O. Mills, J. Tucker Morse, Lewis Nolan, Reba A. Orman, Mary A. Pepin, Allison Pitcock, Carol Ann Seitz, Paula J. Shaw, Barbara Shultz, Richard H. Stowe, S. Tucker Taylor, Irby V. Tedder, Frank L. Watson, Jr., Ed Weathers, and John L. Zorack.

For special counsel and assistance I owe thanks to my colleagues at Memphis State University including: Deborah W. Brackstone, Kenneth J. Burns, James R. Cloud, Kent E. Curran, Arthur L. Grider, J. Bernard Keys, Sharon B. Mader, Thomas R. Miller, Janell Rudolph, Jennifer C. Tift, Larry A. Williams, Saundra W. Williams and Thomas A. Wofford.

I am grateful for the assistance provided by the staffs of the Reference and Government Documents departments of the Memphis State University Library, and by the staff of the Memphis and Shelby County Public Library and Information Center. Both libraries are blessed with talented professionals willing to take that extra step to help. I also acknowledge the assistance of the library staff at the Civil Aeronautics Board, Washington, D.C.

And I would be remiss if I did not acknowledge the guidance, and skillful editing craftmanship of Roger R. Easson, Managing Editor of St. Luke's Press. Thank you for your wise counsel.   —*Robert A. Sigafoos*

Contents

Chapter 1

Chicago to Buffalo Via Memphis

Customer Service Agent: "Hello . . . Federal Express . . . Don Bland . . . May I help you?"

Customer: "Yes . . . This is Real Estate Research Corporation . . . 72 West Adams . . . Chicago . . . We need a pickup."

Agent: "Do you have an account number?"

Customer: "Yes, 3Z6039803."

Agent: "How many packages do you have today?"

Customer: "We have eight: four Courier-Paks, two Priority 1 packages, and two Overnight Letters."

Agent: "How much do the Priority 1 packages weigh?"

Customer: "About fifteen pounds each."

Agent: "Where will the packages be picked up?"

Customer: "On the fourteenth floor until 5:00 p.m. After 5:00 p.m. we'll leave them with the security guard."

Agent: "Will that be all today?"

Customer: "How late could we get a pickup today if there are additional packages?"

Agent: "8:00 p.m. will be the cut off point."

Customer: "Thank you."

Agent: "Your reference number on the eight packages is CGX55 . . . Thank you . . . Goodbye."

Young Don Bland is sitting at one of the 148 agent positions which are arranged in a series of what the company calls "pods." Each pod, or carousel, has six positions. Looking the length and breadth of this huge room in the Customer Service Center at the company's new corporate park near Memphis International Airport, it looks as if a colorful patch of electronic mushrooms has sprung up in the midst of chrome and carpet. In front of him is a CRT terminal. When a customer phones in an order, he keyboards new information or summons from the company's records information pertaining to a particular customer's account. He is also answering queries from customers or consignees about the location of packages and letters sent the previous day. "I'm sure your package is in the hands of one of our couriers. You'll have it by 10:30 a.m." he tells a caller. Diplomatically, he soothes another: "No, we don't have service to Jasper, Alabama, yet. You can take the package to our Birmingham station."

As I stood there listening to Don interview the customers in the green light of his CRT screen, I felt the same excitement that had made my 20-year career as an economic and management consultant so interesting. Over the years I've found it important to spend several days "in the plant" observing and talking with workers and supervisors. It allows me to take the pulse, so to speak, of the patient. When I left the consulting ranks in 1973 after 20 years to accept a professorship at Memphis State University, I was glad to leave the frenetic Los Angeles crowd scenes. Frankly, I did not think I would miss the 16-hour days, the constant travel, or the feast or famine nature of that highly competitive business. But here in the Federal Express Memphis complex, I could feel once more all those old longings for the high energy zones of American business. My task: to follow one package through the Federal Express system, and to examine this process first hand.

As I watched young Bland working with the CRT terminal, I realized he was hooked into a vast Federal Express data bank which provides information to customers within seconds of their calls. He is only one of 148 employees called Customer Service Agents answering the phones at 10:00 a.m. in Memphis. Their counterparts are answering the phones and performing the same functions at similar communication centers in Somerset, New Jersey and Sacramento, California.

As Bland finishes his work on the Real Estate Research Corporation account, the pickup request is retransmitted within seconds to the Dispatcher's Office at Federal Express' downtown Chicago Station at 1415 South Wabash Street. The station dispatcher assigns pickup responsibility to a courier, whom I shall call Steve Kabye, and the 72 West Adams Street address is placed on Steve's route for the day. All of the hundreds of pickup requests which have come into the dispatcher's office will form the route plans for the couriers that afternoon during my visit.

Back in April, 1980, when I asked Fred Smith for permission to undertake a study of his company, I was curious to learn more about this man and how he had built this company practically overnight despite what I had heard were formidable obstacles. It was a venture capital success story to rival anything of recent decades in America. Of course, Smith took my request under advisement. The question he asked his senior officers was simply, did they want me poking around the company? Would it serve Federal's interest in any way? After several weeks Smith consented, and asked everyone in the company to cooperate with me. I was to be given access to corporate files, permission to interview any employee, and free run of the facilities. It was an unusual decision and I knew I was being handed an unusual opportunity rarely offered an independent examiner. As I would learn later, Smith was running true to form. The ever-confident Smith felt a fully independent appraisal — without any company controls — would demonstrate what they all knew, that Federal Express was an extraordinary company with a promising future growth potential.

So here I was, a 59-year-old college professor waiting one late October afternoon in an old garage in Chicago to begin the examination of Fred Smith's confident hypothesis about what I should find. At 1:15 p.m. the nondescript office-garage structure just six blocks east of the Loop District where I now stood was beginning to fill with couriers. In this decaying commercial warehouse area, the only retail business nearby is a neighborhood bar and grill. The open parking lot connected to the station is bordered by a chain link fence and barbed wire as if Federal Express were under seige in this grim fringe area of Chicago. Unlike most Federal Express facilities, this one serves no public relations purpose. It is strictly a functional, operating structure.

At first glance this seems to be a miniature United Nations, such is the ethnic diversity of the couriers. There are Bohemians, Chinese, Irish, Italians, Japanese, Lithuanians, Poles, Puerto Ricans, and Scandinavians. In their navy blue pants and pinstriped white shirts bearing the distinctive purple and orange epaulets, they merge into a cohesive, uniformed unit. This uniform, says Federal Express, is to give the couriers the look of "pilots on the ground." The stripes on the epaulets indicate the individual courier's length of service.

They check their trucks, then enter the Dispatcher's Office to check their early afternoon assignments. As the couriers get ready to cover their routes in downtown Chicago, there is lots of friendly banter: "Hey, Mario, do you think your Bears will ever win another game?" asks a young black courier. Mario returns in kind: "Well, what about your lousy Cubs? They haven't ever won anything. They're even afraid to come out at night." The verbal jousting ultimately is lost in the rising mutter of delivery truck engines preparing for an afternoon's work. The couriers know they must be driving out of the garage area at 1:30 p.m. to begin collections.

Couriers assigned to the three other Federal Express stations in the Chicago area are also preparing to fan out over a broad suburban area to pick up packages. Within minutes the bright purple, orange and white vans will be joining the vans of Emery, Airborne, Burlington Northern Air Freight, Purolator Courier, United Parcel Service, and the Post Office in the competition for packages and express mail envelopes in Chicago. These 42 Federal Express vans based at the South Wabash station represent only one percent of the fleet of over 4,000 such vans in service each day throughout the United States and Canada.

This particular afternoon at the Wabash Avenue station, Carol Jeselski is the supervisor responsible for courier operations. She is efficient and tough as she provides the backup administrative support at the station, and the couriers respect her leadership. When Carol asks Steve Kabye if he would take a special visitor with him on his route, he readily accepts. He seems to sense this is a vote of confidence in his work.

I was anxious to get started, anxious to observe first hand Federal's pickup and delivery operation in Chicago and, let's face it, it felt good to be in the field gathering material again.

A quick look at my guide tells me Steve loves this hard, competitive work. He is the smallest courier, probably weighs 140 pounds, a leather-tough facsimile of Carmine Basilio, the old time boxer. Although he is about 50 — at least 25 years older than most of the couriers — he keeps the pace with the others, day after day, knowing that any slowdown would probably mean replacement.

Today he has one of 42 routes in the downtown Chicago Network; this one shifts in and around the south side of the Chicago Loop. Steve's route this afternoon will cover part of a grim warehouse and manufacturing district, and a small part of the high-rise office district between LaSalle Street and Michigan Avenue. At 1:30 p.m. Steve turns us north out of the parking lot on to South Wabash and heads for his first stop, a turn-of-the-century building on Federal Street where a wholesale sheet music firm has a fourth floor office. After a halting ride on an aged freight elevator, Steve and I are met by a thick-hipped teenager whose equally thick manners fail to respond to Steve's cheerful greeting. While the boy goes to get the package, Steve delivers a conspiratorial whisper, "We don't pay any attention to jerks like that." Then Steve picks up the package and we brave the freight elevator to return to the street. Meanwhile, his truck is blocking the entrance to the building's loading ramp. Steve exchanges a few "Chicago street courtesies" with the irate truck driver we have been delaying. The ritual expletives enjoined, the matter ends quickly, and neither seems very perturbed. Obviously, Steve has met this situation often.

His next stop is the Printing House District, a picturesque collection of nineteenth-century loft buildings still occupied by printing firms. On the first level of several shops in the District, Steve moves quickly through the back door of an old loft building, runs up one flight of stairs, and gets in the freight elevator to go up to the third floor. The trip is fruitless, however. After Steve's long walk to the back of the building, the manager tells him that the company is not shipping anything today. Over the racket of the presses Steve hollers: "O.K., I'll be back tomorrow." He is unflustered because they are good customers, he tells me later.

Back in the truck Steve gets a message on the screen of his truck's CRT terminal to pick up a package on Michigan Avenue. As we turn the corner of Harrison and Clark streets in his van, he sees a half-dozen men hanging around on the corner. All are dressed in colorful, bizarre garb, including some outlandish hats perched like cormorants on their Afros. "Look at those 'hopheads' over there! They wouldn't know a job if they fell over it," Steve comments disgustedly. And as he drives on toward Michigan Avenue he continues a running monologue on hopheads and then, discovering a relevant theme, begins to editorialize on how lazy Emery Air Freight's drivers are. "You know," says Steve, "those Emery guys are Teamsters. I once held a card in the Teamsters, but I feel I'm much better off with Federal Express even though they pay us a dollar or so an hour less than those union guys. I don't like the unions." He does not expand his lecture to identify the source of his hostility with the unions. But he seems to be expressing his honest feelings, apparently unaware that he is supposed to represent Federal Express' public relations staff today in handling my questions. He is too preoccupied with the full-time job of running his route efficiently to be merely pushing Federal's public relations line.

The Michigan Avenue office building where Steve stops next is a gem of 1920's Art Deco architecture. Fortunately, Steve finds a parking space in front of the entrance. This time he is not double-parked or blocking an alley or ramp entrance. As we walk briskly over the marble tiles of the cathedral-like lobby, a security guard gives Steve a condescending stare, but fortunately we are not told to use the freight elevator. "If I carry in an armload of packages or use a hand truck, they'll make me use the freight elevator," Steve advises me as though I were his understudy. "We work hard to get on friendly terms with building security people, doormen, elevator starters, and secretaries. Otherwise, we waste a great deal of time taking the freight elevator. These people can make you or break you."

On the sixteenth floor Steve finds the office listed on his ticket and pushes a doorbell. Moments later, someone peers through a small window in the door and says suspiciously: "What do you want?"

"Federal Express, lady. We got a call to pick up a package," Steve replies politely.

"All right, mister, come on in, but I don't know if the package is ready yet. I don't know anything about filling out these forms," she says nervously to Steve. He winces visably, but he is extremely courteous to this elderly lady as he undertakes to fill out the Federal airbill forms for her. Finally, he hands her the customer's copy, thanks her, and leaves quickly package in hand. "We lost 15 minutes in there, but we'll make it up. We've got to get moving before the 4:30 p.m. start of the rush hour in the downtown Loop area." His tone is urgent now, but confident.

Steve takes us onto Adams Street. After a few seconds he realizes he made a mistake choosing this street. Traffic is blocked. Angry drivers are leaning on their horns, venting their frustrations at a Mayflower moving van which has become stuck backing out of an alley onto Adams. Steve is surprisingly patient, but he keeps a close eye on his watch. As the traffic clears, he proceeds to the Federal Express Customer Convenience Center at 2 North LaSalle. When he double-parks there, five minutes later he worries out loud: "I may not get a traffic ticket here if I'm lucky. That's a big problem for us drivers. Some of the guys in the company tell me the cops are really rough in New York . . . something like $50,000 a year in traffic fines for Federal Express."

The LaSalle Street Convenience Center is within short walking distance of the Chicago Board of Trade. Customers from several of the major banks and many of the high-rise office buildings can drop off their packages and envelopes as late as 9:00 p.m. and still get Federal Express' promise of delivery by 10:30 a.m. the next day. Like the company's other drop-off locations, this one has the flashy, contemporary look with its Federal Express scheme of purple, orange and white. A passerby has no problem recognizing the company.

One of the countergirls waves at Steve, and he gives her a perfunctory nod. "Look, I'll take what you've got here now, and I'll be back later. I'm late," he tells the clerk. He is in the Center no more than two minutes.

As we run back to his van, I realize how out-of-shape I am, and I marvel at what energy Steve must have to keep up this pace. It is 4:20 p.m. now, and downtown Chicago's traffic is classic chrome to chrome. Thousands of office workers will soon be on the streets, adding to the confusion. Steve knows the next hour will be the daily test of his nerves. As he drives into the congestion near Adams and Wells streets, he shrugs and says, "Thank God it isn't snowing or raining. You oughta see this place in the winter." It could be much worse. At least today he will be back at the company station on South Wabash just after 5:30 p.m. in time to begin the early sort of the packages picked up.

Steve will eat after he sorts the packages, and then get ready to go out on the street again. He will go back to many of the same buildings we visited earlier. This time, however, the packages and envelopes will have either been left with security guards or placed in the company drop boxes located in the lobbies of most of the major downtown Chicago office buildings. Before he finishes, Steve will stop to pick up the remaining packages and letters at the Convenience Center.

It is almost 9:30 p.m. when we drive down South Wabash at a speed exceeding the posted limit. Steve knows the final sort is well underway, and there is not much time to get his packages out of the van and on the conveyer belt.

The principal sort had actually gotten underway at 8:30 p.m. At least 50 couriers, cargo handlers, and supervisors are busy unloading trucks adjacent to the conveyer belt or up on the catwalk along the conveyer belt preparing the packages for hand placement into the cargo containers. Others are preparing plastic bags to hold the Courier-Pak envelopes and the Overnight Letters. Very few of the packages are heavy, most are under ten pounds.

Nearby a part time worker, Lloyd, who is a Chicago public school teacher by day and now wears the regulation white shirt and tie of that profession, is also working a furious pace. He is the designated "Restricted Articles Specialist" in charge of the handling of hazardous items. He has been working like a machine since 7:30 p.m., handling special containers and boxes labeled "Toxic Chemicals," "Hazardous Materials," and "Flammable." The principal items requiring his special attention are radioactive shipments, poisons, acids, and anesthetic substances. He treats these items with respect, taking great pains to check the required paperwork as he goes. Despite his white collar worker appearance, he has an easy rapport with the others.

There are now just 45 minutes to go before the 10:15 p.m. deadline when the large cargo van, called a Cargo Transport Vehicle (CTV), must leave for its rendezvous with the Memphis-bound DC-10 at O'Hare Airport. All of the supervisors are pitching in to help. "Let's go!" one of them pleads. "That CTV has got to be out that door on time! Don't screw around! Those packages have got to be in Memphis, or it's going to be our ass!" Someone else bellows, "Hey, don't stop that conveyer belt!" And another yells, "Hey, Chris, move your truck! Steve's got to get his van in here to unload."

Kika and Josephine, two attractive high school girls wearing the required tight T-shirts and jeans of their species, hired as part-timers to help the sorting of the Courier-Pak and Overnight Letter Envelopes, are part of a half-dozen teams scanning the bar codes on the affixed copies of the airbills. The scanning device is a miniature handheld computer which looks like a thick fountain pen. The information recorded by the wand-scanners will help track these envelopes during their movement from the sender to their destination. The Priority 1 packages which can weigh up to 70 pounds are also scanned at the station before being sent on to Memphis. One efficient person can scan over 800 packages per hour with this equipment.

The cold October evening air has permeated the garage sorting area, yet no one seems to notice it. Most are sweating liberally. One young handler named Hector is soaking wet. Despite being grossly overweight, he is moving at a faster pace than most. Searching for additional packages, he runs and puffs along the conveyer belt network. Sideliners in the garage are betting Hector will collapse before 10:15 p.m. The competitive spirit has infected this 18-year-old just as it has everyone else in the garage.

Although Carol Jeselski has been here almost 10 hours, she still manages to retain her composure in this confusion. She keeps her eyes sternly on the progress of the final sort and on the clock.

David Chung, another supervisor, is leading by example. He pitches in wherever there appears to be a lag. One courier comments "David is gung ho Federal Express." When asked how he likes Federal Express, Chung replies, "Look, I joined Federal Express in Los Angeles and I liked it there. They transferred me to Chicago, and this is even better. This company is on the move."

At 10:05 p.m. there is a final charge to meet the deadline. The CTV has been backed into the garage, and several of the huge heavy aluminum cargo containers are immediately rolled into the large van. At 10:10 p.m. the final containers are sealed. Then, with an enormous burst of energy, two cargo leaders push the containers across the ball bearings of the platform into the van. At precisely 10:15 p.m. the huge van moves out of the garage onto South Wabash Avenue heading for the Kennedy Expressway and O'Hare, some 28 miles away.

Most of the couriers and handlers depart at 10:15 p.m. Carol Jeselski has also gone home at last. A few stay around. The last person will check out at 1:15 a.m., and for the next five hours the dispatcher's station will be quiet.

The CTV arrives at O'Hare to meet the DC-10 at 11:20 p.m. and the CTVs from the other Chicago stations and from Milwaukee and South Bend arrive at about the same time. The cargo containers are consolidated onto this one DC-10 for the flight to Memphis. Although the DC-10 has a net payload of 105,000 pounds of cargo, it will carry only 78,000 pounds this night.

I am introduced to the crew, Captain Jim Burton, and First Officer Don Wilson, both ten-year veterans with Federal Express, and four-year veteran Charles Tewksbury, Second Officer. At 11:40 p.m. we take off from O'Hare. As the DC-10 reaches an altitude of 39,000 feet in the clear October evening, they know we will be in Memphis on time to get their packages into the sort. The flight is uneventful, and the plane touches down at the Memphis International Airport at 12:38 a.m.

As Captain Burton taxis into what is called the "Courtyard" area near the Hub building, he notes that the DC-10s have already arrived from Boston, Newark, and Los Angeles. And most of the Boeing 727s and the tiny Falcons are on the ground. Some 52 planes have suddenly arrived in Memphis between midnight and 1:00 a.m. In a time span of just over two hours they will be unloaded and refueled —

and checked mechanically if there are reported problems — and reloaded. By 3:00 a.m. almost all planes will be ready to make the return flight to some ninety-three airports located throughout the United States and Canada. The Chicago-bound DC-10 is scheduled to leave at 3:44 a.m.

About half of the 727s, which the company calls the backbone of its fleet, are at nosedocks at the principal unloading and reloading area of the facility dubbed the "Super Hub." The other 727s are in the Courtyard area being loaded or unloaded because the fleet of 727s has already outgrown the number of available Hub nosedocks. The Hub, a large L-shaped structure, has some 500,000 square feet of area under its roof. The elongated portion of the hub where the 727s are lined up is 1,200 feet in length. Inside this huge complex are 17½ miles of automated, high-speed conveyer belts.

One observer has described this scene of the 727s with their nose ends nuzzling against the Hub as resembling the nightly lineup of dairy cows in a milk barn. But no cows, however decorated or dressed up, would be as colorful as this fleet of purple, orange, and white planes sparkling under the bright lights of the Courtyard area in the early hours of the morning. They have the look of power, the smell of success, the aura of money. Lots of it.

Two of the large DC-10s are nosedocked at the far west end of the Hub away from the 727s. The other two DC-10s, including the one which came from Chicago, are parked on the ramp area about 100 yards beyond the western end of the Hub. So far the company has not built nosedock accommodations to serve these particular planes. These DC-10s are being unloaded and reloaded using huge mechanical lift equipment to expedite the handling of the 22 containers in the upper compartment and the nine smaller containers in the lower compartment of each plane.

The tiny Falcons, with their limited payload of only 6,500 pounds each, are parked in a separate Courtyard area. They are being unloaded and reloaded by hand. Until 1978, all packages were handled this way. Hand processing now seems an anachronism with the advent of state-of-the-art advanced mechanical handling equipment at the Hub. The Falcon fleet has been reduced from 32 to just 10 and further reductions are planned until this aircraft is phased out of operations.

Numerous tugs, forklifts, and fuel trucks are moving in and around the planes. A supervisor comments, "The people operating these ground vehicles have to know what they are doing. Geez . . . if a forklift runs into a DC-10 on the ramp, some 10,000 to 11,000 packages get stranded. We give these people special training, and they know if they hit a plane they 'take-a-walk.' "

Security guards keep a close eye on the activity. Persons without a Federal Express I.D. badge, or visitors without their special lapel badges, are stopped and questioned. Tight security is necessary to prevent theft. Tonight some 189,000 packages and envelopes are going through the sort and Federal Express does not want to lose a single one of them to thieves.

The cargo containers from the DC-10s and the 727s are quickly unloaded. For those planes which are nosedocked, it takes about one minute per container to roll it out of the plane and onto the platform adjacent to the elaborate conveyer belt network. A supervisor standing near a 727 yells: "Let's get these containers emptied onto the belt. We're holding up the sort flow!" Several handlers, most wearing Memphis State University sweatshirts, are working furiously, tossing packages onto the fast-moving belt. They take no offense to the pep talk. It is just the kind of normal admonition they expect.

Most of the 800 part-time handlers, keyers, and sorters inside the Hub are young college students who report in around midnight and work an average of just over three hours Monday through Friday. Their starting pay is $6.91 per hour. Experienced workers get $9.00 an hour. They are guaranteed 17½ hours of work a week. Not only is there an equal mixture of young men and women in the crew, but also there is an equal number of blacks and whites. Very few of them expect permanent jobs with Federal Express when they finish college. To most, this part-time work will simply help them out financially until they can finish school. A big fringe benefit is the privilege of filling their cars at reduced prices from the company-operated gasoline pumps near the Hub's entrance.

Thousands of packages move rapidly on the conveyer belt into the main sort area which is designed for a volume of up to 205,000 items per night. More spaces can be added to the modularly designed Hub facility to increase the ultimate handling capacity to 300,000 items.

The key to the sorting system is the U. S. Postal Service ZIP code identification on each package or envelope. This eliminates hand sorting. The ZIP code on each item is keypunched into small computer terminals as the items move along the belts. This causes each of the items to be routed automatically to the specific area of the Hub where it can be reloaded into the correct cargo container.

The sort has gone well tonight. No planes have been delayed by weather or by the failure of any of the city stations in the Federal Express system to get their packages and letters to the planes on time. And there have been no mechanical failures. During the winter months there is always the threat that a major snow or ice storm will cause a delay somewhere in the system. Memphis is particularly blessed with good year-round weather conditions at its airport. Rarely has the Memphis International Airport been closed down, even temporarily because of fog or snow.

"The Hub has got to work 100 percent of the time, all of the time," Federal Express spokesman Armand Schneider tells me. "We have developed backup, contingency systems to adjust to problems like bad weather and late arrivals. We even have an earthquake contingency plan, too. If our computer system got knocked out even for a short time, we'd be in real trouble. We were really prepared back in 1981 when the air controllers went on strike. This is the only Hub we have, and it is the key to the success of our unique hub-and-spoke distribution system."

Somewhere in the pile of 189,000 packages are the eight items sent out just hours earlier by Real Estate Research Corporation in Chicago. Three of the items are going to the Philadelphia area; two to Buffalo; and one each to Providence, Houston, and Los Angeles. All of the items have come through the Hub in Memphis. "The shipper doesn't care where his package is at 2:30 a.m.," explains Schneider. "All he cares about is that his package gets delivered by 10:30 a.m. today."

One hour before the DC-10 flight to Chicago is scheduled to take off, Captain Ralph Boen, First Officer David Wayham and Second Officer John Hutchinson are checking on weather in the Flight Control Center and preparing their flight plan. Out on the ramp the plane is being reloaded and checked in preparation for the 3:44 a.m. departure.

The first plane takes off at 2:50 a.m., and the next at 2:51 a.m. In the next hour one plane a minute will take off. It's reminiscent of a massive strike force of fighter bombers and B-52 stratofortresses taking off from Da Nang Air Base to hit targets around Hanoi and Haiphong at the peak of the Vietnam War.

Most of the other planes have already left. All evening long personnel in the control room have been coordinating flight and trucking operations, making any adjustments dictated by weather or special mechanical problems on any of the aircraft which need correction.

By 3:00 a.m. the part-time Hub workers have gone home. One observer says, "It's like a miracle the way it comes together. At midnight there's nothing much going on. Then for about two and one-half hours the Hub pulsates with action, with life. And then long before the sun comes up, it's over. The last plane has flown away. Everybody goes home. Calm comes with the early morning. You wonder if it all really happened." But this is a repeatable miracle, a performance which reoccurs five nights each week.

Captain Boen lifts off on time. At 5:15 a.m. the DC-10 taxis to a stop at O'Hare where it had left just 5 hours and 35 minutes earlier. The cargo van destined for the downtown Chicago station is waiting nearby. The van is loaded with the packages and letters sorted in Memphis for downtown Chicago consignees. The CTV pulls in at the South Wabash Station at 6:20 a.m. The morning courier crew arrives minutes later, and the packages are sorted by individual delivery routes at 6:45 a.m.

Courier Phil Beckman, a veteran Federal Express employee, still in his twenties, is one of those quickly loading his truck. He has about one hour and 35 minutes to get his packages lined up so he can coordinate his route plan. Another courier yells at Beckman: "Hey, Phil . . . with that visitor with you this morning, are you going for Vic Babel's record today? That'll really impress the professor from Memphis. He'll tell Fred Smith about you." Phil nods calmly and says: "We'll see."

Vic Babel's name is on the wall, indicating he holds the station record to date for the most stops and on-time deliveries. Petro, a thick shouldered courier cuts in: "Babel was lucky. All the stops were close and there wasn't much traffic."

"Babel won it fair and square. You guys are all goof-offs," the other replied.

On the same wall is the vehicle accident record to remind the couriers to be careful. "If you have an accident and it's your fault, a report goes into your file," Phil tells me. "Some of us make around $30,000 a year with overtime, and you sure don't want to be sacked because of careless accidents."

Promptly at 8:20 a.m. Beckman and I pull out of the garage to start his deliveries. The first stop is under the elevated transit structure on Wabash. Phil pulls out a package, locks the van, and runs into a street level office. He makes a few more stops as he works his way toward the Palmer House Hotel. After a stop near the hotel, he drives to 231 South LaSalle Street to get his van as close as possible to the Continental Illinois Bank because he has a big load of Courier Pak envelopes and Overnight Letters for the bank. The Courier Paks are 12 inch by 15½ inch envelopes with an enclosed maximum permissible weight of up to 2 pounds per item. The Overnight Letter product is a 6⅜ inch by 11 inch envelope with a maximum permissible weight of 2 ounces.

As we hurry, Phil talks, "The Continental Illinois Bank is a big shipper and receiver of Federal Express packages. I sure try to take very good care of them. Here I gotta use the freight elevator down that alley over there. If I had only a few packages, I could go through the lobby but with this hand cart there's no way they're going to let us go on the passenger elevator."

This time it is a challenge for us to get into the building. We reach Continental's freight elevator by first descending a crude sidewalk-to-basement lift, obviously a relic of an earlier building, then negotiate several turns in a cavernous and dirty basement filled with trash cans and scattered debris, to reach one of the internal freight elevators. It takes nearly ten minutes to reach the bank's upper floor mail room. While we're waiting for the elevator, Phil does some paperwork. Once we reach our destination several security guards say hello. Phil is a regular here each business day, and he has good rapport with the bank personnel.

The bank stop consumes about 30 minutes. Phil carefully checks his deliveries and completes his documentation work on all of the

Courier Paks and Overnight Letters he has brought into the building.

Once out of the bank, Phil does not have to move his truck to make the next several deliveries. He is fortunate today to have found a good parking spot along the curb. "This doesn't happen too often," he observes. "It must be my lucky day."

Phil explains, "Downtown Chicago is a vertical market. The bulk of my deliveries are in high-rise office buildings or in factory lofts where movement is up and down by elevators. Those guys out in the suburbs operate in a horizontal market. Their deliveries and pickups are usually in single-story office buildings or office-warehouses stretched out for miles. Geez, those guys drive a lot of miles covering their routes." Obviously impressed with Federal's planning, Phil continues his lecture: "The company has really worked on the problem of increasing the efficiency of our pickup and delivery system. As business has grown, our stops are closer together and the packages per stop have increased. But we're not like United Parcel Service. Those guys are tightly engineered in the way they handle their pickups and deliveries. Each of their stops is timed. Per package handled, UPS is really cost-conscious. Federal Express, on the other hand, is not nearly so tightly engineered. That's because we're more price/value-oriented."

I was struck by his comparisons, so I ventured to ask if there were other differences. Phil says, "Sure there are. Both UPS and the U. S. Postal Service guys don't give the customer as much attention as we do. Federal Express customers expect more because they feel they are paying for this service. We're the only outfit that traces a package every inch of the way from the time it is picked up until it is delivered. That's just one example."

His comrades in the garage were right: Phil was a real competitor. So I asked him if he thought he were brain-washed by Federal's hype. "No," he responded, "I don't think so. We have been an innovator in improving service levels in the small package express business. Most of our competitors, like Emery, Airborne, and the others, try to copy everything we do. All of the people at the station think they are working for the best company. They'll tell you that."

Phil continues his deliveries in and around the Financial District. At 10:10 a.m. he is down to his last few packages. "I'll make it by 10:30 a.m. easily," he remarks. "That new 10:30 a.m. delivery cut-off point is sacred with us. That's what we promise the customer. That's why we get the business and can charge more."

By 10:45 a.m. Phil Beckman is back at the station, as are most of the morning couriers. All of them are working on their paperwork, and getting ready to go out on the streets again to deliver the packages sent by the shippers using Federal Express' Standard Air Service. This is a service for which the company charges the customer far less than the Priority 1, Courier-Pak, and Overnight Letter services, because it commits to a two-day service, and not the "next morning by

10:30 a.m." service for the three higher-priced products. The couriers are also assigned to deliver what the company calls "starter kits" to new customers so they can begin using Federal Express' services. Once these particular deliveries are completed, and Phil and the other couriers are back at the station finishing their paperwork, the Federal Express Package Cycle is almost complete. They will clean out their delivery vans, then go into the small lounge for a cup of coffee or a candy bar from vending machines before checking out to go home. Soon the afternoon crew will report in, and the cycle begins all over again.

It had been a tiring 24 hours as I had pursued this particular 24-hour cycle beginning and ending at the station in downtown Chicago. I was impressed by the technical performance Federal's fleet of trucks and planes exhibited but, more to the point, I was impressed with the people who manned that technology. It would have given Fred Smith absolute confidence that his admonition to "treat each package as if it were the last package Federal Express will ever handle" was being respected by his employees. "We do pretty good," says supervisor Carol Jeselski. "Except when we have a winter snowstorm in Chicago, we meet our service commitments to customers about 99 percent of the time. That's a far cry from the Post Office and the other package outfits."

There is, however, more to this Venture Capital story than technology and employees.

Chapter 2

Big Satin Mama

"If Fred Smith lined up all 13,000 Federal Express employees on the Hernando de Soto Bridge in Memphis and said, 'Jump!' 99.9 percent of them would leap into the swift Mississippi River below. That's how much faith they've got in this guy," says Heinz Adam who is in charge of Customer Service.

"You've seen that poster, 'The Marines are looking for a few good men,' where the troops are dressed in combat fatigues. That's Federal Express," says Art Bass, who served as Federal's president from 1975 to 1980. Bass goes on to add, "This company should have died five or six times in its first three or four years, but Fred refused to give up. Boy, was he tenacious. With sheer bull and courage he pulled off a miracle. That's the only way to express what he did." This same opinion, although phrased in somewhat different words, was expressed by dozens of Smith's employees, from senior officers down through the ranks of the veteran couriers.

Fred Smith had suddenly emerged as one of the new glamour symbols of the entrepreneurial business world. What he had accomplished was considered brash, daring, and highly creative. *Barron's, Business Week, Dun's, Esquire, Financial World, Forbes, Fortune,* and *Nation's Business* all featured articles on Fred Smith and Federal Express. Smith was watched closely by the authoritative publication, *Aviation Week and Space Technology*, and most of the other aviation and transportation trade publications. Federal Express was newsworthy. The *Washing-*

"Get off your dead butt and come up here. We're about to have a damned fine war."
—General Patton's telegram to his nephew, Europe, 1945

ton Post and several other major metropolitan newspapers ran featured stories on Smith in their Sunday supplement sections. Television could not overlook Smith either. Segments on "Fred Smith and his Federal Express" appeared on NBC's "Prime Time Saturday," and on Bill Moyers' "Creativity" series developed for public television.

Smith became the centerpoint of the public's attention to this flashy company for which its dramatic color scheme of purple, orange and white planes and trucks serve as a moving billboard. Moreover, its sometimes provocative and always entertaining television commercials all helped create an enormous corporate identity practically overnight. He still receives the credit for the company's success despite the huge contributions of a loyal and talented group of senior officers and managers, as well as the dedicated rank-and-file employees. And, to be fair, he admits that. His people stood in admiration of him. They willingly accepted a secondary role when the publicity started flooding the media about Fred Smith and *his* Federal Express.

A few of his critics fault Smith for not extending himself to gain more visibility for his key associates. "Art Bass and Roger Frock, two guys who were with Fred from the start, really never got the credit they deserved from the various media and the financial community for what they did to build this company," says Charles Lea who was heavily involved in the company's startup. "Some of these guys around Smith also had strong personalities and egos like Fred's, but they seemed willing to play subordinate roles and stay out of the limelight. I guess they rationalized it away. After all, he made several of them millionaires."

The emergence of Fred Smith, of his company, of the corporate culture which Smith has created should suggest a series of questions which need answers. Who is Fred Smith? What kind of background created his drive? Is this successful Southerner a one-of-a-kind entrepreneur who has emerged from a region of the country not generally known as a spawning ground for founders of large nation-wide corporations? Or is he simply a new version of an old breed? Is Federal Express really the forerunner of a new generation of company? Or is it the same old "Dark Satanic Mill" William Blake identified at the beginning of the Industrial Revolution, albeit now dressed in high-tech finery? Who is this dynamic young business leader who conceptualizes his company as an heir to military strategist Von Clauswitz and the Marine Corps? Is he the prototype for a new generation of American business man? Or is he the rich kid, born to the purple, as the saying goes, managing an electronic plantation where cotton — now transformed into Courier-Paks, Priority 1 packages, and Overnight Letters — is still king?

* * * * *

On August 11th, during the summer, 1944, Frederick Smith, then

49, and his 23-year-old fourth wife, Sally Wallace Smith, were visiting one of their Northern Mississippi farms when their son, Frederick Wallace Smith, was born in nearby Marks, Mississippi.

The elder Smith had achieved considerable success as a businessman. He was founder and chairman of Dixie Greyhound Bus Lines, and chairman and president of the Toddle House restaurant chain. The bus company Fred's father had built from pluck and determination was one of the largest bus lines in the South until it was purchased by Greyhound Bus Lines. Not only had he personally built his first bus by using the body of a truck, but he was also its first driver until he started adding new routes. As his father had been a steamboat captain plying the Mississippi and Ohio rivers, the elder Smith was the second generation in the transportation business. Little did he know that his new born son would extend this transportation dynasty into a third generation.

The elder Smith had an uncanny ability to recognize a business opportunity. In 1934, at the depth of the Depression, he put venture capital into a small, struggling quick-service restaurant chain specializing in hamburgers, chili and pies. Called the Toddle House — because the pre-assembled buildings tended to toddle somewhat as they were hauled to the site — Smith quickly built a national chain of these units. When the Toddle House company was sold in 1961, the estates of the elder Smith and his brother received stock reported to be worth $22 million.

Once he had achieved success in the Depression-wracked 1930s, Smith became an active sportsman, buying surplus U. S. naval vessels and renovating them into pleasure boats. He was an outgoing, flamboyant individual; he was a southern son of Horatio Alger. Failure in life was impossible for him; it simply was not one of the options he allowed himself. During the Great Depression he said, "Many a man is struggling along on a small salary a week because he doesn't realize he can earn ten times as much." At that time a Memphis newspaper editorialized in admiration of the elder Smith, "The reputation of this man is that of a hard hitting, determined executive, who knows what he wants and is willing to pay the price — no matter how big."

Despite his gregarious nature, the elder Smith was somewhat of a loner. After his financial success he never found his way into the closely knit, xenophobic Memphis social structure. The insulated, old Southern gentility entrenched in Memphis since the mid-nineteenth century did not accept him, and he did not seem to care — at least externally. His reaction to these backward looking, wealthy and socially established families was clear; he despised them. Smith despised anyone with money who would not put it to work, and who would not sustain charitable and cultural causes. Just prior to his death in 1948, at the age of 53, the elder Smith wrote a letter to his young son to be opened on his twenty-first birthday. The long letter concluded with a request that young Fred put his inheritance to work and use the funds held in trust as a foundation for greater wealth. "My father didn't want me to be a fop," explained the younger Smith years later when he was being questioned at a Chancery Court hearing in Memphis by an attorney representing the financial interests of his half-sisters, Fredette and Laura.

After his father's early death, young Fred was raised by his mother in Memphis. Although he was born with a birth defect — a bone socket hip disorder called Calvé-Perthes disease — she encouraged him to enter into all sorts of physical activities. Throughout grammar school he wore braces and used crutches, but nothing really slowed him down. According to his mother he was an extraordinarily active child. Perhaps the first index of his future prowess as a leader came when his teachers recognized his organizational skills. When they wanted something done right, Fred got the assignment. Fred was a friendly youngster and an excellent student.

Like many small boys in the South, Fred became very interested in military history, especially in the history of the Civil War. As a small boy toting crutches under his arms, a holstered gun on his hip, he went to a National Guard summer camp. But for a small boy surrounded by that "damned yankee" attitude so thick in Memphis during the last days of Boss Crump and in the flurry of desegregation orders, there was only one real war, the Civil War. He and his mother often visited the Shiloh battlefield on the Tennessee River. And he had a huge collection of toy soldiers with which he exercised his ripening imagination by re-enacting the pitched battles he had read about. His mother encouraged his interest in the military because of the strong military tradition in the family.

Following grammar school, young Fred enrolled in Memphis University School, a fine privately financed preparatory school with a good reputation for offering its students a solid academic training. As he matured his Calvé-Perthes disease was cured, so that he was able to distinguish himself not only in academic work, and as a student leader, but also as an athlete. Where before he had lumbered around on crutches, at prep school he played both basketball and football. In his senior year, Fred was voted "Best All-Around Student."

During this period two watershed things happened: at the age of 15 Smith learned to fly and that same year he and two of his tenth-grade classmates organized a business, the Ardent Record Company — a company still flourishing in Memphis today. They set up a fully equipped studio in a garage, and there recorded rock 'n roll bands using talent from Memphis and the surrounding region. Their first release on the Ardent label, "Rock-House" and on the flip side, "Big Satin Mama," broke even. Young Smith withdrew from his first entrepreneurial venture when he entered Yale in the fall, 1962, but he carried with him the lessons learned there and, of course, continued his enthusiasm for flying.

His first two years at Yale were a sobering educational experience for Smith. At prep school he had been a high-ranking student academically and a class leader. But at Yale he found the competition much more difficult. He held only a B minus average during these years while majoring in economics and political science. Smith was later to confess, "I was a crummy student."

The Yale student body was captivated at that time by President Kennedy's "New Frontier" program. It was a heady time to be a college student. Kennedy and his advisors had articulated a set of challenges for the 1960s which boldly focused on the need for a new breed of pioneers to face the challenging times and revolutionary technologies coming. It was a period replete with a new breed of heroes, too, as astronauts, Alan Shepard and John Glenn seemed to provide new role models for Kennedy's call to a new frontier.

But Fred Smith was not caught up in any momentous cause of the day. He studied economics with a top rate faculty who had survived a devastating case made against them by William F. Buckley ten years earlier in his book, *God and Man at Yale*. Buckley had accused Yale of harboring a faculty "agnostic as to religion, Keynesian as to economics, and collectivist as applied to the relation of the individual to society and government." Although he lived in a heady atmosphere, Smith seemed unaffected. He was a fraternity man, a campus disk jockey, and with the help of two professors, organized the Yale Flying Club. In so doing they revitalized this long defunct club which had been originally organized after World War I by no less than Juan Trippe, pioneer aviation executive and founder of Pan American World Airways. All of this campus activity got Smith elected into Skull and Bones, the prestigious senior secret honorary society organized at Yale in 1832. He may not have been a card carrying New Frontiersman; he was not equipped with all the fashionable theories and postures; but he was in another way following pioneers like Trippe. And he was a certified "Big Man On Campus."

Student radicalism started slowly at Yale, beginning mildly in 1964, and reaching the proverbial "fever pitch" in 1969 and 1970. Consequently, Fred Smith had graduated in May, 1966, and was in Vietnam when the student activist movement picked up velocity on the Yale campus. Seemingly, he was carrying no deep convictions about any domestic social causes. He was not angry about anything. He had enrolled in the U. S. Marine Corps platoon leaders program while still an undergraduate, so he knew military service was awaiting his graduation from Yale. As a result, at graduation, he was commissioned a second lieutenant, Marine Corps Infantry, and sent into active duty.

At 21, Smith was now ready to experience the reality of war. He was going to have the opportunity to know it from an angle different than that found in books, different even from that to be found in dioramas of lead soldiers, and so utterly different than those shards of war left in museums, or those monuments standing alone in fields where the battle had once been. At 21 he was assigned to the First Marine Division, Fleet Marine Force in South Vietnam, after finishing a program at the Defense Language Institute, Monterey, California. At 21, the man left behind the boy.

When asked later why he had joined the Marines, Smith replied: "I had a typical Southerner's viewpoint of the military. I knew I had to go." Smith recalled his military experience during his first of two tours of duty in Vietnam observing: "I joined the First Marine Division and went to the Third Battalion, Fifth Regiment, where I was assigned as a platoon leader in India Company of the battalion. I served as a platoon leader for approximately six months and after a brief three-week stint on the battalion staff, I was assigned as a company commander and put in command of K Company, Third Battalion, Fifth Regiment. The previous commander of K company was killed in action shortly before I took over. I participated in 27 named operations, either amphibious or ground launch."

His first tour of duty in Vietnam lasted seven months. He returned to Memphis on leave before beginning a second tour. In October, 1968, when asked by a reporter for the Memphis *Commercial Appeal* why he was going back for a second time, Smith told him, "It's not that I'm more patriotic than anyone else, but there are 500,000 Americans over there now and there is a job I've been asked to do. I'm not being conceited, but I have had a year's experience and I know I can do it better than any new officer they might send in to replace me."

Smith won his wings and went back to Vietnam. He was assigned to fly A4D Skyhawks and OV-10 Broncos as a forward air controller and spotter. He flew reconnaissance missions in the I Corps area just south of the DMZ in Quang Tri Province, scene of some of the heaviest and most costly fighting of the war. He could not have found more action anywhere else in Vietnam. When he was discharged on July 21, 1969, he had attained the rank of Captain and been awarded the Silver Star, Bronze Star, two Purple Hearts, the Navy Commendation Medal, and the Vietnamese Cross of Gallantry.

Vietnam had been an awakening for Fred Smith. If in Memphis and New Haven he had associated with the youth of privilege and wealth, in Vietnam he led less privileged men, watched their courage, shared their agony. He credits a black platoon sargeant — a veteran of 14 years in the Marines — for helping him to understand what enlisted men think and want. Reminiscing about Vietnam, he credits the lessons he learned from this sargeant with enabling him to understand the concerns of the rank-and-file Federal Express employee.

He developed compassion for the Vietnamese peasants; he admired the determination of Ho Chi Minh. He learned to honor the ancient landscape and its cradled culture which were being savaged and brutalized by military confrontation. Trying to describe that bizarre quality of Vietnam and demonstrating his flair for phrase making he recalled of the war that there "the real was the unreal . . . the unreal was the real. There was an incomprehensible aspect to it all, like a bad but fascinating dream."

At Yale he had not known what he would do after the Marine Corps; he had even considered attending law school or graduate school. Byron Hogue, Smith's personal aide at Federal Express, knew him in Vietnam. Hogue maintains that the legacy Vietnam gave Smith was an essential toughness which sustained him and the company throughout the serial crises Smith confronted from 1973 through 1977. Fred Smith once expressed something of that legacy when he observed after suffering a major setback while trying to arrange financing for Federal Express, "It isn't the end of the world. It's not like getting killed or maimed in Vietnam." It's a kind of perspective that cannot be gained from a Business School MBA!

But perspective was not the only legacy of the Vietnam War. In Hawaii, on his way home, Smith married his high school sweetheart. A month later at 25, in August, 1969, he began to put his inheritance to work, by purchasing controlling interest in a Little Rock company called Arkansas Aviation Sales. His stepfather, a retired Air Force General, had taken over the company, a fixed base operator which provided maintenance services for turbo-prop and corporate jet aircraft, in 1967. Fred Smith had kept posted on the operations of the company while in Vietnam, so he knew the company was losing money. Once back in Little Rock, Smith took control and changed it into an aggressive business buying and selling used corporate jets. Smith was an unusual figure in this very competitive business. Whereas the typical airplane broker was usually thin on cash and had to finance his acquisitions with short term loans, Smith used his own money to buy many of the planes. Financial success was quick to his new Arkansas Aviation Sales. And Smith himself made a lot of money dealing in corporate jets. But he observed: "I really didn't like this business. It was full of shady characters. I just didn't feel comfortable dealing with a lot of these people."

Little Rock is a small, quiet and conservative city in central Arkansas. It is a community where religion is big business, where it is as common for prominent businessmen to quote the Bible in their dealings as often as they quote the stock market. He had established a good credit relationship with the local banks while he was building up profits at Arkansas Aviation Sales and his real estate portfolio. They knew Smith was independently wealthy and that he had inherited a sizeable fortune from his father. Some wanted him as a board member of their institutions. In him they saw a financial golden boy, bright, handsome, wealthy, self-confident, a battle-decorated leader possessing a proven business record — even though that record was less than 36 months old. The Little Rockers smelled money; he was someone they felt they could make money with as a customer.

Fred Smith was piecing together the structure which would become Federal Express. The maturity, the financial backing, the corporation. The missing element still unexamined is the financial legacy.

The inheritance, except for the funds he acquired at age 21, was held in a family trust called Frederick Smith Enterprise Company, Inc., for which the National Bank of Commerce in Memphis acted as trustee. His late father had formed this vehicle in the early 1940's to hold certain properties, which under the elder Smith's will, would pass into certain trusts for the benefit of his three children, Fred, Fredette and Laura. The Enterprise Company was merely a corporation which owned securities of other corporations, and certain real estate located in Memphis. Its principal assets were 164,800 shares of Squibb-Beechnut preferred convertible stock, stock whose value was estimated to be $13.3 million in 1971. Fred's share of this fortune was 38.5 percent. Both Fredette and Laura had slightly smaller shares.

In 1965, when Smith was 21, he had gone on the board of directors of Enterprise. Enterprise was then, as it had been since the elder Smith's death in 1948, a passive trust. The bank trustees neither bought nor sold any of the trust's assets. Fortunately, the Squibb-Beechnut stock — the primary asset — proved to be a good investment. When Fred Smith returned from Vietnam, he began offering new ideas to the board members, urging them to take a more active stance in its investment policies. Initially, his efforts did little to deploy Enterprise's assets more imaginatively and aggressively. Fredette and Laura did not like the bank's long time trust officer because they felt he had been too protective of the assets. They wanted to realize more income from the annual distribution of dividends.

In 1971, the Enterprise Company's investment strategy changed; Fred Smith became board president. He believed he had the support of Fredette and Laura in changing Enterprise from a passive entity into a more aggressive operating company. And he had very good reason to feel he was undertaking to follow his father's wishes as well. Consequently, when Fred and his business advisors came to Enterprise board meetings quite excited about an idea to start a special type of air cargo airline, Fredette and Laura willingly gave their assent to explore this venture by authorizing a modest sum of Enterprise's funds to be used as seed capital. The fact that Fred Smith was willing to match the Enterprise investment with his own personal funds was as well-received then as it would be later. The financial base seemed within reach and Smith was ready to move.

Chapter 3

The Yale Term Paper

"I just knew it was correct, but there were only a few believers at first," reflects Fred Smith. "The overwhelming body of opinion said it wouldn't work, or that we couldn't raise the money."

The idea for Federal Express did not emerge fully battle clad from the head of Plutus — the blind Greek god of wealth — though it may have seemed so to the public. As a Yale undergraduate in 1965, he wrote one of those student exercises in futility and haste, an artificial crisis theoretically designed to induce thought, a term-paper. In it he shaped crudely an idea from which the purple, orange and white elegance we know as Federal Express emerged. Looking back on it from the surety of success, he confessed: "It was just a term paper. You know how it is in your undergraduate days. You leave everything to the last minute. That's the way this paper was written. But I sure had the right idea in pointing out that the air freight industry's future was by no means assured. The passenger route systems used by most air freight shippers were totally wrong for freight distribution. The costs would not come down with volume. It was a technical, an economic impossibility. Air freight would only work in a system designed specifically for it, not as a simple add-on to passenger service." His Yale professor was not impressed. A gilt-edged concept, a hasty preparation: Smith received a humiliating "C" for his inspiration.

His professor's main criticism of Smith's idea was that it did not have a chance because of the

"The man with a new idea is a crank until the idea succeeds."
—Mark Twain

heavy regulation of air transportation by the Civil Aeronautics Board and intense competition. He was right about the heavy regulation. Federal Express' package volume growth was almost capped in 1975 and 1976 when the Civil Aeronautics Board refused to allow the company to fly larger and more efficient aircraft. The regulatory laws, backed up by a hostile commercial airline industry, were there to block Smith's "irrefutable logic" from being proven outright.

And to be fair to this Yale red-pen-wielder, Smith's late-night-wonder did not spell out any details of a grand design for a specific type of airline network with technical and administrative support systems. The general theme of the paper was that there was a huge market out there in the economy for an efficient service for moving high priority, time-sensitive small shipments like medicines, computer parts, and electronics. The American public was not being well served. He observed an inefficient delivery system where he said packages were "hippety-hopping around the country from city to city and from airline to airline before reaching their destination." And he observed that there was no control over the packages by the originating air carrier if the packages had to be carried by additional airlines before reaching their ultimate destination.

That Smith's concept found voice so early, survived initial humiliation, and persisted through two tours of duty in Vietnam is frankly amazing.

It would be impossible to write the history of the early days of the air freight business because no one really knows when the first box or package was transported by an airplane for delivery to what the business designates as a "consignee." The Post Office began regular mail service between New York and Washington in 1918, but it did not handle larger parcels. Juan Trippe, founder of Pan American, had mail contracts in the early 1920s along the East Coast. As early as 1925 Ford Motor Company was flying freight between its plants and, for a time, Ford had seriously considered creating its own airline for freight. At about that same time, the Railway Express Agency started an air express service. By 1925 at least four firms were operating air package services.

The air freight industry was a dull and unpromising business until the 1960s when commercial airlines jumped into the competition in an all-out effort to attract business from the nation's industrial firms. During that period in the late 1960s when Smith was in Vietnam, the air cargo picture began to worsen for the commercial airlines. They struggled to make a profit. The huge jet aircraft brought on-line to compete for both passenger and cargo business simultaneously looked like the perfect answer to their problems. They were convinced that putting cargo in the extensive belly space below the passenger deck could be a lucrative profit center. Delta, Eastern, United, and others continued their all-cargo service during the remainder of that decade despite questions about the profitability of such service. The commercial airlines had $400 million invested in their all-cargo services, and in addition they had huge capacities in their fuselages for freight. But the struggle for profit failed. United lost $19.8 million in its air cargo business in 1970. Eastern and American were also losing heavily. Most of the carriers lost money continuously from 1961 through 1973 and largely abandoned their all-cargo carriers.

The large jumbo jets purchased to compete in the passenger market did not contribute much revenue from hauling freight in their underbellies. The cubic capacity in the bellies of the 747s, the L-1011s, and the DC-10s was so adequate that management of these airlines felt this was an efficient replacement for the space foregone by the abandonment of the all-cargo planes. Deep down, management was discounting freight and treating it as a by-product or appendage. These wide-bodied jets were designed first and foremost to serve passengers. Ironically, the enormous increase in size the jumbos represented had exactly the opposite effect management sought. They made freight handling more difficult, not less.

Most airlines finally discouraged the small package business in the early 1970s. They were not equipped to handle small packages. In fact, small packages were a headache; they were an unprofitable headache because the cost of shipments was considered high. What the airlines thought they wanted was freight weighing over 100 pounds, so they left the responsibility for handling small items to Emery and all of the other freight forwarders. "Let them worry about that part of the market," concluded the airlines' management. "Besides," they rationalized, "the forwarders are our largest customers, contributing 40 cents out of every dollar of our freight revenue."

The airlines had their troubles in the early 1970s, and the small package problem was not a particularly urgent one with most of them. Hundreds of flights were canceled. Service as it had been known in the 1960s had changed for a number of compelling reasons. First, the huge wide-bodied jets increased seating capacities so that flights were consolidated to increase economic efficiency. And additionally, many night flights, or off-peak-hour flights, were cut back to save money. Then the Arab oil embargo, and rising fuel costs, put a real scare in airlines insofar as their expense structures were concerned. In fact, during the fall 1973, the federal government began allocating fuel to airlines in order to protect domestic supplies.

This decline of off-peak-hour service hit the air freight forwarders hard. Old veterans in that industry were fond of saying, "Air freight is basically a night animal; passengers are day animals." Most air freight items were picked up from shippers in the late afternoon or early evening and taken to the airport for flights leaving after 10:00 p.m. for overnight delivery to the consignee. Freight forwarders could not use much of the belly space in 747s or DC-10s leaving

O'Hare Airport in Chicago at 5:00 p.m., or Los Angeles International Airport at 6:15 p.m.

In the early 1970's, service was also cut to many of the smaller regional cities, like Chattanooga and Reno. Some small cities lost half or more of their scheduled flights as airlines made decisions to concentrate their attention on the major metropolitan air transportation hubs.

This was the state of the freight forwarding industry when Fred Smith took over Arkansas Aviation Sales. With the elimination of passenger service by the major trunk carriers, the difficulty of getting packages and other air freight delivered within a day or two after being picked up was escalated. Smith's Arkansas Aviation Sales was one of the victims of this deteriorating air service. It was causing him problems in operating his firm; so he decided to become an activist to do something about this inefficient distribution system. Smith reflects, "I became infuriated that I could not receive on any timely and reliable basis air freight shipments from places around the United States. Sometimes it might be two days, and sometimes, five days, before you could get a part delivered in Little Rock. It was unpredictable." From that point on he stepped up his research to find a way to close what he called the most classical gap in the transportation system. He considered what he was experiencing as a perfect example of the American high-tech industrial base not being able to find solutions to the most obvious economic problems. This is certainly one of the reasons Federal Express' cargo sales force received such a good response from Midwest industries in 1972. They were eager for a fast, reliable air freight system to replace the erratic ones they were used to since the late 1960s.

The small package express market had been growing rapidly measured on an annual percentage basis. Still, in 1970 not many had really given much thought to the market potential for items that could be classified as high value, time-sensitive packages or documents requiring priority service. The growth of this segment was hidden deep in the national freight volume figures representing small shipments moving between the various cities in the United States.

Conceptually, Smith had identified an opportunity. The great unknown to him was how he would work out the mechanics of implementing his idea. Since he was both optimistic and naive, there was no chance that he was going to worry himself to death over a lot of details. Over all, he thought of himself as an idea man, not a detail man. He seemed to believe things would work out.

Chapter 4

Federal

Federal Express faced a big challenge at the start. How was it going to convince customers it could deliver what it promised? That was also what the initial venture capitalists and the lenders wondered. Once the reliability of the service could be established with customers, Smith and his close associates felt the package volume would skyrocket and the profits would flow in rapidly. But little did they realize it was not going to be an easy task.

The company had to impress enough prestigious companies at first in order to get the endorsements or referrals needed to add additional customers. It had to convince the 3M company in St. Paul, Minnesota, for example, that a courier could pick up 35 packages and documents at corporate headquarters at 7:00 p.m., and then have them transported to 35 customers of 3M located in 35 different cities by 6:30 or 7:30 a.m. the next day, and then these same packages delivered by other Federal Express ground couriers to the designated consignees that morning.

To make this point in dozens of formal and informal presentations in New York, Chicago, Baltimore, St. Louis, Little Rock, and Memphis before prospective investors and lenders, Smith was openly critical of the marketing strategies of the air freight industry. He characterized the management of the airlines and the air freight forwarders as slow-witted and unimaginative.

"They have been notoriously bad planners," Smith emphasized to his audiences. "The public's image of the industry is often one of

"Failures are skinned knees — painful but superficial"
—H. Ross Perot

a ragged band of firms wrestling with sacks of potatoes and groceries. They don't see these outfits as transporters of medicines, vital computer parts, architectural drawings, legal documents and other high value, time-sensitive items," added Smith. "The public isn't too impressed when they have to deal with an overweight, gruff, shabbily dressed character chomping on a stale cigar in some seedy shed near an airport or on the back of some loading dock. If the opportunities were going to be fully exploited," continued Smith, "the public's image had to be changed."

Smith then would broadly outline his plan to turn this image around and to capitalize on what he felt was a huge untapped market in the American business community for a superior service. Art Bass would follow Smith with more technical presentations as to the details of the Federal Express operating plan. "He was more articulate in explaining the details of the Federal Express concept," says Charles L. Lea, Jr., then executive vice president of New Court Securities. "There were always some detail-oriented bank or investment house technicians in the audiences who had to be satisfied the logistical system proposed by Smith to move the packages would work."

To succeed with the investors, the superconfident Smith had to convince enough of them to back their belief in his plan with funding. They had to be convinced that Smith had indeed found a hole in the market, and that such a company specializing in transporting time-sensitive, critical packages and documents could capture the higher-income-yielding segment of the air express market and make a profit. What Smith had done was, on one hand, to recognize that high-technology processes often need critical parts and supplies on a "must-have" time-sensitive basis, and on the other hand to recognize that for all the electronic information media hurtling messages and documents from machine to machine, we were still not ready to dispense with paper. As long as American businessmen wanted to create a time sensitive "paper trail" recording transactions and instructions, there would be a place for a special service such as Federal Express had to offer.

Fred Smith defined a time-sensitive item as "one for which the consequences of failure to deliver within a specified period of time would far outweigh any consideration of reasonable rate comparability. If you offer two services and one of them is 15, 20, 30, 40 percent higher on one hand and it gets the documents or items there on time, and a cheaper service whose reliability is not nearly so great, the shipper will always take, if it is time-sensitive, the more reliable method, rather than the cheaper method. This is the essence of the definition of time-sensitive."

The period from 1969 through 1972 was spent in market research. Fred Smith and Joe Golden, one of his Arkansas Aviation Sales employees, investigated the needs of the U. S. Postal Service for air taxi service. Golden spent time in Washington researching this possible opportunity. Later, in 1972, as an interim service to generate cash flow for Federal Express, Smith signed contracts with the Postal Service for carrying mail overnight on several routes.

The initial idea that excited Smith was the possibility of contracting with the Federal Reserve System and its member district banks to move cash letters within the system on an overnight basis. The logistics of the check clearing process in effect in the early 1970s was cumbersome and inefficient. It often took two or more days to get checks sorted and distributed back through the system to the correct Fed district. This time lapse between the receipt of checks and the crediting of accounts, Smith calculated, caused a float problem of about $3 million a day.

At that time Federal Reserve banks were handling annually almost eight billion checks and non-cash items. Smith tried to sell them on his idea for an efficient overnight check clearing service within the Federal Reserve System. His planes could pick up the cash letters each night from some 36 points in the United States, and then fly them to a central sorting hub. Then, on an overnight basis, the sorted items would be flown back to the appropriate drop-off point. Smith seemed to think his contacts with Federal Reserve officials had created serious interest in his proposal. He was optimistic about the chances of it being accepted. He did not have the fleet of aircraft at the time, but he believed that equipment could be leased or purchased on short notice if he were awarded a contract.

Smith assembled the Enterprise board members on May 28, 1971, for the purpose of discussing the status of his contacts with the Federal Reserve. Irby V. Tedder, a retired Air Force colonel and Smith's vice president and controller of Arkansas Aviation Sales, joined in with the board members to discuss some of the details of the proposed distribution network.

The real purpose of that meeting, which Smith presided over as board president, was to request the board members' endorsement of the Federal Reserve plan and to ask them to agree to an investment by Enterprise of $250,000. Smith agreed to match this sum with his personal funds. It was a 50-50 arrangement that the board willingly agreed to accept.

With this approval, Smith incorporated on June 18, 1971, in Delaware, a company he named Federal Express Corporation. The word, "Federal," was the direct result of Smith's expectation that he would soon be under contract with the Federal Reserve System hauling cash letters between the various district banks. Later, after the rejection of Smith's proposal, he felt that the name Federal Express was a particularly good one for creating public attention. There was a patriotic meaning associated with the word, "Federal," and it also suggested an interest in economic activity nationwide.

On June 28, 1971, Smith wrote a letter to the other Enterprise board members, giving them a detailed explanation of the status of his discussions with the Federal Reserve officials. He concluded, "I feel that our chances of getting this contract are extremely high at this point. I had a conversation with the chairman of the Committee on Collection last week, and they are most anxious to receive our proposal."

This letter was written the day before another board meeting of Enterprise to prepare them for his additional request that the members approve a guarantee of a $3.6 million loan from the National Bank of Commerce of Memphis, the same bank serving as trustee. "This loan," Smith told Enterprise, "was needed to purchase two Dassault Falcon 20 Fan Jets from Pan American World Airways. Pan Am was hesitant to enter into a sales contract without any capitalization or commitment on our part."

Smith persuaded the other board members that negotiations had reached a critical stage with both the Federal Reserve and Pan American. Pan American had agreed to give Smith an exclusive right to other Falcon aircraft at a fixed price Smith considered very attractive. He wanted these planes because they fit into his plan for the nationwide small package airline he intended to launch at a later date.

This was his great opportunity, Smith felt, to pull everything together. He sensed the two Falcons were a key to the Federal Reserve contract. And then, if he could get a five-year contract, that would permit him to acquire the additional Falcons. "This was the scheme," he explained, "to get the Federal Reserve to provide the credit."

Backing up his arguments further, Smith reassured the Enterprise board that they were taking no risk. He told them that even if the Federal Reserve deal collapsed, he could sell these Falcon jets on the open market for a profit. And this profit would be over-and-above the sum of their investment, the interest on the loan, and the costs of modifying the planes so they could haul cargo.

Smith's half-sisters and the other Enterprise board members gave him their blessing to the loan by resolution. Two weeks later the National Bank of Commerce loan was secured with collateral of 50,000 shares of Squibb-Beechnut stock worth $4 million.

The euphoria of midsummer, 1971, when Fred Smith appeared to be on the verge of launching his airline, collapsed weeks later. The Federal Reserve told Smith they couldn't do it. Each of the District banks in the Fed system was highly competitive with the others. They could not reach a consensus on Smith's proposal. Each wanted to arrange for its own transportation network. Federal Express was hardly birthed before it had received its first setback.

Reflecting on these events years later, Smith explained to me, "If the Federal Reserve contract had materialized, Federal Express probably would not have become what it is today. But that's a hypothetical question."

So in the summer, 1971, Federal Express was still a shell organization which owned two Falcon jets. Smith and Irby Tedder were the whole staff with an occasional assist from Joe Golden. Cash was not yet a problem. Arkansas Aviation Sales, Smith's principal business endeavor, was doing well financially.

Smith refused to abandon his idea, and he did not sell the Dassault Falcons. The French planes were built to carry passengers, so during the fall, 1971, Smith concerned himself with plans to modify them into cargo planes. More importantly, he had learned some things in developing the proposal put before the Federal Reserve System. He understood more clearly the concept of the hub-and-spokes system for distributing the future nightly haul of packages and documents. Everything could be picked up from customers in big and small communities alike, flown to a central point, sorted as to flight route and destination city, reloaded on the planes, and then flown in reverse. But he continued refining his plans and contacting an assortment of people on whom to try out his ideas. Some six years had passed since the Yale term paper for which he had been awarded the humiliating "C" grade.

Chapter 5

The Truck Line With Wings

"What business are we in? What business should we be in?" These are questions some corporate executives never answer. They either do not understand the significance of answering these questions, or they do not allow themselves the time to do it.

They may assert selfrighteously: "We know what business we are in. That's what we do!" Or they may bristle: "What the hell, that's a ridiculous question. It's what we do. It seems to us that is one of those 'who am I' riddles so popular with intellectuals."

Fred Smith, assisted by key aides, in the 1972-73 period had pretty well defined the business they wanted to be in and had developed the mechanics needed to operate it.

After the rejection of his original air express proposal by the Federal Reserve System in mid-1971, Smith struggled for several months trying to find his exact niche in the air cargo field. During this period he called on numerous air transportation people to discuss his ideas. A friend in Little Rock introduced Smith to New York investment banker Harmon L. "Buck" Remmell of White, Weld & Company. Buck Remmell, after listening to Smith discuss his concept, advised, "Do your homework on the front end. Have some independent research done. Try to verify what you think the status of the domestic air freight industry is like."

In December of that year Smith selected the firm of A. T. Kearney, Inc., a national consulting firm with a strong specialization in transportation economics. Roger J. Frock, a 10-year consulting veteran at A. T. Kearney in New York, was project director of the $75,000 market study which Smith subsequently commissioned. "We began as quickly as Fred wanted us to do," Frock later remembers, "but not before we had a chance to check with Dun & Bradstreet about Smith. It was not everyday we signed a large contract with an unknown. Most of our work was with established corporations or the government. We wanted to know Smith's financial status before we did any work."

And in December, 1971, Fred Smith also called on Art Bass in New York as he had promised he would when they had spoken in Little Rock. "I was really surprised when Fred walked into my office," explains Bass. "I was now a full-fledged consultant, and no longer selling corporate airplanes." Art Bass, J. Vincent Fagan and S. Tucker Taylor, all former Pan American Business Jets salesmen, had joined forces to form a small consulting firm in New York with the impressive name, Aerospace Advance Planning Group — a firm which referred to itself as "AAPG." AAPG did a variety of things, including marketing research assignments for aircraft firms, publishing aviation directories, and acting as advertising consultants. It was a maverick group composed of highly individualistic, nonconformist partners.

Smith felt a special rapport with Bass, Fagan and Taylor, and hired them to duplicate the market study A. T. Kearney had just been hired to do. And it was the same fee, $75,000. Neither of these consulting groups knew the other was at work on the same assignment. Asked if Fred Smith tried to influence him to come up with a favorable conclusion, Roger Frock told me, "No, he really wanted to know if his concept was practical." Smith had put up $150,000 to buy this information, although anyone else in Fred Smith's position might have felt a single study was sufficient. My suspicions are, though I have been unable to prove them, that his financial advisors knew it would require two independent studies to convince investors.

When both firms began their feasibility studies in late December, 1971, their assignments were to contact shippers, banks, and brokerage houses, department stores, oil and petrochemical companies and a cross-section of other businesses shipping priority items. They were to explore with the companies their interests in new types of air service and their complaints about existing services.

Smith wanted statistical data on the market for priority air freight to take to the Civil Aeronautics Board when he tried to get their authorization to use the Dassault Falcon 20 to haul air freight. AAPG project team headed by Art Bass undertook a huge mail survey of shippers to develop these data. Smith prodded Roger Frock and Art Bass to get their studies done quickly. Additionally he needed preliminary reports from them to take to investment bankers he was contacting. Investment bankers were not going to waste their time with Smith unless he could document his case.

During early 1972, Smith commuted frequently between Little Rock and New York, and he often brought along his close aide, Irby Tedder; his attorneys, Frank L. Watson, Jr. and William N. Carter of Little Rock; as well as Robert L. Cox, his personal attorney who was also the secretary of Enterprise Company. Together, they would make the rounds visiting White, Weld & Company, A. T. Kearney and AAPG, Art Bass' team, for discussions or update reports.

Frock, shaking his head in amusement, remembers, "These fellows would come up from Little Rock. Fred often didn't bother to introduce them to me by name, so I didn't know who they were. There was a mystery to it all. And there was this urgency to it all."

The AAPG preliminary report was completed in early March, 1972, while the A. T. Kearney report was largely completed in May, 1972, and the final written report was submitted to Smith in early June. Both studies confirmed Smith's belief that specialized services were desired by shippers of priority air cargo. Both consultants concluded independently that there was a large untapped air freight market in the United States and that it represented over a $1 billion annual business. Overnight delivery service between airports was not being provided within a network of at least 100 major cities, the consultants told Smith. And, they also told him the demand for this service appeared genuine. Their findings also pointed out that many shippers wanted this type of priority air service to be integrated with the ground or highway legs of the transportation journey between shipper and consignee.

Federal Express can compete effectively in the under 50-pound market, Smith was told. He could expect initial capital start-up costs to range from $6.5 million to $15.9 million, and could expect to be generating earnings within six to twelve months after inaugurating the package service. The breakeven point was estimated to be 1.6 million packages and 10,000 tons of charter freight cargo annually. To achieve this breakeven level, Federal Express would only have to tap less than one percent of the total domestic air freight market.

In early, 1972, Smith was planning two profit centers for Federal Express. There would be a scheduled air cargo service. Packages would be picked up and flown to the central hub, then flown to the destination city for delivery to the consignee. "We will provide overnight delivery service," Smith explained. "We will have 23 planes in service with three backup planes. The first planes will arrive at the central hub at 11:30 p.m., and the last planes would depart by 3:00 a.m." Initially, Smith planned to build his central sorting hub at Little Rock's Adams Field.

But Smith also wanted to be in the charter business. During the daylight hours Federal Express would offer an expedited charter service to industries seeking fast same day service between two points. Operating these two systems would permit maximum use of the Falcon aircraft fleet Smith was assembling.

By late spring, 1972, Smith, armed with his two feasibility reports, felt he had the concept fairly-well refined. He was ready to try to raise the funds to launch his innovative airline-truck express venture. He was positive he knew what segment of the transportation business he was going into, and he knew how it was different from anything else around at that time. Additionally, he concluded he would have to differentiate this service he was proposing from the general hauling of air freight, if he were to attract any interest from investors and customers.

One of Fred Smith's catchy definitions of his business which he used to attract attention was: "We're a freight service with 550-mile per hour delivery trucks." Another definition was: "We're an intermodal transportation system using jet cargo planes." And later, after the company was established, Smith told the business world that Federal Express was in the "transportation, communication and logistics business."

In defining what he thinks is Federal's unique role in the daily business economy, Smith has offered this rather visionary observation: "This company is nothing short of being the logistics arm of a whole new society that is building up in our economy — a society that isn't built around automobile and steel production, but that is built up instead around service industries and high-technology endeavors in electronics and optics and medical science. It is the movement of these support items that Federal Express is all about."

The general public has continued to think of Federal Express as a very aggressive cargo airline. Early television advertising featured the colorful purple, orange and white Falcon aircraft awaiting the arrival of the company's trucks and vans with that day's collection of packages and documents. At first attention was focused primarily on the fleet of airplanes.

One early print media ad covered two pages. One page carried, in large bold letters the following statement: "When the airlines are in trouble, we're bound to be affected." — President of Emery Air Freight. Then on the opposite page there was the equally bold print: "That's exactly why we bought our own planes." — President of Federal Express Corporation.

Federal's plan to build this priority small package firm around planes and trucks was greeted skeptically at first. Some of its competitors did not believe one could combine successfully an airline with a trucking company. They claimed they were completely different businesses. Smith felt this criticism was idiotic. "Look," he argued, "a plane and a truck are both vehicles. One has a pilot, and one has a driver. What's the difference?"

"Why just small packages?" Federal Express was asked by financial analysts and others. "It's a matter of economics first," replied

Smith, "and equally important, it presents a clear, unambiguous image to the public. We found our niche in the market. We're not carrying mice and elephants on the same plane like a lot of cargo outfits such as Airborne Freight, Emery Air Freight and Flying Tigers. We carry what a person can lift."

The Federal Express approach to presenting potential customers with a more efficient, quicker and often cheaper small package service was to adopt a systems approach to a systems problem. When he was asked, as he often was, by skeptics why he felt his fledgling Federal Express could do better than the great airlines in handling small packages, Smith would reply: "What makes us better is that we aren't affected by the tunnel vision of most airline managements. Let me give you an example. The airlines' solution to the nagging baggage handling problem is to let the passengers carry their own bags on board." Since Smith had no intention of entering the passenger business at that time, Federal Express did not have the problems of dealing with people and handling their baggage. "People can squawk, while packages can't," explained Federal's planners. These particular differences made it possible for the company to implement a logistical system designed to serve shippers of packages, not passengers.

Federal Express, if it could solve the logistical problems blocking the way of providing efficient overnight nationwide service, at least had an opportunity of becoming a successful transportation entity. The challenge to Federal was developing a system which could provide next day service at a reasonable price. A good portion of the nation had not previously been well-served. Could this idea of Smith's work? Could he really provide air shippers and consignees overnight jet service between most American cities, not just the major metropolitan markets? And could it be profitable?

Since World War II, industry and people had been dispersing away from the older industrial centers of the East and Midwest. Many regional cities and towns in the South, Southwest, the Pacific Coast states, and in the Rocky Mountain area had been attracting industry since the 1950s and 1960s, or giving birth to their own home grown firms. Quick, efficient transportation was an important ingredient to successful economic development in these new, emerging regions. If a firm were located in New York, Chicago or Los Angeles it had good air freight service. But if it were located in Albuquerque, Reno, San Antonio or Wichita and dozens of other regional cities, then delivery dates were not on next-day basis. Two and three day delivery dates were common for priority air cargo. And service? Service was totally unreliable.

These changes gave Federal Express its chance to fill a void. No one wanted to wait very long for anything if it meant loss of productivity and profits. If any transportation or communication company could find ways to reduce the time gaps between requests and delivery of parts, computer tapes, blueprints, contracts, radioactive isotopes and other high priority, time-sensitive items, they would find eager customers.

Federal's supreme logistical challenge was to find a way to serve these widely-dispersed regional, outlying cities and towns while also competing for business against the commercial airlines and the freight forwarders such as Emery. If Federal could provide overnight service to regional cities like Albuquerque, Charlotte, Jacksonville, Portland — whether in Maine or in Oregon — and to smaller cities like Fort Smith, Macon and Williamsport, then tie them all together with the big metropolitan cities in a nationwide network, the company had the ideal support system for America's emerging high technology and service industry economy.

Smith, Frock, Bass and the others knew from their market research that throughout the United States each day there was a quantifiable demand for so many computer parts, for so many pieces of diagnostic medical equipment, and for so many sets of architectural plans. Of course, the mystery — that is the source of the demand — was the unknown.

The demand was quantifiable, but the distribution random. It was not possible on a daily basis to know precisely how many units of a radioactive substance or blood serum might be shipped from a pharmaceutical firm on Route 128 in suburban Boston to Rochester, Minnesota for Mayo Clinic use; or how many Courier-Pak tube containers with engineering blueprints might be moving between Morrison-Knudsen's world headquarters in Boise, Idaho, and a construction project site in Baytown, Texas.

In solving this distribution problem, Federal Express planners borrowed ideas from package distribution systems used by the United Parcel Service — better known as UPS — and some of the interstate trucking companies. They also borrowed from the telephone company's switching system to come up with its "hub-and-spokes" concept. All packages and documents would be flown nightly, Monday through Friday, to a central sorting hub before being transshipped to their ultimate destination. As far as the customer was concerned, it really made no difference that his package was not flown in a lineal fashion, or directly, from City A to City B. Since the package was an inanimate object which could not complain during its journey between pickup and delivery, the only concern originated with the customer who wanted Federal Express to deliver it to the consignee the next day on time.

The non-linear system permitted service to a far greater number of points with fewer aircraft. And in addition, the central hub system helped reduce mishandling and delay in transit, because Federal Express kept total control over the packages from the pickup point through delivery. The system also permitted Federal Express the opportunity each night to match aircraft flights with package loads and re-route flights when the load volume required it. This flexibility permitted considerable savings in operating costs. Late in 1972, Smith made the decision to locate the sorting hub — the center of Federal's radial distribution system — at the Memphis International Airport.

Smith's decision to relocate to Memphis, his home town, was made for several reasons. Little Rock could not justify a huge capital outlay on airport improvements for a company which at that time in late 1972, had not inaugurated its priority package airline operation. Smith knew the key people heading the Memphis and Shelby County Airport Authority. Surplus hangar space was available, and the Authority agreed to issue bonds to provide the improvements Smith needed to start operations. Fortunately for Fred Smith, he came to them at exactly the right time. The favorable lease terms provided by the Airport Authority to an unproven company with very limited capital was a stroke of good fortune for Smith and his associates. It is doubtful that any other major metropolitan airport would have made such a similar generous deal to an unproven company run by a 28-year-old with limited business experience.

Memphis as a geographic location for Smith's "hub-and-spokes" system, was considerably east of the geographic center point of the country. But in 1973, at the time of the company's formal beginning of the small package service, Memphis was close to the center of gravity of the initial target market cities for small packages. Moreover, the weather conditions in Memphis were considered excellent from the viewpoint of uninterrupted service. Rarely had the airport been shut down because of fog, ice or snow. Cities further north and east of Memphis had considerably greater problems in the winter months keeping their airports operational.

Federal's Falcon jets flying east to Memphis from the western states would have a westerly tailwind and fewer stops offsetting the two hour time zone disadvantage from the Pacific coast, and one hour from the Mountain states. The Falcons returning west then would have a one to two hour time advantage to offset any unfavorable wind conditions.

Smith's refinement of his concept had picked up momentum. Armed with his consultants' reports, and some new friends in Roger Frock, Art Bass, Mike Basch, Mike Fitzgerald and the White, Weld investment bankers, Smith prepared to implement his Federal Express which he described as "a special expedited service where the packages never stop moving with the primary conveyer being the airplane."

Chapter 6

Y'all Come Down to Little Rock

In late 1971, Fred Smith was 27 years old and he was less than two and one-half years removed from Vietnam, and five and one-half from Yale. A brief stint selling corporate jet aircraft was the sum of his business experience. But he had an idea for a small package airline, an idea which he felt had great promise if only he could obtain financial backing. In those days he was always trying out his ideas on anyone who might be interested.

Pan American Business Jets, the business aircraft sales subsidiary of Pan American World Airways, offered Smith a friendly ear — although it was not a selfless friendship. Pan Am held the exclusive U. S. distributorship rights for the Dassault Falcon 20 twin executive jet, a plane Smith thought to use for his Federal Express fleet. Since 1965 Pan Am had been marketing the French-built plane, with only mixed success, a success particularly jeopardized by the recession of 1969 and 1970, which flooded the American market with corporate jet aircraft. Consequently, in 1971, when Fred Smith seriously began to consider using the Falcon 20 as the foundation of his proposed fleet, Pan Am's Business Jet Division was losing a substantial amount of money.

In the mid-1960s Pan Am had considered organizing its own air taxi fleet using the Falcon 20s. At that time, it also had tried to sell the idea to Executive Jet Aviation, a subsidiary of Penn Central. By the time Fred Smith visited Pan Am, they had had considerable time to think about the commercial uses of the Falcon.

So when they sat down to talk, Fred Smith and Pan Am had a strong mutual interest. Federal Express became a prime customer prospect for Pan Am; Pan Am became a major ally in the creation of Federal Express.

Smith had been looking at the potentials of different aircraft since 1969. He had taken serious looks at the Gulfstream G-1s as well as the Falcon 20s, but he had zeroed in on the Falcon 20s in 1971 because they had a bigger cubic capacity in the fuselage and the greater flight range. The Falcon had an overall length of approximately 56 feet and a wing span of 50 feet which allowed it to carry either ten passengers or three tons of freight. But Smith was also impressed with the strong airframe and undercarriage of the Falcon since it suggested the plane would be a good fleet workhorse.

The Falcon 20 was the plane Smith wanted, if it could be modified from its physical configuration as a 12-seat corporate passenger jet to a cargo plane capable of hauling at least a three-ton payload. Smith thought he needed an aircraft with a payload at least that large if he were to enter the corporate freight market. If this modification could be made, then he would have a small, fast all-weather jet with the proper width and height for freight. The only other plane around in 1971 which could carry a similar payload was the slow, short-range 35-year-old DC-3. The Falcon, when modified would have a speed of 540 mph and a range of 1,400 to 2,000 miles.

In August, 1971, Smith and Pan Am agreed to put a Falcon 20 into modification to serve as a prototype for his proposed minifreighter fleet. The board of the Smith family-controlled Enterprise Company agreed to guarantee a loan for $3.6 million to buy two Falcons.

A major problem arose with the choice of the Falcon 20, however. The gross weight of the Falcon exceeded the limit permitted by the Civil Aeronautics Board for air taxis. Pan Am made suggestions for lightening the plane, but even with these changes, the plane's weight exceeded the Part 298 limit for air taxis. In order for Smith's plan to work, it would be necessary to get the CAB to change its regulations to permit a larger payload.

Because Fred Smith was reasonably confident the CAB would make the change sometime in early 1972, in early December, 1971, his plan called for a fleet of 26 Falcons. He already owned two; he would lease the other 24. Of this proposed fleet, 23 would be in service with three in backup or in maintenance. The leased aircraft would cost about $6.6 million a year.

"If we could fill the airplane each night, we could produce $66.8 million, providing before tax profits of $42.4 million," Smith concluded in his financial plan prepared in late 1971. "This doesn't even include revenue we earn from charter flights carrying cargo."

Between November 9, 1971, when his tentative operating plan

called for the lease of 24 Falcons, and December 16, 1971, when he signed the contract with Pan Am to buy 23 Falcons, Smith changed his aircraft acquisition plan. What caused Smith to change his plans? It was Pan Am's decision to sell the planes it had been reluctantly storing out in the desert near Roswell, New Mexico, while waiting for the market to improve, a decision created by Pan Am's desperate need for cash to save its Business Jets Division from bankruptcy.

On December 17, 1971 — the day after Smith signed an option to purchase 23 Falcons from Pan Am for a purchase price of $29.1 million — he got the Enterprise board to guarantee a $1,150,000 loan needed to secure this option. As the CAB's Part 298 economic regulations stood in late 1971, the Falcon 20 would not be feasible for Federal Express to use in its proposed small package business. Consequently, Pan Am had agreed to refund this option fee if the CAB refused to relax its cargo payload restrictions.

Early, 1972, Smith went out on the open market and bought eight used Falcons. With the two initial Falcons he had purchased outright in 1971, the 23 he had under option with Pan Am, and the eight used planes, Smith had a fleet of 33 aircraft. But since the final planes did not join the fleet until 1974, it took some 30 months to assemble it. Including costs of modification, plus interest charges, the total cost was $56.1 million.

Smith was elated. He felt he had cornered the market for Falcons, and had purchased the planes at bargain rates. If his plans for his air freight operation collapsed, they could be sold at a profit. Selling corporate jets was a business Fred Smith knew well; he had his emergency exit covered.

Pan Am, which had been so anxious to sell Fred Smith its surplus inventory of new Falcons in late 1971, exerted tremendous pressure on Federal Express in the fall, 1972, and early winter, 1973, to take delivery of the planes and to pay up. Originally, Smith had agreed that Federal Express would accept delivery of one Falcon per week beginning September 28, 1972. Federal Express requested a delay on this original commitment and agreed to pay Pan Am an increase in price as a penalty. On November 1, 1972, a second delay was negotiated, again with financial penalties. And then, because of its further deepening financial crisis, Federal Express had to request a further delay on January 31, 1973.

Negotiations between Pan Am and Federal Express on this issue were at times bitter because Pan Am desperately needed the cash. Its Business Jets Division was bankrupt at that point, and it was in no mood for further compromise. "One of those senior vice presidents at Pan Am was a real S.O.B." remembers Frank Watson, counsel at that time for Federal Express. "I spent 23 days in New York trying to work out a deal to keep Pan Am from selling the Falcons out from under us. This guy was unyielding and unpleasant. We had to play real hardball to keep the agreement alive. At times it was all but dead. Federal Express almost died at these bitter meetings."

The final head-to-head negotiations with Pan Am resulted in Federal Express agreeing to issue Pan Am warrants to purchase common stock. Federal Express under this new agreement in January, 1973, was permitted to take all of the planes on or before May 15, 1973, subject to a price increase on each aircraft of $1,500 for each day delivery was delayed beyond March 31, 1973. May 15th became the most critical date in Federal's history up to that point. It was a "do-or-die" target date.

Banks in Little Rock and Memphis helped Federal Express finance the purchase of the used Falcons purchased on the open market with short term, demand notes. Worthen Bank in Little Rock financed six planes in early 1972, and was so proud of its association with Federal Express that its television commercials showed Federal Express Falcons blasting off into the sunset with captions: "Worthen helps a good idea fly."

A year later, in the summer and fall, 1973, Worthen Bank wondered whether it was a good idea after all. By that time Worthen and some small town Arkansas banks that held participations in the $8 million indebtedness were gravely concerned. Said one close Federal Express observer: "Those little banks over in East Jesus, Arkansas, were really sweating those loans. They were more than happy to lend Fred Smith the money back in 1972. Here was young, successful Fred Smith with a fat family inheritance to backup his ventures. They didn't think they had a thing to worry about. It never dawned on them that Fred might have trouble getting his permanent financing to help pay off the short term loans on the two original Falcons he bought from Pan Am, and the eight used Falcons he had purchased on the open market."

During this period Smith called on Commercial Credit Equipment Corporation — known as CCEC — a subsidiary of Control Data Corporation headquartered in Baltimore. CCEC had known of Fred Smith since his service days in Vietnam. At that time, Smith had used some of his funds from his inheritance to help his stepfather purchase controlling interest in Arkansas Aviation in Little Rock. Afterwards, when Arkansas Aviation got heavily into debt, Smith — still in Vietnam — arranged to make good on a deficiency of $100,000. As a result CCEC, one of the creditors, was particularly impressed with him.

In May, 1972, Smith outlined his ideas for his priority small package airline with the CCEC staff. He gave them copies of the A. T. Kearney and the Aerospace Advance Planning Group consultants' reports in which both firms concluded there was a huge, unserved market for priority air cargo.

Meanwhile, the board of the Enterprise Company resolved to purchase $2 million of Federal Express common stock, and to guarantee $2 million of a proposed $13.8 million loan from CCEC. The assets of Enterprise were to back up this $2 million loan guarantee. On July 8, 1972, CCEC signed the agreement lending Smith and his Federal Express $13.8 million. The 10-year note on the ten Falcons was secured by a first mortgage, a $2 million pledge of collateral by Enterprise, as well as by the personal guarantee of Fred Smith.

The Part 298 matter still had to be resolved if Federal Express were to fly the Falcons as cargo freighters. The CAB strictly forbade any air taxi operator to put a plane in the air that had a maximum takeoff weight exceeding 12,500 pounds. Since the Falcons far exceeded this weight limitation, Federal needed relief from the CAB if Smith's plan was to proceed.

Federal's plan required it to be classified as an air taxi operator under Part 298 regulations. Air taxi operators, under the law, could fly when and where they liked throughout the United States. They were a special class of carriers existing outside the basic certificated structure that had been in place since the Civil Aeronautics Act of 1938. This freedom to fly where and when it wanted was essential to Smith's operating plan.

Oral hearings on the subject of revising Part 298 began at the CAB in January, 1972, but no one really expected a final decision before fall, 1972. Fred Smith nonetheless proceeded with confidence that the issue would be resolved in his favor so he could use the Falcons. The proposed change for air taxi operators was to eliminate the 12,500 pound takeoff weight limitation and replace it with new regulations permitting air taxis to fly aircraft with a 30 passenger seat limitation and a payload capacity up to 7,500 pounds.

There was considerable opposition within the certificated carrier group to the proposed change. They felt that any significant expansion of Part 298 authority would be a threat to them. Perhaps, they were right, since they were tightly restricted as to routes and to tariffs. The opposition was particularly strong from several certificated local service airlines who claimed any change would create unfair competition for them from air taxis operating legally outside the certificated structure.

Fred Smith was advised to seek experienced Washington counsel on the Part 298 matter, because, he was told, the CAB rules were complicated and it was important to get direction from someone who knew the ropes in Washington. Consequently, Smith retained Ramsey D. Potts, a respected Washington attorney, and his firm. After examining the status of the Part 298 regulation, the firm advised Smith any change in Part 298 would probably be challenged in the courts. It also foresaw problems for Federal Express further into the future, even if Part 298 were changed to permit a maximum 7,500 pound payload. Counsel felt if Smith carried through in his plan for a large-scale air operation, Federal Express would be forced to seek CAB certification status later on.

On July 18, 1972, Part 298 was amended by the CAB which permitted the 30-passenger seat, or the maximum 7,500 pound payload — effective September 17, 1972 — the Falcon 20 was now qualified and Federal Express was on safe ground. In late 1972, petitions for review of the CAB's order were filed in the U. S. Court of Appeals, District of Columbia Circuit by Hughes Air Corporation, North Central Airlines, and the Air Line Pilots Association. With the Court's announcement on December 5, 1973, that the CAB had acted properly in liberalizing Part 298, a dark cloud which had hung over the first eight months of the small package business was dispersed. The decision not only meant Federal could proceed safely but also the company could purchase the remaining Falcons to complete its fleet.

"If the court had ruled in favor of Hughes and the others, there wouldn't have been a Federal Express," concludes Nathaniel P. Breed, Jr., the company's Washington-based legal counsel. "The certification process would have had a crushing effect on the company's ability to obtain the financing which it desperately needed to survive and put its system in place."

Early in May, 1972, Smith announced that Federal Express had its operating plan and personnel in place, and was going to hire new employees. Heretofore, his staff had been Irby Tedder, his right hand man at Arkansas Aviation Sales, and several of his corporate jet salesmen. The first people he hired were mostly people he knew, or friends and relatives of people Smith and Tedder knew. Smith had no sophisticated hiring plan in hand, but he had an approximate idea of the type of people who were needed and he set out to find them.

Tucker Morse, for example, only recently relocated to Little Rock and only recently out of law school, was hired more or less over the backyard fence. He was visiting his parents who lived next door to Smith. When Smith suggested to Morse that he needed an attorney, Morse jumped at the chance. At the time the 27-year-old Morse was clerking for a law firm at a non-existent salary in order to gain experience.

Word got around Little Rock and Memphis that Smith was hiring for Federal Express. One applicant is now his senior vice president for operations planning, Ted Weise. Weise had once worked for General Dynamics as a flight test engineer on the F-111 attack bomber program and had been out-of-work for a year before he went to see Smith in Little Rock about a job. Weise remembers the initial meeting as follows:

Smith: "Why do you want to work for me?"

Weise: "I like airplanes."

Smith: "Hell, don't you want to make some money? I like airplanes too, but I'd like to make some money, too."

The money Smith was referring to was obviously not the initial salary of $700.00 per month he offered Weise. Weise was happy with the job, and the $700.00 was a welcome sight.

Smith appealed to the entrepreneurial spirit of most of those he hired. He particularly wanted his key management positions filled with what he called "entrepreneurial-types." He was looking for the same "right stuff" competitive qualities and toughness that, according to author Tom Wolfe, NASA officials sought when they screened the ranks of the jock fighter pilots and test pilots to come up with John Glenn, Alan Shepard, Wally Schirra and the other members of the original astronaut team.

"He was very persuasive," recalls Roger Frock (B.S., Engineering; MBA, Michigan), who quit A. T. Kearney in May, 1972, to join Smith in Little Rock after completing the Federal Express study. "Fred gave me an oral commitment. He said if Federal Express succeeded, I would get stock. There was nothing written and I didn't expect anything written. I took a big pay cut going down to Little Rock from New York. But I was 35, and I wanted to take the plunge in a risk venture."

Frock was appointed general manager at a salary of $36,000, a figure $1,000 more than Smith himself made. The 10 years of experience Frock had at A. T. Kearney conducting distribution logistics and cargo handling studies for transportation clients made him a key employee. He was well-organized, a good technical planner, and he could prepare the type of in-depth reports Smith needed for presentations to potential investors and banks.

Smith used executive "headhunters" to find many key technical personnel. "If anyone he wanted showed a reluctance to accept his offer, he'd really go to work on them," says Art Bass. "Fred's face would light, and he'd paint this glowing portrait of how Federal Express was to be a giant *Fortune* 500 corporation, and that they ought to be part of this adventure. Of course, Little Rock was the end of the Earth to some of these fellows and their families, but Fred Smith successfully overcame most of their concerns." A wife of a prospect from Connecticut was reported to have told her husband: "Why I wouldn't be caught dead in Little Rock."

Arthur C. Bass (B.S., Middlebury), then 40, joined Smith in the Fall, 1972. About Art Bass it may be said that not only did he have the reputation as a resourceful conceptual planner with special talents in marketing, but also he had the good looks of the pilot adventurer to project the image Smith sought in those days — tall, handsome, lanky build with a broad boyish smile. In short, "the right stuff." His early assignments at Federal Express were in developing the marketing plan and handling industrial relations. Three years later, in 1975, he would be elevated to the presidency during a brawl within the board of directors over Smith's performance. One insider says admiringly of Bass, "He's one of the few top guys Fred hired who did not have a big ego problem. Many of those other guys at times were insufferable. Art isn't a numbers guy, or an MBA-type running around with fixed solutions to every problem. He can grasp and handle a broad range of ideas and sort them out. He was the most popular fellow in the company."

Michael D. Basch (B. A., Clarkson Tech) another key aide hired by Smith, had extensive experience at UPS in sales, planning and industrial engineering. Basch, like Art Bass, was equally handsome, personable, easy-going and related well with the staff Smith was assembling. At first he was assigned to sales and customer service; then later put in charge of planning the central hub in Memphis where all of the packages collected throughout the system would be sorted each night.

Basch convinced a friend from his UPS days, Mike Fitzgerald (B.A., Northeastern) to join Federal Express. Fitzgerald, another of these handsome store-window barn-stormers, knew the small package distribution system well from his experience at UPS. He was 36 when he came to Little Rock to take over as head of sales and customer service.

S. Tucker Taylor (B.A., Yale) and Vince Fagan (B.A., Hofstra; M.S., New York University) closed their consulting firm, AAPG, and also an advertising agency they were running in New York in 1974 to come to Memphis to complete Smith's initial management team. Taylor and Art Bass had done much of the primary research work of the AAPG study Smith had commissioned in late 1971. And both Taylor and Fagan had done some advertising and promotion assignments for Smith in 1972 and 1973. They had intimate knowledge of what Smith hoped to accomplish in this package airline.

"Come to Federal Express and I'll pay you a salary," Smith told them. Chuckles Taylor, "We came down to Memphis in 1974 because Smith owed us so much money. That was the only way we were going to get it. There was a lot of macho there and that appealed to Vince and me. We had jock mentalities and we thought we'd be happier there than working for some conservative corporation. We didn't know what convertible bonds were in those days and we wore cheap suits." Taylor, then 34, was known as a free spirit. He admitted he knew very little about running a business. Smith viewed him as having a creative mind and assigned him to tough, demanding special corporate projects.

Vince Fagan admitted he surprised himself by joining Federal Express as senior vice president for marketing, a company which was by then headquartered in Memphis. Fagan was a native New Yorker who felt uncomfortable living anywhere else, and Memphis was not his idea of a cosmopolitan city. Fagan, then 38 when he joined the team, brought to Federal Express many years of experience in the advertising industry as well as significant contacts since a number of his clients had been aviation firms.

Smith needed good people willing to take risks like the ones these men were being asked to accept. These were the individuals who stepped forward. None had any extensive corporate managerial experience to contribute. They were mostly individuals with a strong entrepreneurial interest which Fred Smith was able to cultivate. Several thought the experience would be fun working in what Smith told them would be an atmosphere where they could be iconoclastic about existing traditions in the air freight industry.

What Smith had done with some skill was to bring together in one group air transportation talent and mix them with experienced, rough-and-ready ground trucking people. Of these early years of the company Art Bass remembers: "I am not sure of the ingredients that made a good cake, but the one that fell off the shelf was a good one. This assemblage of creative talent at the outset is what distinguished Federal Express from many contemporary companies."

Smith hired many people with extensive technical experience with airlines or with aircraft maintenance firms. The first pilots hired were often former military fliers, or corporate jet pilots who knew the operational qualities of the Falcons. There were far more job seekers for pilot positions than there were positions in the 1972 and 1973 period. Fred Smith consciously made an effort not to hire commercial airline pilots, because he said adamantly, "I don't want steely, blue-eyed executives with pilots' caps." He also knew he couldn't pay them going airline salaries.

Federal's Veterans Administration-approved Flight Training School started at Little Rock in October, 1972, to train pilots for the Falcons. The federal government paid most of the $8,800 tuition for the intensive two-week course, producing an excellent double benefit for Federal Express; on the one hand, Federal received a pool of pilots trained to fly the Falcons, and on the other hand, the company received a source of revenue badly needed in late 1972 and 1973. Over one year's time some 273 pilots were trained there. Federal gave up the program after a little over a year when it could no longer offer jobs to those graduating.

Managing the company efficiently proved to be difficult that first year, 1972. "Smith and his key people didn't know how to manage anything," says Irby Tedder smiling wanly, the company's original financial officer. "They all came in with a lot of wild ideas of how to put Federal Express together, and only a few of them made any sense. They were an impetuous bunch."

Early internal policy and administrative decisions were often hammered out in "knock down-drag out" meetings extending late into the night. Sixteen hour days were common. Bitter disputes would sometimes occur, and Smith would lose his temper. As Tedder remembers, "Fred would get real tense. Once in a while he'd throw something against the wall. So we would try to get him drunk at some bar, hoping it would relax him, and perhaps keep him away from the office the next day. But he'd come bouncing back early the next morning ready to take on the world again, and get back in the thick of everything going on."

Norman Timper, who had retired from United Airlines and who was used to the way things were done in operations there, would get very upset with Smith and his key aides because he felt they were devoting too much time to studies about how they could improve the cockpit instrument equipment in the Falcons. "Top management is too hard pressed to devote time to these evaluations," Timper pleaded with them. "These decisions should be handled by the Engineering Department."

The Accounting Department was a disaster area. There were no formalized, internal controls. Haphazard records caused reports to be late. Cash flow was hurt by the lag in billings. "Instead of concern about this serious problem, Fred would often worry about some minor office problem," reports one of the early accountants. "He was a real nitpicker in those days. He had his hand on everything."

Winning major contracts became the company's mission in the early part of 1972. Smith did not necessarily want to fly mail for the U. S. Postal Service, but he realized Federal Express needed to develop credibility if it were to sell the priority small package airline concept. The company also needed cash flow during this interim, buildup period. Federal Express was low bidder on six mail routes. Smith shaved the bids as low as he could to win these contracts. "We low-balled them in order to win these routes," Watson confessed. "Fred cut the bids under what his close associates recommended. He really wanted these contracts." Mail service to routes, primarily in the Midwest, started on July 10, 1972, under three-year contracts providing for service five nights a week.

The charter air cargo service for industrial clients began unofficially on June 30, 1972. The CAB had not yet ruled on the petition to change Part 298 to permit up to a 7,500 pound payload for air taxi operators, so Federal Express could not legally charge for any freight service.

As a result of the company's selling efforts in Ypsilanti, Michigan, Ford Motor Company agreed to try Federal Express by asking it to fly a shipment of auto parts from Ypsilanti to Kansas City. Legally, Federal Express could not accept this order because the CAB petition was still pending. So rather than lose Ford as a prospective customer, Fred Smith personally picked up the load and flew it free. Ford wanted Federal Express to bill it, but Smith refused to do so. As much as he may have wanted to, he could not legally bill them.

The charter sales approach was to tell prospects Federal Express, rather than offering the customer set schedules and routes, could offer them a service custom tailored to their needs. During the 1972 charter cargo period, however, Federal Express offered no ground delivery service of its own. Instead, it contracted with local drayage firms to perform this task.

The mission of the sales force in 1972 was to sell Federal's service to large industrial shippers. Smith decided to convert his Arkansas Aviation Sales corporate jet salesmen into freight salesmen. This proved to be a mistake. "They were a flamboyant, unruly group who found it difficult to identify with the problem of selling charter freight services," recalls Bill Arthur, a former marketing director. "They were used to selling million dollar aircraft and living it up on big expense accounts. They were out of their element."

Even so, Smith had anticipated initial losses in 1972. The profit picture finally looked like this: the three original profit centers — air mail, charter cargo and pilot training — yielded $2.8 million in 1972. Just over half came from the Postal Service contracts. Total expenses for that year were just over $3.7 million in 1972, so that the actual operating loss was $927,845. The total debt, on the other hand, at the end of 1972, was $21.7 million. But Smith and his staff felt 1973 would yield far better results.

At the beginning of 1973, Smith bought Little Rock Airmotive, Inc. — a firm often referred to as "LRA". LRA had been Federal's prime contractor for performing modification work on the Falcons which included installation of the cargo doors, revamping the cargo interior, installing the avionics, and painting the exterior the distinctive eye-catching purple, orange and white with "FEDERAL EXPRESS" spelled out boldly across the length of the planes. When Smith's first Falcons arrived in Little Rock in 1971, this firm was given the tough job of finding ways to reduce the bulk weight of the Falcon 20 while leaving the plane's operational efficiency intact. As passenger aircraft, the Falcon's door was only 59 inches wide and 31½ inches high. In order to be able to ship bulky items like mainframe computers and palletized loads, which helped speed the turnaround time to load and unload the Falcons, a much larger door measuring 60 inches wide and 74 inches high was installed by LRA. LRA clearly had a major modification project in hand.

Smith paid $2.5 million for LRA, even though at the time of the sale to Federal Express it had a net worth of only $1.2 million. Why was it, then, that Smith agreed to pay substantially more for this firm? Nearly $1.3 million more? The reason was that LRA was going bankrupt, because its major customer, Federal Express, had not paid for the extensive modification work on the Falcons. Smith announced the acquisition was a perfect adjunct to Federal's business. Now it could perform all its own modification work on the remaining Falcons to be delivered, plus undertake general corporate aircraft customizing for clients beyond the company as an additional source of income. Smith borrowed the money for the acquisition from the same Worthen Bank in Little Rock which had lent him the money to purchase some of the Falcons.

Stephens, Inc., a diversified and powerful Arkansas-based investment banking firm and the parent organization of LRA, was very
concerned about the huge debt Federal Express had run up. "We
had Jack Stephens over a barrel," muses Frank Watson. "He had to
sell LRA to us or see it go bankrupt. In effect, with the Worthen
Bank loan, we wiped out our obligation, and eliminated the possibility of a severe drain on our cash flow. We played a lot of hardball with the people to whom we owed money in those days to
stay alive."

Equally important, this acquisition gave Federal complete control
over the modification of the remaining Falcons, and it provided the
company with a modern fully-equipped hanger at Adams Field in
Little Rock for its own maintenance center, its flight school and
office space.

Early in 1973, Federal Express shifted its base of flight operations from Little Rock to Memphis. The city of Little Rock had
been asked to construct various physical improvements at Adams
Field to accommodate the company. At the same time, the Memphis
and Shelby County Airport Authority had agreed to lease Federal
Express hangar facilities and to provide bond funds for renovating
hangars, building an administrative building and a cargo sort building. Memphis had a large modern airport with an aggressive management interested in promoting additional revenue generating
activities.

Smith gave Little Rock the opportunity to match this attractive
offer from Memphis. This was a sensitive matter. Congressman
Wilbur Mills who had helped Smith was unhappy about Federal's
plan to leave Little Rock because the company was providing badly
needed jobs. Mills tried to persuade Little Rock public agencies to
spend the funds to improve Adams Field, but they showed no
interest. Mills later told me in his Washington law office he realized
why Federal chose Memphis and held no animosity toward it.

Work started in January, 1973, and by early March a system
capable of handling 10,000 packages per hour was completed. This
early hub was a primitive structure by later standards, but at least
it was capable of helping Federal Express get started in its small
package service.

March 12, 1973, was selected as the inaugural night of service.
The operational test took place in an 11-city network extending
from Dallas on the west to Jacksonville and Atlanta on the east.
Kansas City, St. Louis and Cincinnati were the northernmost cities
in this initial system. Reports from the salesmen in the field the
afternoon of March 12 were very optimistic.

That night Federal Express employees and their families gathered
near the sorting facilities looking up into the midnight sky waiting
for the Falcons to come in. Henry W. "Brick" Meers, representing

White, Weld & Company — the investment banking firm — was there to observe the results of the first night of service. "I saw the anguish on their faces as they waited," reminisces Meers. "Most were very worried about their future. It was a critical moment for all of them as they finally crowded around the Falcons and the cargo doors opened. But as they gazed inside, there was bitter disappointment. There were only six packages and one of them was a birthday present Fred Smith sent to his close aide, Irby Tedder."

In looking back on that disappointing night, Mike Fitzgerald who was in charge of the field sales force lamented, "We realized then that we didn't have enough cities and people hadn't heard of us. This introduction was a bust."

The March 12th disappointment forced the company to go back and re-structure its network. Art Bass and Bill Arthur of the market planning group, and Charles Brandon, who had just recently joined Federal Express to head the operations research program, locked themselves in a room at the Union Bank in Little Rock where Smith still had his office. Here without benefit of computer assistance — Federal Express still could not afford to lease such assistance — they rebuilt the distribution network.

On the second try, the night of April 17th, the network had been expanded to a 25-city system and the plan was to add four additional cities every two weeks for the next several months. The northernmost point in the April, 1973, network was Rochester, New York; and the southernmost point, Miami. Dallas and Kansas City were geographic limits of service to the west of Memphis.

During the late afternoon of April 17th, the projected package count called in to Mike Fitzgerald from the field stations was 163. Actually, when the cargo doors opened there were 186 packages. There was an air of optimism that night. An internal memorandum circulated to employees the next day announcing proudly, "We are launched!" The horrible memory of the night of March 12th had been erased. Not only does Federal Express never mention publicly this fatal night but also the public relations staff has always claimed April 17, 1973, as the night Federal Express started operations. The image makers would never again admit Federal Express had ever known such an initial failure. To do so might make Federal Express seem a less heroic venture than it was, might make it seem a more human one.

The May, 1973, nightly package count averaged 473, but in the later part of July the nightly count moved over the 1,000 mark. And by October, 1973, the month just prior to the $52 million credit agreement, the nightly average was 2,517.

The program of matching Falcon flight schedules with loads kept planners busy each night revising route patterns. The market research staff tested package counts for the various cities with the data produced by their package forecasting models to check their accuracy.

The period May to October, 1973, was one of trial and error as workable systems for handling packages, for billing and for attracting business were developed. Federal's operation seemed to be consciously patterned after that of the United Parcel Service. The price schedules, the report forms and even the selling techniques were the same initially. Even the conservative dress code and "no beard" policy of UPS for sales people and executives were implemented by the company. Federal had hired many UPS people in the beginning, and they brought the UPS system with them.

Reflecting on these days some Federal Express veterans have admitted they placed too much reliance on the UPS techniques. "We didn't have much time to experiment on our own," says one veteran. "We were trying to survive the best we could. And UPS was the best at handling small packages on the ground."

Getting Federal Express known to the business public, and converting prospects into sales, was a hard struggle during the summer and early fall, 1973. On August 1, 1973 — after almost three and one-half months of operations — the daily package count was only 112 for New York, 91 for Chicago, 52 for Philadelphia, 19 for St. Louis, 13 for Detroit, and 9 for Denver. The company was still unknown.

In September, 1973, Ted Sartoian, a former UPS salesman, was brought in to head the sales force, replacing Bill Lackey whose experience had been as a corporate jet salesman. Almost immediately Sartoian introduced the approach used by UPS successfully, team selling. He led sales teams of eight persons into different cities to contact in a one or two week period all the big shippers in those cities. It was a quick-hitting, saturation campaign designed to get immediate results.

Sartoian, a colorful and enthusiastic, energetic motivator, fired up his salesmen with such statements: "The name of the game is packages, boxes and bundles and service," or "Get the Elephants, the rabbits will come automatically." Of course, the slogans were trite, but they were standard motivational fare for those doing direct selling.

In late 1973, Federal Express, after much experimentation with its sales promotion program, concluded that its backbone accounts should be those industrial customers who could not afford to duplicate inventories in warehouses located all over the country. Company planners realized perhaps they should have been trying to attract the same type of customers as Emery Air Freight instead of those using UPS. Emery had traditionally done a heavy volume of business with industrial customers. UPS served a much different clientele and carried primarily consumer-oriented, non-priority-type parcels. Federal Express identified its target market as some 37,000 businesses and industries located in the 100 leading U. S. metropolitan markets, markets which were then accounting for 84 percent of all domestic air shipments.

Chapter 7

The Jackals of Wall Street

Financing Federal Express did not seem to be an insurmountable hurdle to Fred Smith when he started acquiring Falcon 20 fan jets from Pan American. Local banks readily provided him with interim financing in the Spring, 1972, and CCEC, the Baltimore-based finance company, had made a 10-year loan on his initial fleet of ten Falcons. But to succeed in assembling the entire Falcon fleet of 33 planes and ground support equipment and operating funds, Smith needed equity capital. Enterprise Company, the family's private trust, had the resources to invest heavily in Federal Express, but not nearly to the extent of the total equity required by the venture. Smith needed to raise considerable equity funds and long term loans.

From the date the CCEC loan for $13.8 million was made, July 7, 1972, until November 13, 1973, when the $52 million financing package was signed, Fred Smith's enormous energy was almost totally consumed trying to get commitments from groups of venture capitalists and lenders. At the same time, Smith held at bay a legion of creditors demanding payment and threatening foreclosure, or its equivalent — confiscating the Falcons.

When asked to describe this period by attorneys representing his two half-sisters, Fredette and Laura, in a 1976 deposition hearing in Memphis, Fred Smith fired back: "No man on this Earth will ever know what I went through during that year, and I am lucky I remember my name much less the details that you are trying to ask me. With the trauma that year, the pressure

"Nine days of ceaseless rain for one day of fine weather! Really the sky above must be a pitiless thing. My shoes are in pieces, the muddy road soils my feet, but, however, it is done, I have to keep on moving."
—Ho Chi Minh, *Prison Diary*

was so great on me, and there were so many events that went on, and so much travel and so many meetings with investment bankers, General Dynamics, and a hundred different people who came down to Memphis, I just don't recall specifics of virtually anything during that period of time, in addition to trying to run a company at the same time."

Fred Smith had made some preliminary contacts in November, 1971, with White, Weld & Company, the old and established investment banking firm based in New York and Chicago. He was introduced to several partners by Buck Remmell — the officer in White, Weld who had been introduced to Smith by a mutual friend in Little Rock.

White, Weld, part of the establishment in investment banking, was a leader in managing corporate underwritings and in securing private placements for companies seeking capital. White, Weld was the firm, for example, which had arranged a number of private placements for Jim Ling in the late-1950s when this well-known Texas industrial entrepreneur was putting together Ling Electronics.

Smith kept in close touch with White, Weld during the spring, 1972. Progress reports were sent to them by Smith's research consultants, A. T. Kearney and AAPG. "Third party opinions greatly soothed the trepidations of venture capitalists," Smith had been told by White, Weld officers. According to Smith, White, Weld senior officers were extremely enthusiastic about this proposed small package airline and expressed an interest in helping to raise sufficient capital to start the company. In September, 1972, White, Weld wrote Fred Smith outlining the steps necessary for them to secure the financing. The plan called for Smith, or the family's Enterprise Company, to invest $3,250,000 of their own funds.

White, Weld had become very serious about Federal Express in late 1972. It sent Homer Rees, one of its key people, to Little Rock for an extended period so he could assemble the operational and financial details of the company, and examine Federal's corporate plan. This information was needed to include in an offering brochure to be circulated among a group of potential investors White, Weld felt might be interested in Federal Express. This was to be a private placement which meant White, Weld did not have to register the securities with the Securities and Exchange Commission. The resultant offering brochure contained this encouraging statement: "Starting in 1974, Federal Express expects to begin generating substantial surpluses." But at the end of January, 1973, Federal Express was absolutely broke. Smith later admitted all it would have taken then was "just a little push," and the company would have collapsed. White, Weld contacted Smith on February 2, 1973, to request that he put another $1.5 million equity into Federal Express. This amount — White, Weld told Smith — was needed to trigger the deal. Up to that point, Federal Express had a paid-in capital of $3,250,000. With this additional equity, the figure then would be $4,750,000. The company desperately needed another cash injection, and Smith knew if he did not come forward with more money then Federal Express was out of business.

On February 5, 1973 — three days prior to Smith's signing the agreement with White, Weld — Smith borrowed $2 million from Union Bank in Little Rock. To authorize the loan, he gave the bank a copy of a resolution of the Enterprise Company board signed by Memphis attorney Robert L. Cox, board secretary. The document certified that the debt would be secured by an assignment of a stock repurchase agreement between Fred Smith and the Frederick Smith Enterprise Company. It also certified that Fred Smith's financial statement reflected a net worth of $7.2 million.

On February 8, 1973, White, Weld and Smith signed an agreement. White, Weld agreed to try to place $16 million in equity securities and $4 million of 8½ percent second mortgage notes due in 1980, with warrants attached. The funds were to be used to support the permanent, long-term-debt financing necessary to acquire the Falcons plus provide the company with working capital. White, Weld agreed to use its "best efforts" to secure this private placement and they had optimistically expected to raise this $20 million by March or April, 1973.

Smith and his staff were now confident Federal Express would get the financial foundation they needed. Significantly, the White, Weld agreement to undertake the raising of $20 million also helped reassure several Little Rock and Memphis banks holding short term loans, or personal notes, from Fred Smith.

Later, it was discovered that not only was the resolution Smith had presented to the Union Bank on February 5, 1973, fictitious, but also that just an hour or so before he sat down with Union Bank officers to sign the loan papers, Smith had the document typed and then took it to his office upstairs at the Union Bank where he forged the signature of attorney Robert L. Cox. The details leading up to the loan came out in the federal trial in December, 1975, in Little Rock before the U. S. District Court for Eastern Arkansas. Smith was on trial there for violating Section 1014 of Title 18 of the United States Code for defrauding a bank by using false documents.

Prosecutor: "Were you pressured enough that you would do anything to get some money?"

Smith: "I wouldn't kill someone, no, sir."

Prosecutor: ". . . but you would submit a false and fictitious statement on a document to a bank to get it, wouldn't you?"

Smith: "I have never denied that . . . and that is correct, sir."

Smith was acquitted. His defense was that he had acted on behalf of Enterprise Company on previous occasions with the apparent approval of his sisters and other board members. He had a 38.5 percent beneficial interest in Enterprise, and at the time of the Union Bank loan he was president of the Enterprise board. Smith maintained he and Enterprise were virtually one and the same. And Smith insisted at his trial that the banker handling the loan knew he had signed Robert Cox's name to the Enterprise Company resolution.

With the $2 million loan Smith immediately bought $1.5 million in Federal Express stock as requested by White, Weld and used the balance to pay off some bank loans in Memphis and to cover several overdrafts. There can be no doubt that without the Union Bank loan Federal Express would have collapsed in early February, 1973.

Financial crises came with increasing speed, each hard on the heels of the next. By January, 1973, the agreement with Pan Am on the Falcons was also in default. Federal Express had negotiated a third delay on January 31, 1973, and had agreed to a penalty schedule to take effect in 60 days if it could not accept delivery of the Falcons on schedule. Until this revised agreement was struck, Smith feared Pan Am might sell the Falcons out from under Federal Express. This also would have sealed the company's doom. Replacement Falcons could neither have been found quickly, nor on such favorable terms as had been granted by Pan Am.

Smith continued his pursuit of short term loans in the first part of 1973 to meet the payroll and to keep Federal Express solvent. And once again, in the case of a $1 million short term loan from the First National Bank of Memphis, he had provided bank loan officers with a fictitious Enterprise board resolution as evidence of an Enterprise Company loan guarantee.

Fred Smith might have remembered the cartoon in his 1962 Memphis University School *Yearbook* which showed him stranded on a tropical island with a smashed propeller in his hands; nearby a plane is sinking in shark infested waters. Now, 11 years later, he was truly on that cartoonist's island awaiting his fate.

White, Weld had arranged for Fred Smith to make numerous presentations before venture capital groups all over the country. In March, 1973, Smith made at least a dozen presentations to solicit interest. Most listened attentively, then wrote Smith politely: "We 'pass' at this time." Prudential Insurance Company informed Smith: "When Federal Express reaches the point of seeking more traditional financing, do keep Prudential in mind." And Prudential ultimately became a major part of the Federal Express venture capital consortium.

Discouragement set in by April, 1973, when White, Weld was unable to attract enough interest among venture capital groups. The Dow-Jones Industrial Average had slid from near the 1,000 mark in January, 1973, to the lower 900 range in April. Venture capitalists as a group had been gun shy about new venture start-ups since the late 1960s.

Smith and his Memphis advisors were critical of White, Weld's efforts, because they thought White, Weld would be able to deliver without any difficulty. Charles Lea of New Court Securities faulted Smith for not understanding the difference in the financial meaning of the word "undertaking" and the word "commitment" as used by White, Weld. "They didn't guarantee to deliver $20 million as Smith believed," Lea said. "Fred should have known that a private placement is an agency transaction. White, Weld agreed to undertake a search for this capital. They couldn't commit to it." Smith was greatly distressed because White, Weld and others like Prudential had been so euphoric. Explained the disgusted Smith: "Everybody was saying this is the most classical gap in the market. This is the next Xerox. I don't think we thought it was speculative at all. We naively thought this was a sure thing."

At the end of April, 1973, Federal Express had a deficit of over $4.4 million. Total stockholders' equity had sunk to only $289,000. Most of what Fred Smith had personally invested, as well as what Enterprise Company had invested, was gone. Once again, the end appeared imminent.

It was during this dark period that Fred Smith received a telephone call from Henry W. "Brick" Meers, who was White, Weld's resident partner in Chicago as well as vice chairman, asking him to come to Chicago. Meers, then 65, was not only a leading investment banker, but also active throughout Chicago in many industrial and civic organizations; he was also a trustee of the University of Chicago. So when he told Smith he had arranged an appointment on Friday, May 4th, for the two of them to see the legendary industrialist and financier, Colonel Henry Crown, Smith realized this might be the last hope to keep Federal Express alive.

Henry Crown was then 77 years old, but still very active managing his enormous holdings of industrial and financial enterprises as well as his real estate interests, which included large investment positions in General Dynamics and in Hilton Hotels Corporation. Crown had been known for half a century as a shrewd, opportunistic entrepreneur. He had gotten his start in the rough and tumble sand and gravel business in Chicago, then moved on in later years to a variety of profitable investments. One of his biggest coups was buying a controlling interest in the Empire State Building in 1952 for $3 million, and then selling the building in 1961 for $65 million, free and clear of mortgages. At the time of Smith's meeting with Colonel Crown, Crown was the controlling stockholder of General Dynamics, a major industrial conglomerate with one major component being in the aerospace industry, and which in 1973 had sales over $1.6 billion.

Crown has been described as an "urbane, articulate, well-dressed and remarkably well-preserved" gentleman whose wealth was estimated to be well beyond the one billion dollar mark. This is the man who was once heard to remark, "Owing money has never concerned me, so long as I know where it could be repaid from."

When 28-year old Fred Smith and Brick Meers sat down with him, Crown listened to Smith's presentation and seemed genuinely interested in helping. There was a problem, however. Crown said his financial man was in the hospital recovering from a hernia operation, so he could not do anything until his aide reported back to work in a week or so. This was Crown's style. He had never been known for making quick deals. "Fast deals are for suckers," Crown once commented. One observer of the legendary Crown claimed, "When the Colonel gets into your deal, he knows the size of your underwear."

Time was of the essence to Smith. On May 15, 1973 — just 11 days hence — the option to purchase 18 Falcons plus 36 jet engines from Pan Am was to expire. Brick Meers called the hospital and asked the bedridden aide if it would be all right for Fred Smith and him to visit his hospital room that afternoon. So while the patient was flat on his back, Smith and Meers spent that afternoon and evening filling Crown's financial aide in on the details of the Federal Express proposal.

On Monday, May 7th, Crown arranged a meeting for the next day in his office. He asked General Dynamics' executive vice president for finance, Gorden E. MacDonald, and the corporation's general counsel to meet with Fred Smith and Brick Meers to work out the arrangements. This was the first of several meetings that week in Crown's office. Conference calls were arranged so that General Dynamics' chairman, David S. Lewis, could give his approval to the arrangements. During the discussions it was pointed out that the Section 408 provision of the CAB regulations might prevent General Dynamics from taking control of an air carrier. Colonel Crown responded, according to Smith, that he could accomplish anything he damn well pleased in Washington and that Section 408 was the least of his concerns. And in addition, Crown felt Fred Smith was too young and inexperienced to be heading Federal Express and he told Brick Meers in Smith's presence someone more experienced should be brought in. But Crown did not insist Smith step aside.

On May 12, 1973, General Dynamics and Federal Express signed an agreement providing for financial assistance. General Dynamics agreed to guarantee loans to Federal Express totaling $23.7 million. For this accommodation, General Dynamics was granted an option to acquire 80.1 percent of Federal Express stock for a price of $16 million. The agreement also provided that Federal Express was to repay the working capital loan and was to secure alternative financing for its aircraft to release General Dynamics as guarantor if the 80.1 percent option was not exercised. And in the event it did not exercise its option, six percent of Federal's stock would revert to General Dynamics as consideration for the loan guarantee.

In an awesome display of power, Henry Crown, in Smith's and Meer's presence, called a top official at the First National Bank of Chicago, and asked him to make the $23.7 million loan to Federal

Express. The bank officer agreed over the phone to do it. Crown had been a major customer of the bank since the 1920s and any request he made carried a lot of weight. But David Lewis said he preferred the loan be made through General Dynamics' own corporate bank, Chase Manhattan.

The short term loan came from the Chase; its due date was September 17, 1973 — a scant four months away. According to the agreement with General Dynamics, Federal Express was prohibited from converting 14 of the 18 Falcons covered by loan guarantee, pending final completion of Federal's financing program. Four of the Falcons had already been delivered to Little Rock Airmotive and were undergoing modification.

Chase Manhattan assigned one of its younger loan officers to check periodically to see that Federal Express would not attempt to convert the 14 Falcons in violation of the loan agreement. But "as soon as these planes were delivered 'green' — that is unmodified to serve as a cargo freighter — to Little Rock, Dick Yarmowich, one of Federal's key aircraft technicians, would go right down the line cutting holes in the fuselages to start the cargo door modification work," chuckles a veteran officer. "Dick was a real wild man with that torch. We needed these planes in the air soon." Notwithstanding these prohibitions, as far as Federal Express was concerned, the loan from Chase Manhattan was authorization to proceed rapidly with its total development program.

As Fred Smith remembers the restrictive terms of the agreement with General Dynamics achieved through Henry Crown's intervention: "There was nothing else I could do but to agree to give General Dynamics controlling interest. We were in the soup. I really didn't think it would exercise the option because of the CAB's regulations against air framers controlling airlines."

General Dynamics sent a 15-man technical team to Memphis on May 21, 1973; and for the next month these technicians put in some 3,056 man-hours examining every aspect of Federal Express. The team interviewed all of Smith's key people, examined the company's plans, and prepared "best case," "middle road," and "worst case" forecasts for their superiors at corporate headquarters in St. Louis. General Dynamics' engineers spent hundreds of man-hours testing the landing gear and the cargo handling capabilities and dozens of other physical and operational characteristics of the Falcon aircraft. This testing was vital to Federal's success in raising venture capital, because investors insisted on having this technical detail before committing themselves one way or the other.

On July 12, 1973, the report was completed and copies sent to General Dynamics' chairman, David Lewis, and to Gorden MacDonald. The conclusions were generally favorable. The General Dynamics project team reported that Federal Express had achieved some excellent results for such a new company. It was impressed with

Federal's ability to respond quickly to problems and to react to opportunities. And financially, the team expected Federal Express to be a profitable operation in fiscal year 1974.

Even though the General Dynamics option to acquire Federal Express had technically expired on July 16, 1973, three days later, on July 19th, the General Dynamics board of directors — largely through the influence of its outside directors — turned down for the second time the opportunity to purchase Federal Express.

This was a setback for both David Lewis as well as Fred Smith. Lewis had recommended to his board favorable action, because he liked the Federal Express venture and wanted it to be part of General Dynamics. He had several sons Smith's age and discovered they had a lot in common. They were both Episcopalians, Democrats, and Southerners, though Lewis was a native of South Carolina. He genuinely like Fred.

General Dynamics gave several reasons for the board's negative decision. First, it was worried about Section 408 which required any person or organization with a controlling interest in an air carrier be subject to CAB approval. Secondly, General Dynamics had just reopened its Quincy Shipyard in Massachusetts, and had imposed financial restraints on itself due to previous losses with that operation. Brick Meers observed, "General Dynamics' plate was full. They had too many other worries on their minds. And several of David Lewis' key people wanted to get rid of that 'tar baby' called Federal Express."

But General Dynamics did not totally abandon Federal Express. It agreed to continue as guarantor on the Chase loan. And later, in order to mollify Worthen Bank, on August 28, 1973, General Dynamics agreed to purchase one Falcon for $1,550,000 and then lease it back to Federal Express. As a result, the Worthen Bank in Little Rock temporarily cancelled its threat to call its loan on Federal Express, an action which probably would have caused a shutdown of operations.

When Fred Smith left the final General Dynamics board meeting on July 19, he was very discouraged. He told Jessica Savitch of NBC News in an interview: "I was in Chicago when I was turned down for the umpteenth time from a source I was sure would come through. I went to the airport to go back to Memphis, and saw on the TWA schedule a flight to Las Vegas. I won $27,000 starting with just a couple of hundred and sent it back to Memphis. The $27,000 wasn't decisive, but it was an omen that things would get better." In those days, even Fred Smith the former financial golden boy, needed an omen in the face of what must have seemed to him to be an irrational universe.

On July 23, 1973, another attempt was made to find a source of capital. Brick Meers and Gorden MacDonald contacted New Court Securities Corporation, a New York-based investment banking and venture capital firm organized in 1967 by the European-based Rothschild international banking dynasty. This was the second time in 1973 New Court Securities became part of the drama. In March, 1973, New Court had received a copy of the White, Weld private placement offering. Charles Lea, then executive vice president of New Court, and his colleague Richard H. Stowe, went to Memphis to see the Federal Express operation first hand. Lea was again in Memphis on the night of April 17, 1973, and was a witness at the sorting hub when the Federal Express planes brought in a combined yield of only 183 packages. This meager yield was a sobering sight for Lea. "We didn't think Federal Express was living up to its plan, and we lost interest," Lea explained when he told Brick Meers and the other White, Weld people New Court was not interested in pursuing the Federal Express matter further.

But New Court changed its mind in July and agreed to co-manage the search for capital with White, Weld. By that time both New Court and White, Weld felt Federal Express was coming closer to its volume forecasts and its prospects were more promising. There was also an indication Prudential would invest $5 million and that General Dynamics would also put up $5 million. If these two sources came through, then the goal at that time was to raise another $10 million.

Prudential's interest was a surprise on two points. First, it was rare for Prudential to put an amount as large as $5 million into a venture capital deal. And secondly, just a few months earlier it had written Fred Smith that it was not interested in being a participant. But here was another instance where Wilbur Mills had come to Fred Smith's rescue. Mills, when I asked him about his role, replied: "Sure, I knew the people at Prudential, and I called them on Fred's behalf." It was also Mills who had called Henry Crown earlier to put in a good word for Smith.

General Dynamics still wanted to help Smith, and the $5 million commitment did not put it in conflict with Section 408. As long as it had no controlling interest in Federal Express, it did not need CAB approval.

"After Brick Meers and Gorden MacDonald called New Court in July, we jumped on the assignment immediately," recalls Lea. "Rick Stowe along with Brick Meers of White, Weld called everybody they knew. They had calls out to the venture capital groups at Citicorp, Bank of America, First National Bank of Chicago, Prudential and a whole bunch of venture capital fellows like Allstate's Dave Seidman, Ned Heizer in Chicago, Phil Greer in San Francisco and a whole lot more."

Those showing an interest were invited to come to Memphis one week later for a formal presentation by Federal Express, and by the General Dynamics project staff who had just recently completed the full scale feasibility study of Federal Express. This meeting was followed by a bigger one in St. Louis at General Dynamics. While these presentations were impressive to the potential investors in attendance, several were very concerned Federal Express might not survive until the financial package could be put together by White, Weld and New Court.

Heavy losses continued through the summer months and the early fall: Fred Smith and the family-owned Enterprise company had seen their investments vanish. By September 30, 1973, the deficit had reached $7.8 million. By that date liabilities exceeded $46.7 million. Federal Express was just barely alive, and living from day-to-day.

Lenders grew very nervous. Chase Manhattan Bank wanted to get out of its loan even before the due date. By September 14, 1973, the $23.7 million Chase loan was in default, and by that point several major loans from Memphis and Little Rock banks were also in default. Moreover, Federal's working capital loan from General Dynamics was past due. To say that things looked very bleak for Federal Express in September would be classic understatement. Lenders had good reason to be seriously concerned about their loans.

The most nervous lender of all was Worthen Bank in Little Rock. It had loaned Federal Express nearly $8.7 million, and the loans were all due on October 31, 1973. The Bank's loan limit was $2.5 million so it had syndicated out parts of its loans to several small town Arkansas banks. Almost weekly Worthen Bank would send Pete Maris, a young loan officer, to Memphis to talk with Fred Smith and try to encourage him to reduce the outstanding balance. "He didn't pay any attention to us," recalls Maris. "There really wasn't anything he could do until the company got its permanent financing and the equity funds New Court and White, Weld were trying to raise."

Smith was able to convince Worthen that if it foreclosed, it faced several years of litigation, plus its action would cause the total collapse of Federal Express. "It was a close call," Federal's Irby Tedder told me. "Every time Worthen's people came around, word was passed to keep the Falcons from landing. If they had chained the planes that would have been the end of Federal Express."

Delays in the arrangement of the financing package were causing turmoil. There were mounting vendor suits against the company. Accounts receivable from suppliers exceeded $3.6 million at the end of September and, to make matters worse, the State of Arkansas was pressuring the company for sales and use taxes it claimed were owed it. Creditors were literally everywhere.

The company was having trouble meeting its payroll. In a memorandum dated September 14, 1973, from Fred Smith and Roger Frock to Federal's employees, was the following request: "With the most profound regret, we would like to request from each of you that you do not cash or deposit your payroll check until next

Monday, September 17, at the very earliest."

Federal Express was not only in danger of losing its planes but, if payroll funds were not forthcoming, possibly its employees as well. One memorandum, dated August 20, 1973, had been sent to employees telling them permanent financing should be completed by the first week in September. Another memorandum, dated September 24, 1973, told them the closing was scheduled for no later than October 15.

If the company were to go bankrupt, Fred Smith and the Enterprise Company stood to lose $7.9 million. Fred Smith had invested $2.5 million and the Enterprise company $2,250,000. In addition, Enterprise company had guaranteed $3,150,000 of Federal Express indebtedness.

Federal Express hung by one of those proverbial threads as Brick Meers, Charley Lea and Rick Stowe tried to hold together the venture capital group they had assembled, and to solve major concerns of the lender group. There were 23 venture partners lined up in October, 1973, pledging a total of $23 million. New Court Securities and the investments groups it represented were committed to just under $3.3 million. There were two groups pledging $2 million each — the venture capital arm of Allstate Insurance and the Heizer Corporation. The rest of the equity participants, including two bank SBIC venture capital groups, pledged smaller amounts.

E. F. "Ned" Heizer, who headed a venture capital firm located in Chicago, vacillated in October. "First Ned was in; then he was out; then he was back in again," said Rick Stowe. The Arab oil crisis made Heizer nervous, as it did several others of those whom New Court had lined up. The Arab nations told the world on October 19, 1973, they were going to cut off oil exports to force a change in the Middle East policy of the United States. They were upset about the pro-Israeli policy of the United States and about our sale of arms to Israel.

Heizer's commitment of $2 million was a particularly large one for a non-institutional venture capital group in 1973. The plunging stock market and the debacle among ill-conceived high technology and service ventures in the period after 1969, had scared off most venture capitalists. Heizer's concern was probably justified. One of the venture capitalists said of Heizer, "Ned is a stubborn German. It's difficult to get him to change his mind. He's tough, and at times, irrascible."

Meers, Lea and Stowe were on the telephone continually in New York, or in Chicago, or in Memphis trying to keep the venture capital group together and to hold on to the $23 million it had pledged.

A venture capital unit of a small Chicago insurance company backed out, but despite all of the concerns brought forth by the various equity participants, this was the only group to withdraw.

In late October, 1973, Chase Manhattan disrupted the credit financing plan. It did not want to make the loan to Federal Express unless General Dynamics agreed to maintain the $23.7 million loan guarantee it had made with the Chase on the 18 Falcons. General Dynamics, however, was hesitant. General Dynamics; White, Weld; and New Court tried to persuade the Chase, the First National Bank of Chicago and the other banks in the lender group to make the loan to Federal Express without the General Dynamics guarantee, but with no success. Without the General Dynamics guarantee the credit rating on the loan went from a prime status to a very hazardous one. Chase Manhattan wanted to syndicate the loan among entirely different lending groups, and agreed to only a $4 million share. Meers and Lea considered this switch in direction by the Chase to be very unsatisfactory and to jeopardize the whole credit plan.

Consequently, in the first week in October, 1973, the credit agreement had stalled. On Friday, October 26th, Fred Smith made a final appeal to David Lewis of General Dynamics to break this impasse. In an impassioned, apparently handwritten letter, Smith told him that Lewis had in his hands the decision which would determine once and for all whether Federal Express would continue to exist or whether next Monday morning would bring "a catastrophic failure." Smith mentioned that many people were responsible for the position Federal Express was in, and that General Dynamics shared in that responsibility. The distraught Smith told Lewis he could be reached by phone Saturday morning at the Union Planters Bank in Memphis and, if necessary, could be in St. Louis on two hours notice.

Meanwhile in Chicago, Brick Meers called A. Robert Abboud, then vice chairman of the First National Bank of Chicago, to tell him about the dilemma with the Chase and that the whole deal to finance Federal Express was about to collapse. Abboud asked Meers if he could call him back because he wanted to talk to his loan officers. Meers replied to Abboud: "You'll get the whole horrible story from them, not only the fact that the General Dynamics loan guarantee was being eliminated, but also the facts on the performance of Federal Express." When Abboud called Brick Meers back, Abboud groaned: "The story on Federal Express was much worse than you described it. . . . How much money do you want?" Meers told him: "We need $10 million which we'll use to try to get the Chase to match your $10 million, giving us a total of $20 million." Abboud asked Meers if he would stay on top of the situation, and Meers promised he would. Abboud finally announced: "O.K. you've got it." Meers was to remember this decision as one of the most courageous moments in this long and debilitating process.

Yet Abboud's help did not finally resolve the impasse. The Chase insisted that Smith or the Enterprise Company come up with an additional $4 million investment to make the deal go. Smith called a meeting of the Enterprise board in Memphis on November 6th and got it to approve an equity contribution of $1.5 million and a loan of $2.5 million secured by a second mortgage of the Falcons and other company assets. William L. Richmond, board member of Enterprise representing the National Bank of Commerce in Memphis, commented: "Enterprise stood to lose $5.4 million if Federal Express closed its doors. We had a tiger by the tail and we could not let it go at this point."

To resolve this conflict with the major banks, CCEC agreed to give up its $2 million collateralization request of the Enterprise Company on its loan on the 10 Falcons. And it was also agreed that two Memphis bank loans could be paid off with the proceeds of the permanent financing.

As a result of this further investment, Enterprise Company's commitment to Federal Express was now up to $6,250,000. Including Fred Smith's own personal investment of $2.5 million, the total family involvement was thus, $8,750,000.

The $1.5 million equity contribution from Enterprise brought the venture capitalists' share to $24.5 million. One half of each of the venture partners, investment was represented by shares of convertible preferred stock; and the other half by subordinated promissory notes due October 1, 1981.

The long term loan funds were primarily from the Chase Manhattan Bank, the First National Bank of Chicago and a group of regional banks. Out of this pool of $27.5 million, Federal Express was given a primary revolving credit sum of $20 million to use. A major portion of the loan was secured by a chattel mortgage on 23 Falcons. The credit agreement excepted the other 10 Falcons in the company's fleet, which were security for Federal's indebtedness to CCEC. The agreement also excepted the stock of Little Rock Airmotive which was security for the indebtedness owed to Worthen Bank. The $2.5 million subordinated term loan of Enterprise Company was subject to the prior interest of the bank lenders, the group which had first claim to the 23 Falcons in case of loan default.

According to the credit agreement, the secondary revolving credit sum of $5 million could not be taken by the company until the first $22.5 million of the $27.5 million loan was fully utilized. The credit agreement stipulated that the $5 million loan could be triggered only if Federal Express were in compliance with the financial covenants contained in the credit agreement. This meant Federal Express would not obtain all of the $27.5 million at once. It had to comply with the strict terms of the credit agreement to get the total $27.5 million loan proceeds. To make this possible Federal had to become profitable ahead of the original company timetable. This stipulation may have been designed to motivate the company, but as things turned out it was not only unrealistic but also it was oppressive.

The final signing ceremony for the credit agreement took place on Tuesday, November 13, 1973, in the offices of the special counsel to the investors, Cravath, Swaine and Moore at One Chase Manhattan Plaza in New York. The dominant headline in the *New York Times* Business/Economic Section that morning was: "Gasoline Rationing Hinted for January 1." The previous day the Dow-Jones Industrial Average was off 10.76 points, and closed at 897.65 in response to the widening energy crisis.

The meeting began at 10:00 a.m. and lasted 5 hours and 55 minutes during which time at least 75 persons moved in and out of the room. "Nothing eventful happened," remembers Brick Meers. "There were lawyers running around the room trying to clean up all of the defaults and get everybody paid off. It was really anticlimactic to what had been going on since early February." One of the bank representatives, however, had a negative reaction to the whole affair. He said ruefully: "It was disgusting. Most of those financial people in that room didn't give a damn about Federal Express. They wanted their money; or they wanted to position themselves to suck some blood out of the victim — Federal Express."

Finally at 3:55 p.m. it was over. He had persevered. Federal Express would survive. Frederick Wallace Smith would be known as a captain of industry, a model of success, a hero. But it had been close.

A day or two later Fred Smith received a letter from New Court Securities with this compliment: "We believe if you are as successful in developing Federal Express as you were in convincing half the venture capitalists in America, we will all get very rich."

In December, 1973, Federal Express issued bonus checks to all employees ranging from $15 to $100. Fred Smith attached a note which said memorably: "Rome wasn't built in a day. Possibly it could have been if Federal Express employees were in charge." The company announced a wage increase effective January 1, 1974, and it promised there would be no layoffs.

The early 1970s were not an optimistic period for venture capital undertakings. Investors with funds ordinarily were not interested in taking the plunge into the unknown when the so called "blue chip" stocks were selling at price-earnings ratios of four, or five, or six. How then did Federal Express defy the odds and succeed in attracting interest from a broad spectrum of investors and lenders? Those involved in putting the Federal Express financing together felt Federal Express' concept was exciting to equity investors. Simply put investors liked what they saw, and they were often spellbound with Fred Smith's dramatization of what could lie ahead for Federal Express. He convinced them that a large, previously untapped market lay out there waiting for his Federal Express to mine it.

In agreeing to finance Federal Express, the venture capitalists involved bypassed several of the principal requirements it is ordinarily said should be satisfied before funds are invested. One was that the potential must exist for an unusually large payoff within a couple of years at most. Two others were that there be quality management, and that the entrepreneurial team assembled be proven winners. Paradoxically, at the time of the decision none of these conditions existed.

"Maybe these investors in an outfit like Federal Express were attempting one last gasp in 1973 before everything went down the drain in the American economy," chuckled Art Bass when asked why. He adds, "It was the Snoopy and the Red Baron mentality of the lenders. They felt they were doing a very heroic thing in financing Federal Express."

Chapter 8

Please Don't Shoot The Piano Player, He's the Only One We've Got

The credit agreement signed on November 13, 1973, provided $52 million, but after all the previous creditors were paid off that day, Federal Express was practically out of operating funds. Survival depended on quickly gaining a strong foothold in the market. As a result emphasis had to be placed on marketing and sales to get the package volume and to get the cash flow to cover mounting expenses. Monthly revenues were falling far short of what had been projected in the company's business plan for fiscal year 1974, beginning on June 1, 1973, and ending May 31, 1974. Barring a miracle it seemed certain there would be a huge loss this first half of the operating year ending November 30, 1973.

But raising sales volume and revenues was not the only problem. A new threat to Federal Express came in the form of an announcement from the federal government that effective November 1, 1973, airlines were to receive a fuel allotment on the basis of their 1972 consumption levels. Since Federal Express did not start operating on a daily basis until April 17, 1973, there would be no benchmark available to determine what volume the company should be given. With a characteristic blitzkreig, Fred Smith and his assistants swarmed on the newly-created Energy Policy Office of the Department of the Interior in Washington to plead for special consideration.

"Prudence is a rich, ugly old maid courted by incapacity."
—William Blake,
The Marriage of Heaven and Hell,
1793

Smith's luck held again. Using his characteristic dogged determination, he and his associates literally camped in the Energy Policy Office's headquarters in Washington until they agreed to grant Federal Express relief. The outcome of this petitioning was that Federal Express was granted a fuel allotment of 40.9 million gallons, an amount which turned out to be far in excess of its actual need. Once more Federal Express had badly miscalculated, and the FEA's generous allotment raised the eyebrows of many in the airline industry. Here, they said, was a company getting special consideration which after eight months of operation had taken in only $2.4 million in revenues. It was not until the late 1970s, after Federal Express had assembled its initial fleet of Boeing 727s, that it would consume this quantity of fuel annually.

While Federal was fighting for survival, it was being subjected to what it considered harassment by Executive Jet Aviation (EJA), an Ohio-based air taxi operator. Through its chief executive officer, Washington attorney Bruce G. Sundlun, EJA complained to the Civil Aeronautics Board that General Dynamics had unlawfully gained control of Federal Express without the CAB's approval. The charge was that General Dynamics' guarantee of the $23.7 million loan by Chase Manhattan Bank on the 18 Falcons was a violation of Section 408 of the CAB's economic regulations. EJA feared that Federal Express — through its connection with General Dynamics — had as its real purpose to get into the executive jet business, not the express mail package business as Federal claimed.

In response to EJA's charges, Federal Express informed the CAB that it had kept the agency informed of the list of investors, and that it had complied with all of the CAB's regulations. It emphasized the EJA's demand for the divestiture of General Dynamics' interest in Federal was a brazen attempt by one air taxi operator, EJA, to eliminate a potential competitor, Federal Express. General Dynamics in March, 1974, held only 8.8 percent of the voting shares in Federal, while in September, 1974, its total shares represented only a 4.9 percent interest in the venture.

Petitions by Executive Jet Aviation and responses by Federal Express flew back and forth; and, when CAB Docket No. 25953 was closed in March, 1979, there had been 34 documents submitted to the CAB by the two parties. EJA's action was considered pure harassment by Federal Express, but, in fact, it had not been harmed by EJA in any way.

Cash flow continued to be the most serious problem in early 1974. Accounts receivable were increasing inordinately in relation to Federal's collections. The "turn," that is to say the time lapse between the service rendered to the customer and the date payment was received, was 54 days — an extraordinarily long time for a company desperately needing funds. Smith explained: "All the packages in the world aren't going to do us any good if we don't get paid. Like most companies, we just wanted to get sales. We weren't spending much time tracking accounts. We didn't know exactly what was owed us." Federal Express had solved the complex transportation logistics problems in moving a package overnight between Point A and Point B via Memphis, but it could not solve its paperwork problems.

Some competitors seized the opportunity to discredit Federal Express by sending to air express shippers copies of uncomplimentary reports, or articles, which reported on Federal's losses. Robert G. Brazier, president of Airborne Freight, circulated a memorandum which scornfully said: "Mr. Smith has an expensive toy in Federal Express. Let's concentrate on Emery. They should be around longer." But even so, John Emery himself was generally complimentary. He said that, considering the declining service of the scheduled commercial airlines, Federal's market timing was good. He could afford to be generous in 1974 since Emery Air Freight was the giant of the industry and therefore it did not worry too much about the small, infant company in Memphis.

The January, 1974, loss was some $12,000 more than the revenue taken in. The financial situation was not much different in February. Federal Express was practically out of money. It needed additional capital quickly. Package volume was growing, but not fast enough to provide any positive cash flow. Ultimately, the company would have to wait 17 more months before monthly revenues exceeded monthly expenses.

Cash for payrolls was short, and some employees complained about the delays in receiving their payroll checks. A disgruntled courier in Kansas City to whom the company owed $300 held his station manager hostage one afternoon. The courier telephoned Memphis to talk with Mike Fitzgerald, head of field operations, and screamed: "Fitzgerald, I'm going to blow his head off and shit in the hole, if you don't pay me what you owe me." After several hours of scrambling around trying to find someone in Memphis to find the funds, the money was dispatched to Kansas City to pay the courier.

The company had one of its employees act as an ombudsman and his assignment was to stall off creditors, or dole out partial payments. "Checks were bouncing all over the country," chuckled Fitzgerald.

On February 12, 1974, there was a meeting of the venture capital group and lenders in Memphis to discuss the company's critical need for more funds. Under the terms of the original November 13, 1973, credit agreement, the lenders held back funds desperately needed by Federal Express to operate. The company had fallen short of its committed objectives, package volume was less than projected, and expenses far outdistanced revenues.

The participants agreed that a financial collapse could be avoided only if $6.4 million additional equity and an additional loan of $5.1 million from the bank lenders were pumped into the company.

General Dynamics and two very minor initial venture capital participants refused to invest in the second round.

"The failure of General Dynamics to come forth was caused by a little bit of several things," says Charles Lea. "It had its own financial problems and it couldn't see putting any more money into Federal Express. Also, there was the problem with Gorden MacDonald, General Dynamics' finance guy and Fred Smith. Fred didn't know much about corporate finance, and he just didn't get on a common wave length with MacDonald. Fred was only 29 years old and didn't always get the best advice. Some of his ideas were off-the-wall and disconcerting to MacDonald."

A surprise event occurred on March 6th, just 13 days before the scheduled completion of the second round of financing. On that day in Memphis the Enterprise board was informed of the nature of Fred Smith's $2 million loan in February, 1973, from Union Bank in Little Rock. The one-year loan was overdue and Union Bank had contacted the Enterprise Company board citing the terms of the redemption agreement. That was the first time Enterprise had knowledge of Fred Smith's loan. On March 11th at a meeting of the Enterprise board, Fred Smith admitted he had forged the documents. The Enterprise board not only agreed to expose Fred Smith's falsification of the document; but it also decided immediately to inform Union Bank of what had happened, as well as to tell the bank's officers there was no redemption agreement.

In the aftermath of this revelation, Fred Smith agreed to inform all of the participants scheduled to take part in the second round of financing about the misrepresentation. In his own defense, Smith wrote to Rick Stowe of New Court Securities the following day telling Stowe he expected to meet his financial obligations as they matured without impairing his ability to run Federal Express. Smith explained that he had been having a running battle with the Enterprise Company board on the matter of its further participation in, and support of, the Federal Express venture.

The second round of financing completed on March 19, 1974, was vital to the company's future. Federal Express had experienced in its brief life an operating loss of $5.5 million on revenues of $10.2 million. There was a real danger of imminent suspension of operations without these second round funds. Nightly package volume was increasing, but not fast enough.

William J. Hewitt, then a partner with Cravath, Swaine and Moore, the Wall Street law firm representing the investors, summoned Fred Smith to New York. Hewitt was reported to be very upset at Smith about the Union Bank loan and because of the bitter complaints of Fredette and Laura about what Fred had done. The sisters had hired a Washington attorney, Robert Molloy, and according to Smith, he was threatening to throw a monkey wrench into the forthcoming second round of financing. Hewitt had a Dutch-uncle talk with Smith about the seriousness of the matter of the forged documents. Clearly, and with good reason, the lenders and the equity investors were very worried about what this might do to the future of Federal Express. In addition, a number of careers were on the line among those professionals who represented the participating financial groups. Their superiors could probably accuse them of ineptness for failure to do their homework handling the Federal Express matter. Financial institutions often deal very harshly with those they think have been negligent. If such men do not get fired, they are at least relegated to positions away from lending or investing money.

On March 12th the investor and lender groups met in Chicago to discuss with an executive search firm a plan for hiring a new chief executive officer to run Federal Express. "Ironically, we met in the Icarus Room of the O'Hare Hilton," an amused Rick Stowe told me. There is a sign outside the door of this meeting room which describes in summary form the fate of this character in Greek mythology, a character not unlike the threatened fate of Fred Smith: "By disobeying his father's orders, Icarus flew too near the sun, with the result that the fastenings of his wings were melted, and he plunged to his death in the sea — the world's first pilot casualty."

The group debated whether Fred Smith should stay or whether he should be fired. They were extremely concerned that Smith's financial problems might preoccupy him and conceivably make him unavailable to run the company. But most agreed the company was not endangered by his staying. After lengthy discussions, the majority in the room supported Smith's continuance because they realized he had a real power base. That is to say they realized that to outsiders Smith *was* Federal Express. Equally important, he had the loyalty and dedication of his employees. Nonetheless, they were still concerned about the company because most of Smith's key people were marketing specialists and because nobody there in Memphis knew how to run an airline.

The general criteria for the search were established at that meeting. The banks were requesting a person be hired with broad general management experience, preferably with a background in airlines, trucking, hotel, or other service business. They wanted someone older than Fred Smith, who was then only 29, and Peter S. Willmott, then 37. Willmott had been offered the job as chief financial officer. He accepted at the April, 1974, board of directors meeting and agreed to report to Memphis on May 6th.

The screening committee for finding a new chief executive officer was Brick Meers of White, Weld and Charley Lea of New Court. They agreed to interview candidates found by the search firm. They later found several prospects, including 59-year-old General Howell M. Estes, Jr. Estes had retired from the Air Force in 1969 after a distinguished career, and had taken the job as president of World Airways, a military and commercial charter airline based in Oakland,

California. "Estes was checked out very quickly by people at the Bank of America, and largely on the basis of this check we hired him," Brick Meers answered when asked how the screening committee made its recommendation.

The new equity of $6.4 million was represented by 64,000 shares of senior convertible preferred stock, with a conversion price of $29.34 per share. The agreement to grant $5.1 million of additional bank credit came only after Federal agreed to issue the lenders warrants to purchase 236,190 shares of stock at a future date at a specified price, called the exercise price.

As of March 19, 1974, the holder of the greatest number of voting shares was New Court Securities and its special accounts with almost 21 percent. Fred Smith had a 9.80 voting interest; and the family Enterprise Company, 9.25 percent. The bank warrant holders had 9.26 percent; and Citicorp's venture capital subsidiary, the FNCB Capital Corporation, 9.24 percent.

Smith and his family prior to November, 1973, had outright control. On March 19, 1974, they held only a 19.05 percent voting share position. They had to give up a major portion of their ownership or risk losing everything.

The strength of the various ownership interests may have looked academic to outsiders when informed of the loss of about $13.7 million for the fiscal year ending May 31, 1974. *Business Week* carried an uncomplimentary article in its June 15th issue titled: "Federal Express Takes A Nosedive." The author of the article pointed to a myriad of mistakes he felt the company had made, including its overly-optimistic volume projections and its inability to control costs. It was a stinging article with strong negative overtones insofar as its effects on the company's marketing efforts in attracting new customers and retaining existing ones.

Federal Express protested loudly that the influential *Business Week* had painted an inaccurate picture of conditions. The company agreed with some of the points but they objected to the "nosedive" conclusion.

The company was developing national visibility. The question was: Would it survive the summer of 1974? Even though industrial shippers were highly complimentary of the service Federal was providing and the rates charged, it did not seem to be enough.

On May 31, 1974, the company was in default on interest due on some $2.5 million in bank debt. The investors held an emergency meeting in Chicago on June 18, 1974, with General Estes to discuss the serious financial condition. Earnings were nonexistent, and there was no cash flow to pay off bank debt. Those in attendance agreed it would be difficult to raise funds to support the company's 1975 Business Plan, but they also agreed an attempt should be made to secure more equity by July. Numerous potential venture capital groups were approached by Charley Lea and Rick Stowe of New

Court, but the response was almost always the same. They either said they were not interested in new deals, or that the Federal Express venture had been very spotty up to this point and much too risky. Some questioned the ability of Federal's new management to perform.

It was September, 1974, before the third round of financing could be completed. Investors put up another $3,876,000 represented by 1,550,400 shares of convertible subordinated notes.

In mid-July, 1974, General Estes and Peter Willmott met with Henry Crown in Chicago to ask his help, but Crown demurred. He told them that General Dynamics had urgent cash needs for its own projects. Be that as it may, General Dynamics did agree to put in a modest investment of $300,000.

The recalcitrant Ned Heizer refused to take part in round three. Brick Meers, Charley Lea and Fred Smith were not able to convince Heizer to stay in. In fact, during heated conversations Heizer is reported to have threatened to sue over the dilution factor. The heaviest investors in round three stood to gain substantial ownership of the company at the expense of the smaller, original investors. Heizer was under some strain from the burden on his private venture firm of its previous investments in Federal Express and its $9.2 million equity investment in Amdahl. Inside Federal Express and among some of the other investors there was a feeling that Heizer had stayed out of the third round in order to improve his equity position by later approaching Chase Manhattan Bank to try to purchase the Federal Express warrants held by the Chase.

In the third round, 17 of the original 24 investors put up additional cash. No new investors were attracted, despite the hard canvassing which had been done among a good part of America's venture capitalists. The conversion price on the 1,550,400 shares issued was $2.50.

It was very painful for those who chose not to take part in round three. New Court Securities, which had invested just $973,000 in this round, received 369,200 shares. New Court and the accounts it represented now owned 16 percent of Federal Express; Prudential owned 10.7 percent; Fred Smith, just 8.5 percent; and the family trust, the Enterprise Company, a meager 0.4 percent.

New Court had put up 13.8 percent of the total equity. But Enterprise now had only a 0.4 percent interest despite contributing 11 percent of the total equity capital. Heizer also saw his position diluted. His group had put up 5 percent of the equity, and after round three his interest was down to 0.5 percent.

The lenders held a 24.8 percent interest. The warrants that had been issued to them represented rights to 669,666 shares of the total of 1,704,562 shares issued or issuable through September, 1974.

Chase Manhattan, the First National Bank of Chicago, and the other participating banks in the Credit Agreement agreed to waive interest on their loans in September, but stipulated that Federal Express must come up with $4 million on these loans by May 1, 1975. Temporarily, Federal was off the hook with the banks, but later in 1976 and 1977 enormous pressure was placed by the banks' lending officers to collect what was owed them. By that time the banks had lost patience with Fred Smith and his company. There were many bitter moments as the banks applied pressure on the company. It was in 1974 and 1975 that Chase Manhattan, the First National Bank of Chicago, and numerous other banking giants were faced with wholesale numbers of defaults on loans to real estate ventures, fast food franchises, and conglomerates made in the late 1960s and the early 1970s. Major banks were accused by analysts of making a lot of stupid loans during that period.

Federal Express, throughout 1974, and well into 1975, was competitively vulnerable. Smith knew if Emery or Airborne were to have gone into aggressive direct competition with Federal for the priority small package market, the company would not have survived. Says Smith: "At that stage we could have gotten our brains blown out." Emery was slow to react to Federal Express' presence. Emery had done well historically in the business of handling general air cargo. It was the established air freight leader and highly regarded by Wall Street analysts. Its price/earnings ratio in the spring of 1974 was 26 to 1.

Federal raised its rates several times in 1974 to try to balance revenues with expenses. Still, it was far below the breakeven point through 1974 and into 1975. The additional investment dollars were drained away quickly, and negative cash flows kept Federal on the endangered species list. The company was facing pressure from every direction. On a daily basis the company faced a multitude of creditors ranging from the City of Detroit to their own employees. Airport officials in Detroit parked a fire truck in front of a Falcon one day because Federal had not paid the landing fee. Couriers often used their credit cards to buy gasoline for their delivery vans and sought reimbursement from the company later. It took a lot of loyalty to be a courier in those days.

On the recommendation of Charley Lea of New Court, Peter S. Willmott (B.A., Williams; MBA, Harvard) came to Federal Express in May from a position as treasurer of the Continental Baking Company. He had at one time been a management consultant with Booz, Allen & Hamilton and an analyst for American Airlines. The tall, serious-looking Willmott wanted an entrepreneurial opportunity, and at 37 he felt Federal Express was his chance.

What Willmott found in Memphis was a chaotic financial administrative mess. "Pete saw a bunch of guys running around seemingly not knowing what to do," says Lea. "He didn't come down hard on anybody because he understood the situation. His job was to straighten out the numbers so we could find out where we stood financially." Brick Meers had been trying for months prior to Willmott's arrival to get a clean audit prepared to present to the lenders. As chairman of Federal's Audit Committee he also wanted to get the company straightened out before an audit by one of the "Big Eight" accounting firms so some of the company's problems would not appear in such a professional audit.

It took Willmott about three months to get the financial numbers the investors could believe in. Contrary to the thinking of Smith and his senior staff, Willmott strongly recommended raising prices. He reasoned that if the company offered a quality service, customers would pay for it. He wanted to get revenues up quickly to close the gap on expenses.

Willmott was a no-nonsense, conservative financial manager given a difficult assignment. Charley Lea told Federal's investor group, "Peter Willmott, who comes from Glens Falls, New York, wasn't always understood by people who came from Arkansas. Financial management is a long way from bean counting." Lea's flippant remark, alluding to the tradition where, in the saloons of the old West, beans were used as poker chips, was meant to draw a distinction between the reckless gamblers of Federal Express and the conservative money managers of the eastern-financial establishment.

General Estes arrived in Memphis on June 1, 1974, to assume command of Federal Express. The company's public relations staff issued the statement that Fred Smith could not handle the task of raising investment funds and running the airline simultaneously, and that Smith had suggested Estes for the chief executive officer's job. This was not the case. Since the March 12 meeting at the Icarus Room in Chicago's O'Hare Hilton, the investors firmly indicated that they were looking for an older, operations-oriented executive with managerial experience either in airlines or a related type service industry. Smith was to remain, but only as Federal's president.

Later, when Lea was asked why Estes was picked, he explains, "We needed to give credibility to Federal Express and to give comfort to the lenders and investors. As it worked out, Estes detached himself from worrying about the deeper operational problems we were facing, and he was of limited help in the crucial financial planning side of the business."

General Estes was paid $75,000 as chief executive officer; Smith, as president received $40,000. "Throughout Estes' nine-month stay at Federal Express, Fred Smith was always respectful of the General," remembers Bill Arthur, one of Smith's aides at the time. "Fred operated as if the General wasn't there. Estes seemed to be so caught up in obtaining the perks of his position as chief executive officer, like insisting on a reserved parking spot for his fancy European model of a Mercedes or ordering a special brand of cigars, he didn't realize Fred wasn't carrying out his suggestions. They never had any open disagreements."

Smith later characterized his relationship with General Estes as "Ho Chi Minh versus Bismarck." Interestingly enough, in the course of this research, I found it nearly impossible to discover either photographic or biographical materials concerning Estes. Apparently, Estes has become a non-person as far as Federal Express is concerned.

A crisis arose on January 21, 1975, and the arms-length relationship between the two ended. Fred Smith informed the board of directors of a federal grand jury investigation in Little Rock concerning the circumstances of his $2 million loan from Union Bank in February, 1973. He mentioned that Fredette and Laura had contracted Federal authorities through their attorneys on the matter of his submitting forged documents pledging the credit of the family-owned Enterprise Company in which they held a major ownership position. Fred Smith told the board: "It is my opinion that the actions of my sisters were designed to discredit both myself and Federal Express in the hopes of influencing the civil action."

On Friday, January 31, 1975, Smith was formally indicted for obtaining funds from the Union Bank by use of false documents. And on Monday, February 3rd, a warrant was issued for his arrest. But this was only part of his trouble: late that same night he had been indicted, he hit and killed a pedestrian who was jaywalking. When apprehended, he claimed he did not realize he had hit anybody, and this was the reason he failed to stop. Smith was charged with leaving the scene of the accident as well as driving with an expired license.

Fred Smith was in serious trouble. Worried that competitors would use the bad publicity against the company, he told his employees: "I do not want to burden you with my personal problems and want to stress this matter of the indictment has absolutely no bearing on Federal Express' operations, but I ask your continuing support in confronting the publicity that may result from this action. An indictment is certainly no proof of guilt or innocence."

The next meeting of Federal's board of directors was scheduled for Thursday, February 27, 1975. Tension had been building concerning Fred Smith's future at Federal Express. The evening before the meeting, Charley Lea, who had arrived in Memphis from New York early, had a long discussion with Smith about Smith's status with the company. Roger Frock and Mike Fitzgerald, two of Smith's key senior officers, saw Smith later that evening in his office before going home. They remember that Smith did not mention anything to them about resigning. But Fitzgerald recalls that as he was getting ready to go to bed he got a call from Roger Frock to tell him Smith had written a letter of resignation to submit the next morning at 10:00 a.m. when Federal's board convened. They both knew Smith was still at the office, so they decided to go back to the office to try to talk him out of it. According to Fitzgerald they "talked for hours."

Early the next morning Fitzgerald went to the Memphis Hilton to talk with Charley Lea. In a heated discussion Fitzgerald announced that if Fred Smith were to be fired, he, Roger Frock, and Art Bass would resign, and in all likelihood Federal Express would cease operations the following Monday morning because of a mass walkout. Lea remembers: "This was real soap opera stuff. The board had a potential mutiny on its hands, and it was totally unexpected."

The board convened just after 10:00 a.m. General Estes, like several others, tried to convince the rest of the board Smith should go. Then, Art Bass asked if he could address the board. In an impassioned plea Bass said: "Fred Smith is our spiritual leader, and those of us who work with him greatly admire him. He has given Federal Express total dedication. He has put everything on the line." And he told the board to expect the resignation of Smith's key officers if Smith were fired.

This threat of a mass resignation of the principal company officers threw the board in turmoil. They knew they were facing a palace revolt so the meeting was adjourned until 4:00 p.m. to give the board leadership time to plan a strategy. The possibility of these resignations was sobering to Meers and Lea and the other board members representing the principal investors. If the company ceased operations, all the time and money they had put into Federal Express would be lost. A lot of professional careers of these board members were at stake; heads would roll if they were the cause of the company's failure.

As a result of this crisis, the board immediately designated a special Ad Hoc Committee on Management and Organization to be made up of board members — Philip Greer, Larry Lawrence, Charley Lea, Gorden MacDonald, Brick Meers and Bartz Schneider — then adjourned to permit the Ad Hoc Committee to meet. Brick Meers, Charley Lea and Fred Smith adjourned to a side room for a long "give-and-take" discussion. "We talked straight with Fred about the situation, and he told us what was on his mind," said Brick Meers. Afterwards Smith left to talk with his senior officers who had been meeting on their own in another room, while Meers and Lea met privately with General Estes for the same type of "give-and-take" discussion they had had with Fred Smith. It was a rough day for Meers and Lea trying to sort out the conflict.

At 4:00 p.m. when the full board reconvened there was a surprise announcement. The board accepted with regret the resignation of General Estes, offering him an option to buy 242,249 shares of Class A common stock at an exercise price of $1 million. The option was in effect between August 1, 1976, and July 31, 1977, but as it turned out Estes didn't exercise it. With the departure of Estes, Art Bass was selected to replace Smith as president and acting chief operating officer, and Fred Smith was appointed to replace Estes as chairman of the board. At the same time the executive committee of the board, with Charley Lea as the chairman, was selected to oversee all major policy decisions while it undertook a search for a new CEO. Smith was requested to work very closely with the executive committee in future policy matters.

No public announcement was made by the company that some power had been taken away from Smith. As far as the public and the rank-and-file of Federal's employees knew Fred Smith was the new chairman of the board. It was supposed to seem as though this was an obvious enhancement of Smith's stature as founder and "guiding light" of Federal Express. General Estes cleaned out his desk the next morning, and quietly left exactly nine months after his arrival in Memphis.

Charley Lea, in summarizing the bizarre turn of events, told the lenders a year later: "We did a strange thing. We fired the most senior man at the top; elevated the founder to the title of chairman; appointed a relatively untried executive to the post of president and chief operating officer; and retained for itself a small committee with no special credentials to function as the executive. The beauty of these profound changes was that the situation permitted no alternative choices at the time. The efficacy of these changes was apparent to no one." This strange episode is reminiscent of the sign on the old western saloon door: "Please don't shoot the piano player, he's the only one we've got." Fred Smith's charmed life had allowed him to escape once again, or at least for a while.

The company was still in deep financial trouble in spring, 1975. For the fiscal year ending May 31, 1975, the loss was $11.5 million. This made the cumulative loss for the first 26 months of operation over $29.3 million, and in addition, it owed its lenders over $49 million. One wonders how many other companies in this predicament would have survived.

Little Rock Airmotive, Federal's aircraft modification subsidiary, was liquidated in 1975 after three years of continuous operating losses totaling about $1 million. It was not exactly a rosy picture Federal Express was giving the investment world, or its concerned creditors. Understandably, two articles in the influential business weekly *Barron's* in mid-1975 questioned whether Federal Express had the ability to survive. The respected Alan Abelson referred to it as "a spunky company," but he expressed reservations about its chances of success.

A serious problem arose in late May, 1975, when CCEC, the lender on ten of the Falcons in Federal's fleet, was showing reluctance to waive the loan default due to occur on May 31, 1975. Federal's management was summoned to CCEC's headquarters in Baltimore for a meeting on May 28th to discuss the problem. John Sheehan, president and CEO, strode into the meeting room to meet with Art Bass, Peter Willmott, and Charley Lea. He asked Art Bass what he did at Federal Express, and Bass told him he was the new president. Turning to Peter Willmott, Sheehan asked him what he did. Willmott replied he was senior vice president of finance and administration. But before he could get to Lea, one of his aides interrupted him. Later Lea recalled: "Look, if Sheehan had asked me what I did, it probably would have been all over for Federal Express. You see, I was a member of the Executive Committee of the board of directors, and we had stripped Fred Smith of policy control in the aftermath of the federal indictment earlier that year and the reorganization that pushed Howell Estes out. We were running the company."

Sheehan expressed amazement at how old the Falcons were which CCEC had been financing. Bass told Sheehan that if CCEC were to repossess these aircraft, it would cost a great deal of money to reconvert the Falcons from cargo aircraft back to their original passenger configurations. But more to the point, it was explained to Sheehan that at that time there was practically no market for Falcons.

Then, Sheehan turned his attention to the company's performance after he was shown the fiscal 1976 Business Plan. He responded with disbelief: "You are still telling us the same optimistic story about Federal's achieving its corporate business plan you told us in 1974." Later, after further discussion, Sheehan told Bass, Willmott, and Lea: "In the light of Federal's new management we will give the company a couple of months." Once more Federal Express got yet another reprieve. If CCEC had seized the ten Falcons, in all likelihood the company would have ceased operations soon thereafter.

A key issue within the company at that time was recapitalization. How and when should Federal Express restructure itself to lift the onerous debt burden off its back? All agreed the company's present capitalization was extremely unwieldy owing to the hodge-podge of different types of securities, and it was imperative steps be taken to make Federal Express more attractive to potential equity investors. The initial target date for holding a public offering was before the end of 1975. There were problems, however. If it were to be successful, the company needed to gain the cooperation of the bank lenders who held 628,244 of the total of 669,666 warrants outstanding. Both Federal's board and management felt it was critical that no third party like Ned Heizer or someone else be permitted to gain control of any of these bank warrants by going directly to the banks with an offer to purchase. If recapitalization were to be successful, Federal Express would have to gain control of the majority of them.

In June, 1975, the board agreed to proceed with preliminary steps toward a public equity financing. Members of the board told the company's staff that the necessary condition for a successful recapitalization would be three or four months of profitable operations. Up to that point the company had failed to break even for any prior monthly period. The first profitable month finally came in July, 1975, when the company netted $55,000. This was the start of what turned out to be the first profitable fiscal year and, when it ended on May 31, 1976, the net income had reached nearly $3.6 million.

The immediate concern, however, was restructuring the debt to lighten the burden on the company while it tried to build its cash flow. Federal requested $5 million in principal deferrals in its 1976 Business Plan so it could expand on its quest for profits. If the banks were unwilling to reshape the loan repayment schedule, then the company might fail before the end of that year.

Fred Smith's future role at Federal Express was also an issue with both the lender and investor groups. Federal's board in fall, 1975, undertook a search for a new CEO. On December 4, 1975, less than a week before Fred Smith went on trial in federal court on the forgery charge, an offer was made to G. Michael Hostage, then a vice president of the Marriott Corporation. Inexplicably Hostage turned them down despite a lucrative offer. Perhaps the waters seemed too rough at Federal Express for a new CEO.

At the trial held in Little Rock, Smith's defense was based on the theme, "I am Frederick Smith Enterprise Company." His counsel was Lucius E. Burch, Jr., a highly experienced Memphis-based trial lawyer with a long record of major victories in tough courtroom battles. Burch had Smith elaborate extensively on his Marine Corps combat experience in Vietnam and on his development of the concept which led ultimately to the formation of Federal Express.

In justifying his actions in regard to the Union Bank loan, Smith testified: "Almost 50 percent of the Enterprise Company is Fred Smith, either personally or in trust for me. And I felt at the time that I was the Enterprise Company. It's as simple as that. And I felt that both of the sisters felt the same way. Both of them had written letters to the bankers that sat on the board saying, 'We support Fred Smith in whatever he wants to do.'"

Smith told the court that, at the time of the Union Bank loan in February, 1973, he felt Enterprise Company would ratify the resolution he had prepared if called upon to do so. After all, he was president of the Enterprise board, and as such, he had the authority to commit the board.

On December 11, 1975, after ten hours of deliberation, the federal jury acquitted him. The heavy strain on Smith personally and the cloud the forgery charge had placed over the company were removed. If he had been convicted he could have faced up to a five year prison term.

Federal Express employees had remained loyal throughout. They thought all along it was a trumped-up charge. Characterizing the mood of those times one aide close to Fred Smith remembered, "We all felt those greedy Little Rock banks knew perfectly well what was happening when Smith borrowed the money. They pushed loans on him; then because of pressure from Robert Molloy, the aggressive lawyer hired by Fred's sisters, they got loosey-goosey."

Earlier Fredette and Laura, Fred's sisters, had brought action in the Chancery Court of Shelby County, Tennessee, against their brother, the National Bank of Commerce of Memphis, certain of the banks' officers, and the Enterprise Company. They sought relief arising from the Enterprise Company's investments of $6,250,000 in Federal Express, alleging violations of the "prudent man" rule and other fiduciary principles. They sought to restore assets of Enterprise Company to the $17 million level which was the worth of its assets prior to the investments in Federal Express. It was their estimate that the Enterprise Company was now worth only $2.5 million. Finally, four years after the original filing, an out-of-court settlement was reached in December, 1978. Fred Smith agreed to buy out his sisters' stock in Enterprise and guaranteed to make complete restitution for any loss in value to this trust.

With the Federal trial behind him, Smith in early 1976 turned his attention to pushing the lenders to reshape the loan payment schedule and to try to recapture the warrants held by the lenders in order to reduce this overhang on the company. Each warrant gave the holder the right to purchase one share of Class A common stock. Considerable effort was made by Federal's management in the spring of 1976 to get the bank lenders to consent to renegotiation of the credit agreement made originally in November, 1973, and amended in March, 1974. The company requested that the banks agree to a debt amortization schedule some $5.5 million less than the $9.5 million called for in fiscal 1977 by the terms of the credit agreement.

Brick Meers, who was observing all of this conflict, remembers: "There was bad blood all around on this issue. A loan officer of the First National Bank of Chicago had brought up the fact that Federal's March, 1976, figures were much worse for the company than expected and that margins were down. The loan officer was quite concerned about Federal's future." His unyielding attitude angered Smith and he said he would never again do business with the First National Bank of Chicago. Later, however, Smith and the bank forgot their differences at the time of the 1978 recapitalization when Federal Express went public and its financial future brightened.

At the height of Smith's bitter fight with the bank lenders in early 1976, Federal's management and board of directors held exploratory talks with Purolator Courier Corporation. Purolator was considering whether it might want to take over despite Federal's serious financial problems. Later, after considerable research, Purolator concluded the acquisition was not a good corporate fit and dropped further discussions.

The issue of the bank warrants, and how Federal Express could get the warrants back from the lenders, occupied Federal's management and board throughout much of 1976. Chase Manhattan declined the company's request to surrender its warrants which would have allowed Federal Express to proceed with plans for a recapitalization and a public offering. Smith questioned the legitimacy of the bank holding the warrants in the first place. He believed that the banks had obligated themselves to return the warrants on a reasonable basis. "Greed seemed to get the better of them when they decided to renege on this deal," grumbled Smith. "If pressed, this issue could be litigated and be won. They took the warrants to allow a fourth financing had it been necessary — not as an 'equity kicker' and there were too many participants to ultimately deny this." Smith hinted that, if the banks were to exercise their warrants, they would be in violation of the Glass-Steagall Act, the law governing national banks. Counsel for the First National Bank of Chicago later did indeed advise his bank that the Act would prohibit it from exercising the warrants.

In June, 1976, Smith called on his friend David S. Lewis, chairman of General Dynamics, asking for help in purchasing and exercising these warrants. He requested that General Dynamics agree to be guarantor on a $3 million, two-year loan. Smith said he needed $700,000 to purchase the warrants, another $1.7 million to exercise the warrants, and another $600,000 to pay off the loans he had personally guaranteed for the company. If he could get these warrants and exercise them, this would give him at least a 25 percent ownership position. He maintained he had the right of first refusal on these warrants if the banks attempted to sell them, and that it was urgent he be able to purchase them. He maintained he had been granted this right to regain a substantial equity position in Federal Express and that it was a concession granted him as a result of what the three rounds of financing in 1973 and 1974 had done to his ownership position. His interest had declined to a meager 8.5 percent as a result of being forced to make concessions to attract desperately needed additional capital to survive in those years.

The squabbling among the lenders and the venture capital group over the issue of the warrants had been upsetting to Smith. In frustration he charged: "There are too many fingers in the pie, and too many misunderstandings. Neither group is focusing on the only real issue — the future of the company. This is absolutely tragic."

In anticipation that he might be unable to purchase the warrants, Smith, in a surprise move in early June, 1976, asked Henry Crown and David Lewis to consider him for a management position with either General Dynamics or Trans World Airways. This was a real turn of events because Fred, Fredette, and Laura still had a substantial sum of money tied up in Federal Express. Fred Smith was obviously aggravated and exhausted. He had been flying back and forth from Memphis to Washington trying frantically to get relief from the Civil Aeronautics Board regulations so Federal could fly on its major routes aircraft with payloads substantially larger than the Falcons.

In 1976, Fred Smith was on good terms with neither the lenders nor the venture capitalist group. The contemptuous expression company senior officers used to describe them during this period was "the Jackals of Wall Street" because jackals hunt in packs at night feeding on smaller prey. Says Lea, "It was an 'us' versus 'them' mentality." Smith and his inner circle of advisors did not always agree with what was happening in the apportionment of ownership shares in the second and third rounds of financing in 1974. They felt the venture capital groups overreached themselves in gaining greater control of the company, particularly in the third round. And they resented the lenders' position. They felt the "jackals" were still at work on behalf of their own selfish interests.

At a meeting of lenders and the investors held in Chicago on June 10, 1976, Brick Meers and Charley Lea discussed the open confrontation which had occurred between Smith and the banks and expressed regret that this conflict had occurred at a time when the future of Federal Express looked bright. They told the group that, unfortunately, the bank's plan calling for a 70 percent warrant recapture from the banks — a substantial equity "give-up" on the part of the present equity holders in favor of their acceptance of subordinated notes and becoming preferred stockholders to permit a possible $12 to $15 million public offering of common stock — had been cast aside by the banks as a frivolous gesture. The banks did not feel the proposal dealt properly with their interests.

Meers and Lea pleaded for goodwill. "Huge sums had been invested," Lea continued, "and many of the investors had seen their equity wiped out." Lea cautioned the banks that if they accelerated their loans, Federal Express would be forced to take the issue to the courts and the company would probably win. To add a final and sobering food-for-thought item for the bankers' consideration, Lea said, "If Federal Express goes under, whatever accolades you may win within your institution will soon be lost in public opprobrium, for you must be aware such events become front page news in the financial press and the fable of David and Goliath seems to have been plagiarized by every reporter writing today."

Negotiations continued through 1976 with Smith and his management standing firm in their resolve to acquire the warrants held by the lenders. Smith was unable to get a loan from General Dynamics, and he continued seeking a co-maker on a $3 million loan a Memphis bank had committed to make so he could attempt to purchase the warrants. He had no luck at all that year. But he continued to speak out loudly of his right of first refusal on the warrants, and declined to compromise his position. He reminded the lenders that the Smith family had put over $8 million into Federal Express, and as of 1976 he held only an 8.5 percent interest, and the family-owned Enterprise Company, only 0.4 percent.

The recapitalization issue dragged on through 1976 and 1977.

Fred Smith suggested at one point, when he was thinking of quitting, that the company create an ESOP — an Employees Stock Ownership Plan — as a means of raising additional capital, while at the same time keeping the company privately-owned. Such a financing vehicle would give Smith's loyal employees "a piece-of-the-action" in Federal Express. Brick Meers felt Smith was getting poor advice, and strongly urged that the only way to make Smith "whole" was through a public offering of stock. This, Meers advised Smith, would enable Smith to bail himself out by giving him collateral, and Federal Express public value and borrowing value.

No action resolving the complex financing issues was made until after the action by Congress in November, 1977, when it passed the Air Cargo Deregulation Act, permitting Federal Express and other similar air taxi operators to fly larger aircraft. Deregulation brought the banks around. These banks viewed Federal Express differently for the first time since they had made the original loans four years earlier.

Air cargo deregulation triggered a positive attitude of all of the parties. White, Weld and New Court Securities were authorized to undertake a public offering. The recapitalization, after three long years in the discussion stage, took place on April 12, 1978. Federal Express sold 783,000 shares at $24 per share, and raised $17,539,200 in new equity. Selling stockholders sold 292,000 shares for $6,540,800.

To activate the recapitalization, the warrant holders agreed to sell for $5.25 per underlying share a total of 444,641 shares having an exercise price of $2.50 per share. For a payment made to Smith by Federal Express of $200,000, he waived his right of first refusal to purchase warrants for 200,000 shares. These warrants were purchased by the company for $5.25 per share. Smith bought the remaining 244,641 shares, also for $5.25 per share. The warrant holders also accounted for 183,603 of the 292,000 shares sold at the public offering by the selling stockholder group.

Federal Express guaranteed a loan of $4.7 million made by the First National Bank of Chicago to Fred Smith. He used $1,284,000 to purchase warrants; another $482,000 to prepay the first year's interest on this loan; and $2,934,000 to pay off his outstanding bank loans and his other creditors.

The April, 1978, sale of common stock reduced the oppressive debt burden and increased the company's net worth. The balance sheet had never looked better, and those loyal Federal Express employees who had stuck with Smith throughout his countless close calls with disaster were given the opportunity to purchase 220,000 shares at a slightly discounted price. They leaped at the opportunity: 56 percent of Federal's employees placed orders for 635,000 shares. Because of this oversubscription, individual orders had to be reduced to fit within the 220,000 share allocation for employees.

After the recapitalization the ownership structure was: company officers and directors, 19 percent; the initial venture capital investors, 49 percent; and the general public, including Federal Express employees, 32 percent.

Fred Smith, age 33, had been through crisis after crisis since June, 1971, when he incorporated Federal Express. The "Arkansas bean counters," as Smith and his close associates were labeled by some Wall Street wags, had defied the dire predictions on the company's lifespan and outwitted a lot of hard bitten, so-called "old pros" in the financial community. Some had attempted to take advantage of Fred Smith, but he had turned the tables on them. And, after-the-fact, they admired him for it. He had played rougher and shown more determination than they had. His unorthodox tactics may have been learned in part from Ho Chi Minh, the fearless old Vietnamese leader whom Smith admired, and in part from the "kill-or-be-killed" lessons learned during his Marine Corps career in the battle zones of Vietnam. He had walked continually on the edge of disaster and survived.

Chapter 9

Mr. Smith Goes to Washington

By mid-1975 two or more flights per night were required to serve Boston, New York, Newark, Philadelphia, Chicago, Los Angeles and San Francisco. "Falcons are flying wingtip-to wingtip over the same lanes at approximately the same hours at night," worried Art Bass, "and this is holding back market expansion and adding greatly to the expense of serving our largest markets."

Costs of operating the Falcon fleet were increasing month-by-month. Fuel costs represented 15 percent of the company's total variable costs and were expected to escalate rapidly. An individual Falcon used 366 gallons of fuel per hour at a burning cost of $140.09 per hour in 1975. The company estimated the burn cost for 1976 would be $156.51 per hour. This was another compelling reason for Federal Express to gain approval from the Civil Aeronautics Board to fly larger, more fuel efficient, aircraft to complement the Falcon fleet.

"Ev'ry time I come to town, The boys keep kickin' my dawg aroun', Makes no dif'rence if he's a houn', They've gotta quit kickin' my dawg aroun'."
—A verse from a political campaign song at the 1912 Democratic Party Convention

Fred Smith went before the Federal Express board of directors in June, 1975, and presented a plan to lease five Douglas DC-9s. His message was hopeful and optimistic as always. As a result of a changing attitude among many legislators toward regulation and even within President Ford's Administration, he felt the CAB might approve the company's request to fly the larger DC-9s on certain major routes to alleviate the nightly lift problems. Smith expected favorable consideration by the CAB if the company applied in the next three or four months.

On September 26, 1975, Federal Express

filed an application with the CAB seeking relief from what Federal Express termed its "critical lift capacity problems." The company requested this relief be granted by exemption from the 7,500 pound limit of Part 298, rather than through issuance of a "Certificate of Public Convenience and Necessity." This process would ordinarily require a very long and drawn out administrative hearing procedure before the CAB could render a decision. The heart of Federal's petition was a request for quick relief from the "critical lift" problem by being permitted to fly five DC-9-15 cargo planes, each with a payload of between 14,000 and 20,000 pounds, on five routes. Federal Express requested an answer by December 1, 1975.

Federal Express argued that its market penetration was so slight and its service so specialized that such an exemption would not seriously affect any of the certificated carriers. Federal's opponents instantly jumped on this application when filed, arguing that not only had Federal Express grown because it had been exploiting a loophole in the law which put it beyond the CAB's control on the matter of flight routes and rates charged, but also that Federal Express could not have reached its present level of growth without this loophole. The worst indictment was that Federal Express was a cutthroat competitor engaged in predatory, below-cost pricing of its services.

When challenged by his critics about the aggressive tactics used by Federal Express to build volume, Smith's rebuttal insisted that the company's business was expanding because it was penetrating a vast market which had not previously shipped by air. "Sure," retorted the self-confident Smith, "we took some customers away from Emery, Airborne, and the scheduled carriers like American, Delta, and Eastern. We were offering a better service." Countering the objections of the Air Freight Forwarders Association, Smith observed that Federal Express was providing reliable overnight express service in many off-line markets not easily reached by air freight forwarders because of their heavy reliance on scheduled airlines for nightly lift.

It was no coincidence, then, that every scheduled airline objected to Federal's request to fly DC-9s, except powerful United Airlines. United was not much concerned about Federal Express because United was in favor of general airline deregulation as it anticipated greater competition would be the result. United saw deregulation as an opportunity for it to out-compete the scheduled airline industry and to earn a better return on its investment. The influential Air Transport Association (also known as the ATA), a Washington-based lobbying group for the scheduled airlines, spearheaded the opposition, an opposition in which Delta and American Airlines were among the most vocal.

On December 8, 1975, the company was dealt a severe blow when the order came down from the CAB denying the Federal

While waiting to take off in a corporate aircraft, Fred Smith, in a characteristic pose, ponders a question. (Courtesy Federal Express Corporation)

Arkansas Aviation Sales, Inc., located at Adams Field, Little Rock, Arkansas, was the birthplace of Federal Express in 1971. (Courtesy Federal Express Corporation)

Arthur C. Bass joined Federal Express in 1972. He served as president from 1975 to 1980. He became vice-chairman of the board in 1980, and held that position until he resigned in 1982.

Roger J. Frock joined the company in May 1972 to serve as general manager. He served in a variety of senior level positions until the end of 1982 when he resigned.

(Courtesy Federal Express Corporation)

Peter S. Willmott came to the company in May 1974 to serve as chief financial officer. He became president in September 1980.

The late J. Vincent Fagan served from 1974 until 1980 as the principal architect of the company's marketing strategy. Fagan died in 1982.

The company's senior officers assembled at the Hub for this group photo in May 1980. Missing are Fred Smith, Arthur C. Bass and S. Tucker Taylor. (Courtesy Federal Express Corporation)

1. Fred A. Manske, Jr., 2. Michael D. Basch, 3. J. Vincent Fagan, 4. J. Tucker Morse, 5. James R. Reidmeyer, 6. Wesley W. Terry, 7. Peter S. Willmott, 8. Michael J. Fitzgerald, 9. James A. Perkins, 10. Brian E. Pecon, 11. Larry W. McMahan, 12. Theodore L. Weise, 13. Francis X. Maguire, 14. James L. Barksdale

Top: An avalanche of packages from all over the United States being sorted at 1:30 a.m. at the Super Hub at Memphis International Airport. Bottom: Portable lights illuminate the unloading of cargo containers from one of Federal's fleet of Douglas DC-10s parked on the ramp just beyond the Super Hub. (Courtesy Federal Express Corporation)

Top: Part of the fleet of Boeing 727-100s nosedocked at the Super Hub while they are being unloaded and reloaded with thousands of packages and documents. Right: A Federal Express courier unloads his delivery van on a congested street in midtown Manhattan preparing to make deliveries in a nearby office building. (Courtesy Federal Express Corporation)

Top: Fred Smith at age two with his mother and father on their way to the Caribbean aboard the Salchanick, a 125-foot World War II Navy vessel purchased and refitted by the elder Smith into a luxury yacht. Bottom: Fred Smith during the summers as a boy visited a National Guard training camp. (Courtesy Sally W. Hook)

Top: Lt. Fred Smith, a 23-year old Marine Corps infantry officer, receiving the Silver Star for gallantry in action in Quang Nam Province, South Vietnam in May 1968. (Courtesy Sally W. Hook) Bottom: Fred Smith in Washington during one of his several appearances before Congressional committees in 1976 and 1977 requesting legislative relief for Federal Express to fly larger aircraft. (Courtesy Federal Express Corporation)

Prior to the phasing out of the Falcon Fleet in 1982, this was the scene at 1:00 a.m., Monday through Friday, as these aircraft rendezvoused in Memphis.

(Courtesy Federal Express Corporation)

Federal Express employees serve as "extras" in the producing of a television commercial. The theme of this ad was: "More and more people depend on Federal Express."

Express request for relief. In denying the request to fly larger aircraft, the Board asserted that the exemption authority in section 416(b) of the Federal Aviation Act was not broad enough to permit it to consider the question of the use of larger aircraft. As a consequence, the CAB's exemption powers were limited to inconsequential air transportation matters. The CAB had been blocked by an outdated limitation dating from the Civil Aeronautics Act of 1938, a limitation which prevented Federal's relief, a limitation only legislative action could reverse.

The CAB told Federal Express the authority it requested was more appropriately a matter for examination under the normal certification procedures of section 401 of the Act. It concluded that Federal's past growth record and its projected growth were proper justification for it to go through the normal certification process. It would be happy to receive a request for certification, the Board said.

Federal Express was clearly in a predicament, and it petitioned the CAB for reconsideration. Strains on company operations from surges in nightly package volume were already apparent even at the end of 1975. REA Express, one of its competitors, after struggling for several years, collapsed in November, and in December the United Airlines strike pushed Federal Express to the limits in handling new business generated from shippers unable to use United.

By 1976, it had gained the dominant position in the small shipment air express market. In total priority air shipments under 100 pounds, Federal Express handled 19 percent; Emery, 10 percent; and Airborne, 5 percent. In Federal's fiscal 1976 Business Plan, its planners wrote that their goal was "to achieve a leadership role in the air freight industry." In terms of the growing nightly package volume, this goal already appeared to be a reality: yet financially, Federal Express was still struggling to survive.

These same planners calculated that the projected package volume would probably exceed the system's capacity in the spring, 1978. And by the time of the CAB rejection this capacity limit was just over two years away. It seemed clear that without larger jet aircraft the company's future growth would be limited. It was a problem which would restrict the number of new markets opened.

The task of analyzing the capacity needs, and matching anticipated demand with the space availability on the Falcons, consumed an inordinate amount of time of the company's technical planning staff. Federal's West Coast service was one of the most pressing of these logistical problems. In order to get the packages to Memphis and back to the West Coast to meet overnight service commitments, Falcons had to take off just an hour or so after the close of the business day in Los Angeles, San Francisco, Oakland, Portland, and Seattle. The resulting earlier customer pickup, and the consequent loss of potential business in the time period from 5:00 or 5:30 p.m.

and 8:00 p.m. would be considerable. The limited lift of the Falcons precluded the carrying of heavier, consolidated shipments and of offering customers special pricing for bulk shipments. If the company had larger aircraft, these additional services could create another opportunity for a strong profit center.

Until a permanent solution could be found in 1976 and 1977, the corporate planners turned their attention to improving the nightly match-ups of the 32 Falcons and the often unreliable smaller supplemental fleet of "wet-leased" DC-3s, Lear Jets, and Twin Beeches to the disparate geographic markets in the Federal Express system. In addition to these difficulties, one Falcon had been wrecked in a crash on the ground in Rhode Island, so there were fewer aircraft to work with. These "wet leased" planes came with non-Federal Express crews and maintenance and were, as a consequence, a ragtag assortment of equipment.

Competition in the air express business in 1976 was preventing desperately needed price increases and this lid on rates was pressuring the company's profitability. Enhancing productivity became an absolute necessity to keep operating margins growing.

As part of the effort to increase efficiency Smith considered the costs and benefits of moving the sorting hub out of Memphis to a site a few hundred miles northeast in order to help save fuel and to permit greater utilization of the planes. "We want to get closer to the market," Smith concluded. "It's a matter of economics." Several logistical solutions were studied. Pittsburgh served temporarily as a mini-hub to "bleed off" some of the East Coast intra-regional shipments during this emergency period.

"We did some excellent planning during the crisis years," says the then head of special projects, Ted Weise. "We considered the 'best case' and the 'worst case' environment. We considered a variety of options which might be opened if regulatory relief was granted or in case it was not. It was a series of 'what if' exercises using computer simulation models. And we worried a lot, too."

While these studies were underway, Fred Smith began the campaign to obtain regulatory relief. From the spring, 1976, until the fall, 1977, he spent considerable time in Washington briefing himself on the laws governing commercial aviation, working closely with Washington-based regulatory counsel, Nathaniel P. Breed, Jr., lobbying government officials and legislators, and testifying on seven different occasions before Congressional committees examining the issue of regulatory reform of aviation.

Because he was considered by the business media as bright, articulate, and very quotable, Smith was asked to give many interviews during this period. He told one reporter: "If ever there was a case where the government is cheating somebody — not by commission but by omission — this is it." To another he lectured: "The government doesn't have to give us a thing. All they have to do is get out of our way."

His preparation on the background of the CAB and the history of the Civil Aeronautics Act of 1938, impressed several of the Congressmen who listened to his testimony at many hearings during his 18-month Washington ordeal. He believed that passenger travel had always been the primary focus of CAB regulations and that air cargo transportation needs had been sadly neglected. "When the original Act was passed," Smith conjectured, "there was no economic incentive to carry property by air. Radioactive isotopes were unheard of. But society and industry have changed. The values of items shipped today are far different than they were 40 years ago. What we have is an anachronistic regulatory framework."

Smith attacked the scheduled airlines for not fully exploiting what he called "the quantum leaps in technology." One failure was their inability to utilize the full potential of the widebodied jet, while another was their failure to accommodate competition. At a symposium concerning the status of the transportation industry he told his audience: "The free enterprise system could collapse, not because of some foreign power, but from the captains of industry whose competitive spirit does not extend to prospective competitors." He took a similar message all over the United States at speaking engagements his public relations advisors had lined up for him. He repeated the message that the scheduled airlines "came off as whining fat cats interested only in preserving the status quo with the appearance of a 'public be damned' attitude."

Delta Airlines was one of the major thorns in Federal's side. Delta's position throughout the period of Federal's fight for regulatory relief was that there was nothing the matter with the present law and it did not need to be changed. American and Eastern also vigorously opposed any change in the traditional system of regulation, charging that those who questioned the regulatory structure were well-meaning but unknowledgeable critics.

Smith blamed the CAB's denial of the company's application to fly the five DC-9s directly on the airlines. Smith charged: "When we applied to the CAB for an exemption, lo and behold, the air transportation industry opposed it. It was like Attila the Hun coming to the frontier, if you grant this exemption to Federal Express. It would be the end of air transportation as we know it. They really wanted to scuttle us." Smith maintained the CAB had consistently denied exemption requests when the certificated carriers opposed them. The CAB was accused by Federal Express of neglecting the air cargo industry and its problems, and devoting most of its time to the air passenger business. In its report to the CAB, Federal wrote: "With this scenario, Federal Express is almost an unwelcome, or, at the very least, an unfamiliar intruder."

Federal Express' entry on the Washington scene was excellent as far as timing was concerned. The issue of deregulation was finally peaking after nearly two decades of general discussion by at least three presidential administrations, several CAB board chairman, and many prominent academicians who had examined the government regulatory structure. In addition, there was mounting concern by critics of the Federal Aviation Act that it was stifling competition and was serving as a wall behind which was hiding the entrenched commercial airlines industry. The consensus was that the regulatory system was obsolete and that it was protecting the inefficient carriers. Be that as it may, the emphasis of these attacks was always on reform of the passenger side of the air transportation industry. Air cargo was seldom mentioned.

The December, 1975, CAB rejection of Federal's request for exemption to fly larger aircraft caused some turmoil in the early months of 1976, among Federal's management and its board of directors. Not only was there the threat of reaching the physical limits of growth sometime within the next two years, but also there was the elimination of any possibility for a recapitalization for the company. Federal Express desperately needed this recapitalization to improve its balance sheet, but it could not realistically take place so long as the Falcons, or any other small jet aircraft meeting the payload requirements of Part 298 of the CAB's regulations, remained the primary operating equipment.

In the months after the CAB's negative decision, there was deep dejection as Smith and the board of directors attempted to figure out a strategy. Those familiar with the operations of the Washington political scene advised Federal Express, "Go to Capitol Hill and get your Tennessee Congressional delegation working for you. Stay away from the CAB. The Board's business is to say 'No.'" Calling on its Tennessee senatorial delegation proved to be good advice. Howard Baker was Senate Minority Leader in 1976, and Senator William Brock was a respected legislator. Federal Express was also advised to retain experienced Washington legislative counsel and Congressional lobbyists to help sell its case. Gary Burhop, who at the time was Senator Brock's chief administrative aide, was later to remember: "The Federal Express people showed their inexperience in maneuvering in Washington in early 1976. If they hadn't been advised otherwise, I really think they would have picked their Washington consultants from the *Yellow Pages*."

The quandry facing Federal Express was whether it should play the "establishment game" and seek CAB certification knowing the pitfalls and the agonizingly slow process, or whether it should seek immediate legislative relief. To represent the company in the Washington regulatory arenas, Smith retained as special aviation counsel, Nat Breed. Breed had been a former CAB attorney and later an attorney with a Washington law firm which represented Delta Airlines. At the same time, the Federal Express investor group retained another Washington attorney — who also represented the legislative interests of General Dynamics in Washington — Lee Hydeman, as special counsel to them.

At the board of directors meeting at Federal Express on January 13, 1976, the various options available to the company were reviewed and confusion seemed omnipresent. Primarily, the discussion was directed to the question of the pitfalls of the certification process. Hydeman, described as a hardnosed, outspoken individual, believed this process could take a minimum of two years and possibly as long as six years. He also thought the hearing and decision process might be dragged out even longer if there were competing applications filed, such as one from Flying Tigers.

Also the group discussed the problems that a certificate, if awarded by the CAB, might restrict Federal's market freedom to select its nightly route patterns and the prices it could charge for its different services. There was also the concern that during the course of the CAB certification process Federal's growth might be seriously restrained if it were denied the opportunity to fly the larger Douglas DC-9s or Boeing 727s during that time period.

The issue dragged on throughout most of 1976, although it was not debated in detail again until after October 2, 1976, when the bill which would have granted Federal Express relief died in a House committee. Fred Smith made his first appearance before a Congressional committee in April, 1976, to testify before the Senate's Subcommittee on Aviation of the Committee on Commerce which was looking into the question of regulatory reform in air transportation. This was Smith's first encounter with Senator Howard Cannon of Nevada, the subcommittee's chairman. His state did not have particularly good air cargo service, and Federal Express was able to make a strong case with shippers in Nevada for the advantages overnight delivery service would bring them if such service were available.

Smith told Cannon's Subcommittee why the airlines collectively opposed Federal's CAB request to fly the DC-9s: "They think they are entitled to the traffic regardless of whether they provide as good a service or as cheap a rate; and second, that they were there first with the mostest and consequently it is their business, and I think that is a very unhealthy attitude."

It must have seemed odd to see the then 31-year-old Fred Smith, attacking not only the established scheduled airlines but also the CAB with a skillfully prepared presentation. It was almost as if he had been involved with the commercial aviation industry a quarter of a century rather than only three years. Smith's good humored but brash articulation of his case brought much needed attention to this aggressive, small package airline.

Smith's second Congressional appearance came several weeks later when he appeared before the House Subcommitee on Aviation chaired by Glenn Anderson of California. At this hearing Smith made clear the inherent differences between people and packages and argued that the Federal Aviation Act did not recognize air cargo for what it is. His nemesis, the scheduled airlines, again came under Smith's attack. When asked why Federal Express did not use the bellies of the airlines to handle packages, Smith identified two reasons: first, the lack of carrier service at night; and secondly, the lack of ability to solve the problem of transporting restricted emergency items. To illustrate his point, Smith shared his recent conversation with the president of New England Nuclear Corporation, a supplier of nuclear generators used in hospitals to save lives:

> *President, New England Nuclear:* "I will go down and testify before the CAB that we have two choices. We can either use Federal Express to ship these nuclear medicines out, or they can bring the patient to us, you know, in a wheelchair."
>
> *Smith:* "No, we should not do that, because American Airlines would call that a diversion. We could not bring the patient in on that sort of thing."

Again, Smith played out his effective role like a bright, eloquent college professor explaining to his class — the Subcommittee in this case — the serious omissions of the Civil Aeronautics Act of 1938, and the Federal Aviation Act of 1958, as amended, insofar as the air cargo industry was concerned. He demonstrated that the law was heavily oriented toward passenger regulation dating from the 1938 legislation. And, as he had done at all of his seven Congressional appearances, he hammered away at the theme that passenger and cargo services were vastly different businesses with different characteristics. Air cargo, Smith argued, was an industry stifled by economic regulation. Federal Express was seeking legislative relief from the rigid limitations of section 416(b) as a remedy to its problem of not being able to fly larger aircraft. Chairman Anderson questioned Smith about this strategy:

> *Mr. Anderson:* "You testify that you fear that a CAB case would take 2 to 10 years to complete. Would you please explain why the time factor led you to a decision not to seek certification? To put it another way, what did you have to lose by trying to get a certificate?"
>
> *Mr. Smith:* "Well, we felt we had a number of things to lose by asking for a certificate. We could easily expend half a million or a million dollars — and we are not a rich company. And then only to find out that the Congress had taken some of these reform measures — and we think you are going to take some of them, certainly as it applies to air cargo.
>
> The second thing, Mr. Chairman, is that it has just been put to us very directly that you get your neck into that certification noose, and we are going to chop you up. And what I am talking about are the opposition counsel for some of the bigger carriers. And they will use the certification process as a weapon of and by itself to delay us from the needed solutions."

Smith and his counsel, Nat Breed, explained that Federal Express was not merely seeking special privilege for itself in seeking modification of the Board's 416(b) power. They told the Subcommittee the CAB was in agreement with them that 416(b) was an outdated limitation on the Board's discretion. And furthermore, they assured the committee they did not mind submitting to the certification process, provided Federal Express was given the breathing room an exemption from 416(b) would provide.

On June 30, 1976, H.R.14623, titled *To Broaden the Power of the Civil Aeronautics Board to Grant Relief by Exemption in Certain Cases*, was introduced in the House of Representatives by a group of 12 members. Three weeks later Senators Howard Baker and William Brock introduced in the Senate S.3684, a similar bill which would grant Federal Express immediate relief pending certification by the CAB. Federal Express would be permitted to operate larger aircraft while it went through the typically complicated and lengthy certification process.

Both bills were labeled by opponents, "the Federal Express Relief Bills." Hearings began in August, 1976, and a long list of witnesses was asked to appear before Congressman Anderson's House Subcommittee on Aviation. The Air Transport Association's Leo Seybold summed up the airlines' opposition, "This little-bitty old bill has caused a lot of waves. The airlines strongly oppose H.R.14623. It was introduced as special interest legislation because of the denial by the Civil Aeronautics Board. It is back door deregulation."

The opposition brought out a variety of arguments why Federal Express should be denied relief, including the one about the hub-and-spokes distribution system which required all packages be flown first to Memphis for sorting, wasting enormous amounts of fuel. The company had heard this same argument from its industry opponents since the fall, 1973.

Shortly before his death, Robert Prescott, founder and chairman of Flying Tigers, came to Washington in August, 1976, to attack the S.3684 bill. Although opposition came from the American Truckers Association and the Teamsters, they did not testify on this bill. It was the executives of Flying Tigers who were most vitriolic in their attacks on Federal Express. Prescott, who was very ill and spoke in a whisper, brought up the issue of foreign ownership of Federal Express, and he claimed it had "money galore" behind it. He was referring, of course, to the European-based Rothschild family's financial interest in New Court Securities, the venture capital group which had assembled the Federal Express investor group along with White, Weld, and had taken a leadership role in guiding the company through its infancy. Prescott's hostility was based on the fact that his Flying Tigers cargo line was regulated by the CAB, and that if S.3684 were approved, Federal Express would be unfairly free of regulation.

Prescott further testified that Federal Express was not doing anything particularly unique, and granting relief "means getting into our cabbage patch that we have pioneered." He continued with great hostility: "They are a specialty carrier. They are serving off-line points, off-line as far as we are concerned, because they are small lines. They are doing it at a very high price, and they now want to trade their motorcycle in for a Mack truck and get into the airfreight business that we are in." The attacks and counterattacks were bitter. In order to counter what he saw as an attack on his veracity when Fred Smith testified before Glenn Anderson's House Subcommittee in late August, 1976, he requested he be put under oath.

During the hearings in 1976, Federal Express was advised by some of its friends to get better known on Capitol Hill, and also to initiate a grassroots campaign across the country to make legislators more aware of the company. So in June, 1976, Washington attorney John Zorack was hired to serve as a lobbyist for the company. He remembered, "Nobody knew anything about Federal Express when H.R. 14623 and S.3684 were being considered. We were small time and insignificant to the power groups in Congress. It was tough getting any real sympathy when we were unknown." Zorack continued, "We lobbied Senator Cannon real hard and worked with the staff people of several senators and congressmen. The Tennessee Congressional delegation was very helpful in our cause."

In addition to Zorack, Charles Schneider, who had been a staff writer for the well-known trade publication *Aviation Week*, was hired to undertake promotion and publicity assignments. The grassroots campaign which he mounted was based on a theme reminiscent of General Patton's remarks against the Russians: "Let's go in and fight the SOB's now because we will have to sooner or later." Some 43,000 Federal Express customers were sent copies of a brochure titled: "Sometimes Free Enterprise Needs A Little Help," designed to help to gain legislative support for the two bills before Congress. As part of the same campaign, 535 members of Congress were targeted with promotion packets so they would be aware of what their constituents were requesting.

Furthermore all company employees were mobilized for an organized letter campaign. Some were even encouraged to phone their legislators. Traditionally, this type of pressure campaign has been considered the least effective way of communicating with Congressmen and Senators, but in this case the company's consultants felt it would be otherwise, and believed constituent mail would make a difference.

Fred Smith, Art Bass, and several other company officers traveled to all parts of the nation soliciting help. They spoke at chambers of commerce, service clubs, and at meetings of transportation professionals. Says Byron Hogue, Fred Smith's versatile special assistant: "We traveled to the home turf of congressmen who held positions on committees important to deregulation. We would go to fund-raising dinners in Montana and barbecues in Texas. We would talk to these people in straight, face-to-face lobbying."

Federal Express undertook a strong direct sales campaign to Louisiana, Texas, Nevada, and several other states where many local chambers of commerce were most anxious to have overnight air express service. Its public relations staff arranged for numerous press conferences in these communities, and prepared follow-up articles telling the Federal Express story which were often published without change by local newspapers.

The climax of this intensive grassroots campaign came just before October 1, 1976. In late September, H.R.15026 — a bill which provided for reduced air fares for the elderly and handicapped — was sent to the Senate for concurrence. H.R.15026 had been co-sponsored in the House by Congressman Glenn Anderson. Just prior to the vote on this bill on the Senate floor, Senator Cannon, chairman of the Subcommittee on Aviation, was asked to tack S.3684 — the so-called "Federal Express Bill" — on to H.R.15026 as an amendment. Congressman Anderson warned Senator Cannon that if he did this, he would let H.R.15026 die in committee when the bill was returned to the House for final approval. Senator Cannon brought the amended bill before the full Senate, where it was approved, 73 to 0.

Congressman Anderson was upset at what happened to his bill. He called the amended bill, "blatant special interest legislation." Consequently, he decided not to bring the amended bill before the House for final action, thus killing it.

Friday, October 1st, was the eleventh hour for Federal Express, and it made one last attempt to get the bill out of Congressman Anderson's Subcommittee before Congress adjourned the next day. Frank Maguire, then just a management consultant hired by Art Bass, had a friend who knew an aide to House Speaker Carl Albert. Maguire asked his help in trying to pressure Anderson to permit the bill to come out of committee. Late that day Maguire received this answer from his friend: "Albert doesn't want to do it. He is stepping down as Speaker of the House, and apparently has lost all interest in the Congress. He is sick and he is tired, and he just doesn't give a damn."

The "Federal Express Bill" was dead. The months of lobbying work had proven fruitless. Smith and his Federal Express had received a major defeat.

Why did Anderson refuse? Flying Tigers had opposed Federal Express, and so had the Teamsters, and so had the powerful Air Transport Association. Many Flying Tigers employees lived in Anderson's district, which was located just south of the Los Angeles International Airport. Moreover, his district was made up of several large blue collar suburbs and his constituents were strongly pro labor. And Anderson was probably sincere in his belief that Federal Express was asking for special treatment in the highly competitive and regulated air transportation industry.

Later, when the shock of this defeat wore off, Smith philosophized, "Maybe it was a blessing in disguise, because the bill dealt only with the company's present situation. We can now try for a broader bill which will change the whole law as it applies to the all-cargo operation."

The Federal Express board of directors convened in Memphis in mid-October, 1976, to discuss the next strategy. The question arose again about filing for CAB certification. Brick Meers felt the company was not strong enough to weather the uncertainties of regulation. "Regulation is a negative," he warned. And fellow board member Charley Lea warned about the "unknown excess costs associated with regulation. The regulators are not interested in profits — they only act as policemen." Not withstanding these complaints Smith wanted to file immediately. He argued, "The company will have regulatory freedom during the pendency of the certificate application. We also have the possibility of seeking an interim exemption utilizing non-controversial aircraft." After extensive discussion, the decision to file was left pending. In point of act, Federal Express did not apply for certification until mid-1977.

Deregulation prospects for the airline industry appeared better than they ever had been before, but action on any proposed bills to bring this about would have to await the next session of Congress and to await the Carter Administration's attitude toward the airline industry which would not be known until it assumed office in January of 1977.

Federal Express did not have to wait long. In February, 1977, two bills were introduced: Senators Cannon and Kennedy introduced S.689, a bill entitled, "Regulatory Reform in Air Transportation," while Senators Pearson and Baker introduced reform bill, S.292. Both bills were directed toward promoting competition and efficiency in the airline industry.

In March, 1977, President Carter asked Congress to support deregulation legislation. Consumer groups and activist academic economists, familiar with the status of commercial aviation, generally supported a major overhaul. But most of the scheduled carriers and labor representatives, as they had done in the past, opposed regulatory reform legislation.

At the Senate hearings beginning in March, 1977, the airline giants — American, Delta, Eastern, and TWA — not unexpectedly, strongly opposed any change. Again United was the lone exception: it continued to support deregulation.

When Smith testified on S.292 and S.689 on March 24, 1977, he continued his attack on the airlines and what he called "bureaucratic red tape." It was difficult, he said — forgetting his own influence peddling of recent months — for an entrepreneur who offers a better mousetrap to overcome influence peddlars and legions of bureaucrats.

The great concern of Federal Express in the spring, 1977, was what would happen if the Cannon-Kennedy and the Pearson-Baker bills were to run aground. Could the air cargo provisions be broken out and put into a separate bill? The company still feared that, if it were to pursue the certification route with the CAB, it would be a two-to-six-year wait at best. Smith, reacting to the possibility of failure of these two Senate bills, started to stress an old theme in his speeches and interviews — the difference between air cargo and passenger service. And again he lectured anyone who would give him an ear: "You cannot lump them together in one regulatory scheme without doing violence to both." He realized air cargo was not of major concern to Congress and that he would have to convince Congress the air cargo industry needed special attention.

The almost always quotable Fred Smith optimistically described his uphill fight by remarking: "If you keep working at it, in the last analysis, you win. We're like the old Ho Chi Minh. They've got to kill us 100 times. All we have to do is kill them once."

Then, on August 13, 1977, Congressman Glenn Anderson introduced his regulatory reform proposal in H.R.8813. His objective was to see not only greater freedom of entry and greater pricing flexibility, but also that airlines be given greater power to operate without government control. Although it may not have seemed like it, Anderson was for change. His refusal to cooperate with Federal Express in September, 1976, was not because he favored the continuance of tight CAB regulation. In that instance he felt Federal Express was asking for preferential treatment.

Cornell professor Alfred E. Kahn, who had by this time been appointed by President Carter as chairman of the CAB, appeared before Anderson's committee in October, 1977, to plead for open entry. In his view open entry would not have an adverse effect on airlines offering combined passenger and cargo services, or on all-cargo carriers like Flying Tigers. But Kahn thought some schedule carriers might have trouble adapting to deregulation because for the previous 39 years they had been protected by law from potential competitors.

Congressman Anderson's bill would have made it relatively easy for Federal Express, or for that matter other all-cargo airlines, to be certificated. Any carrier operating 12 continuous months prior to the date of the enactment of the new law, and carrying at least "20 million interstate freight revenue ton-miles" during the same period, could apply for a license from the CAB to provide all-cargo air service. H.R.8813 proposed the payload weight ceiling on air taxi operators be raised from 7,500 pounds to 18,000 pounds.

In September, 1977, Federal Express and several other carriers who called themselves "The Air Carrier Committee for Regulatory

Reform" published an eight-page tabloid-style newspaper called *The Airline Free Press*. The paper attempted to explain the benefits of regulatory reform. Federal Express ordered 100,000 copies to be distributed to its customers and consignees throughout the nation. A postcard was attached for the signatures of all of those persons or companies who supported the objectives outlined by Federal Express and the other firms distributing *The Airline Free Press*. These results were to be used to generate support for the deregulation bills currently before both the House and Senate.

In the latter part of October there was concern at Federal Express that Congress would not pass any airline deregulation bill in 1977. Senator Cannon, who remained a steadfast supporter of Federal Express, saw this danger too. On October 20th he arranged to have the air cargo deregulation provisions tacked on as an amendment to H.R.6010. This House bill, which had been sent to the Senate for approval, provided for expanding the type of risks the Secretary of Transportation could insure or reinsure.

The House and Senate conferees met on the bill October 26th. On October 28th the Senate approved by voice vote. Five days later the House approved it in similar fashion. There was no opposition. By this action, Congress had changed Section 17(a), Title IV of the Federal Aviation Act of 1958 by adding at the end a new section titled "Certificate for All-Cargo Air Service."

The bill became law on November 9, 1977, when it was signed by President Carter as PL 95-163, the domestic all-cargo deregulation statute. Thus, the air cargo industry had the distinction of being the first industry to be decontrolled by Congress. Competition was opened up by eliminating the CAB's control over market entry and pricing. Carriers were now permitted to use aircraft of any size.

Fred Smith had had a strong hand in bringing about this change. Once more his persistence had paid off. Many of those who observed Smith during the Congressional ordeal believe this victory to be his greatest single achievement in building Federal Express. The company had now become a full-fledged airline free to choose routes, free to set rates so long as they were not predatory, and free to choose its own equipment. Although new firms had to wait one year to apply for a certificate, Federal Express and over 50 other airlines were grandfathered in under the new law because they met the requirement of providing all-cargo service the previous year.

Fortunately for Federal Express, while it battled its way through Congress in 1976 and 1977 to obtain relief, its planning group had been refining its development blueprint on the assumption the company would be authorized at some point to fly larger aircraft.

Consequently, in December, 1977, Federal made its first purchase of Boeing 727-100s. Each of these planes had an effective payload capacity of 42,000 pounds. Soon after this purchase, the acquisition of nine additional 727s brought into reality the tentative decision made earlier to have the 727-100s as the new backbone of the Federal Express fleet. The sturdy old Falcons, which had brought Smith and Federal Express a remarkably long way since the first one began flying in 1973, were now placed in a secondary role to await eventual retirement from the fleet. A crisis filled era was ending at Federal Express.

The board of directors showed its appreciation of Fred Smith's work in securing favorable Congressional action by awarding him a $100,000 bonus. The investors and the bank lenders were obviously pleased the regulatory restraints had been taken off and the company was free to grow. Recapitalization, which had been discussed and fought over since 1975, by Smith, the investors, and the banks now became a realistic objective to pursue. It appeared that, if Federal Express could get the deadweight of debt lifted, it could realize those profits Smith had dreamed about back during 1972 and 1973 in his early plans. Meaningful profits were just starting to surface. For the six months ending November 30, 1977, the company realized almost $8 million profit. At the end of that fiscal year in May, 1978, the profit was $19.5 million.

Without the freedom provided by air cargo deregulation, Federal Express would have faced a flattening of its growth curve within a year or two, and it probably would have remained a small, moderately profitable air transportation company. But the growth limitations imposed by continued reliance on the Falcon fleet would have negated continued interest by the investors and the lenders. Talented staff and technical people would have abandoned the company in droves. But with deregulation, Smith and his bright, entrepreneurally-oriented colleagues were given new motivation to try to take Federal Express to unprecedented heights in the air cargo industry.

Chapter 10

The Bear and the Alligator

"When we started out, Emery could have kicked the crap out of us, but it didn't," Art Bass declared in 1981. "Now it'll have to come into the swamp to fight us — and it's not going to be any contest." Like so many of Art Bass' or Fred Smith's references to warfare to illustrate some competition situation, Bass' reference to the bear and alligator allegory was repeated by other senior officers and lesser-ranked employees as I interviewed them. Bass expanded this allegory when he said: "If there is going to be a fight between a bear and an alligator . . . the outcome is going to be determined more by the terrain than by the individual skill of the combatants. Much of the competition has jumped into the water with us alligators and they are totally reacting to what we are doing. And in marketing, there is nothing I would rather see than a predictable competitor. You can make him do things you wouldn't do yourself." This allegory is now an important part of the company culture. During my research for this book, as I moved through the network of Federal's offices and city stations, I heard references to this allegory at least a dozen times. I even heard it from a CTV driver at midnight standing in the pouring rain at Newark Airport while I observed the loading of a 727 aircraft. It was just another example of how the company culture has been inculcated within Federal's rank-and-file.

This bear and alligator allegory is characteristic of the company's iconoclastic and militant personality. Being attacked was never consider-

"Rapidity is the essence of war; take advantage of the enemy's unreadiness, make your way by unexpected routes, and attack unguarded spots."
—Sun Tzu, *The Art of War*, 500 B.C.

ed anything more than an incentive to engage in hand-to-hand fighting to rout the enemy. Its pugnacious spirit permeates most strategic marketing decisions. Its military metaphors and its Darwinian economic philosophy of "kill-or-be-killed" and "survival of the fittest" are deeply ingrained into both the overt and subconscious actions in daily corporate life. Retaliation is instinctive. Fighting is an heroic exercise helping to keep the competitive spirit nourished.

After Federal's first year, it gained momentum by taking business away in terms of both Emery and REA. It was almost too good to be true. "They were asleep," claims Smith. "They were vulnerable. They didn't realize how much market there was for small packages. They hadn't identified the market at all."

John Emery, Jr., admitted Federal Express had taken business away from his company in the 1974 and 1975 period but, at the time, he was not very worried. He did not regard Federal Express as a long term threat . . . yet. Emery, like so many others involved directly or indirectly in the air freight industry, considered Federal "an expensive toy" and incapable of survival. Few along Wall Street expected Federal to survive more than a few months. And perhaps deep down in their hearts Fred Smith, Roger Frock, Art Bass, and the other key Federal people did not expect the company to survive either. No one expected Federal's gun to be loaded with real bullets; it would prove to be a classic and costly mistake for the competition.

Federal's package volume grew very slowly in 1973, but in 1974 it grew in daily volume, although the yield was well-behind its plan. By 1975, it gained a 10 percent market share and yet it continued to struggle. Each year volume grew. In 1976 the company finally showed a profit. And three years later it not only handled one-third of all of the priority small packages but also it had reached a dominant position in the market from both volume and profit.

From that point the always confident Fred Smith began telling financial analysts and the national business press, "We are much bigger than anyone else. It would take a corporate behemoth to muscle its way into our business." In effect, he was warning competitors and would-be competitors to beware because Federal Express was not going to permit anyone to gain an advantage on them. His company had taken the corporate equivalent of Hill 117 in Vietnam and he was not about to surrender it. Smith's strategy continued to be to put greater distance between Federal and its competitors regardless of what Emery and the others were doing to penetrate the small package market.

Like the effective Marine officer he once was, Smith is an advocate of combat readiness. Competitive challenges excite him and bring his leadership skills to peak energy. When Emery decided to challenge Federal with a full scale attack in 1979 and 1980, Smith had the company ready. And when United Parcel Service announced in 1982, it was going to inaugurate overnight air service later that year with a large fleet of 727-100s, Smith reacted with a vengeance.

No Marine outfit could possibly survive without field intelligence, and similarly Federal Express has perfected its intelligence operation. Every move of its competitors is mapped out like a military G-2 intelligence operation to assess the implications. It carefully monitors competitors' financial and operating statistics. Its marketing staff conducts customer awareness studies of all of the competitors. Since its earliest days its surveillance has also included physical observance of competitors' field movements. For example, in 1979, when Emery set up a central sorting facility for its priority overnight package service at an airport near Smyrna, Tennessee, Federal had people positioned outside of the airfield to observe the nightly movements of aircraft and ground vehicles to get some indication of how well Emery was doing. In addition, Federal's staff observed the actions of UPS carefully during the spring and summer, 1982. As a result, management knew almost instantly that not only was UPS assembling its fleet of 727-100s in North Carolina, but also what color scheme and logo UPS had selected for its aircraft. Federal has consistently used information of this sort to develop a marketing strategy to combat competitive threats.

Smith's Marine Corps experience has served him well. He reacts to competitive challenges as if he were fighting in a military campaign. Competitors who do not understand his psychological makeup will be handicapped in preparing for Smith's certain counterattack. He will storm back. Whether they have realized it or not, Emery, UPS, the Postal Service, Airborne, and the others in Smith's mind are the industrial equivalent of the Vietcong, lurking out there in the field trying to better their positions at Federal's expense.

Until UPS entered the overnight market in September, 1982, Federal's principal competitor was Emery. After REA Air Express' collapse in 1975, Airborne moved into second position. Emery had always been aware of Federal's presence in the market, but it was not until 1977, that it began to take Federal very seriously. Emery finally recognized, primarily as a result of Federal's success in building its market share, that the small package segment of the air freight market was the place to be. After nearly five years of napping, in 1978, with a lot of fanfare, Emery announced it was establishing the priority small package and document business as a separate company profit center to compete head-on with Federal Express. It offered shippers "one-half price" coupons in an effort to build volume quickly. This tactic brought an immediate reaction from Federal Express. "Price cutting doesn't help when you can't deliver the product," Smith observed. "Emery's helter-skelter, often contradictory strategies to try to build its small package volume border on the schizophrenic." He felt Emery had received poor marketing advice. "Emery is making a mistake expanding beyond its traditional air freight business," continued Smith. "They are opting out of their life's work of 32 years." Smith's alligator was luring the bears into the swamp of a capital intensive operation and debt burden. Smith had created a new industry standard and if the competition were to survive it had to come off the hill into the Federal Express swamp.

Federal Express viewed the price cutting as an all-out assault on it by Emery. The threat of a price war clearly worried the company. Federal Express wanted desperately to protect and enhance its operating margins and above all it had to keep the margins attractive to investors. It knew that everybody gets hurt in a rate war. When Emery promoted its new service aggressively for about one year, then backed off, Federal was relieved. It had not been intimidated by Emery's price cutting. As a matter-of-fact, Federal's business expanded during Emery's attack.

Emery was struggling to find a marketing direction. The company apparently did not know the answer to the question, "What business are we in?" In 1980, it retained McKinsey & Company, an international consulting firm, to help it define its place in the air freight market and to draw up an effective organization plan. From 1946 until 1981, Emery had been a highly profitable, low-overhead air freight forwarder. Profits were made by working on a narrow spread between the rates charged by the scheduled airlines to accept shipments tendered by Emery, and the rates Emery charged its customers. Until 1975, it had been purchasing cargo space almost exclusively from the airlines. But that year, it was forced to charter more and more aircraft in order to meet its overnight customer service commitments. And then in 1981, the company made the most critical decision in its 35-year history when it decided to purchase its own fleet of jet aircraft. Although John Emery had earlier scoffed at Federal's fleet calling it "Smith's expensive toy" he finally recognized that, in order for Emery to survive, a similar fleet had to become a crucial element of his company's future. Its days as merely a freight forwarder were over. And its debt-free days were also over as it was forced to become a far more capital intensive operation if it were to continue to compete in the overnight market.

John Emery informed his company's shareholders that in the short run the company would no longer be able to pay out, as it once did, a very high percentage of its annual earnings as dividends. Long term debt jumped overnight from zero in 1980 to $70 million in 1981; and obligations under capital leases ballooned upward from just over $6 million to more than $60 million.

Airborne Freight, in order to stay competitive, also made the same decision as Emery and at about the same time. And in the same way, it suddenly went from being a very profitable, low overhead firm with limited capitalization to one with a large debt structure required to acquire its new aircraft fleet and its central package sorting hub facilities in New Wilmington, Ohio. It spent $70 million on new equipment and facilities over an 18-month period to expand its express business.

Airborne's decision to fly its own planes did not create much of a ripple at Federal Express, but the decision of UPS to do the same thing caused a great deal of excitement. Federal Express experienced some anxious moments in 1982, as it waited for UPS to make its move. The UPS threat gave Smith once more a dramatic cause to assert his leadership among Federal's senior officers and the rank-and-file. As part of the company's culture since the beginning, the focus was on Fred Smith. UPS had long been the dominant firm in the surface parcel business. This employee-owned company — one of the five largest privately-owned companies in America — handled over 6 million packages daily. A small portion of these packages were shipped by air in a two-day service called Blue Label. The bulk of its packages moved by truck. Thus, the UPS decision to operate an overnight air service was considered the greatest challenge Federal Express had ever received.

UPS is a very wealthy company. Its annual revenues approached $5 billion and at the start of 1982, it had available $650 million in cash and short term investments. Because, UPS was almost debt free — unlike Emery, Airborne and Federal Express — the financing of its fleet of aircraft would present no burden.

Smith had always admired UPS because of financial success and its efficient management. During Federal's start-up in 1973, it relied heavily on the technical help of ex-UPS employees. It adopted many of UPS's administrative procedures and selling techniques until Federal had devised its own. Privately, it wished that it did not have to meet head-to-head competition from UPS. But the formal announcement from UPS was in some ways useful to Smith because once again it gave him another cause to rally his company against.

In the summer, 1982, the tension at Federal Express mounted. In early August Fred Smith flew to Europe on a business trip and suddenly disappeared for several days. It turned out that he had gone to the Middle East and had turned up in Beirut during the height of the Israeli and PLO fighting in the heart of that war torn city. He had hitched a ride from Israel with an Israeli army officer to observe firsthand what was going on. His close advisors at Federal Express were convinced Smith went there to get the smell of battle so he could inspire his staff for the upcoming air battle with UPS.

At the Summer, 1982, Family Briefing for employees, perennial master-of-ceremonies Frank Maguire, in the ebullient manner of midmorning television game show hosts, set the competitive theme for the major speeches to follow by Federal's president, Peter Willmott and Fred Smith. Maguire concluded his remarks buoyantly: "The competition is out there, and they are going to try to eat our lunch. The competition is tough, and the outcome is not yet decided.

It's a year of challenge — a year of risk. We face the most challenging and competitive year in the history of this marvelous company. I say bring 'em on. Let's hit 'em between the running lights."

Then Willmott, the company president, followed Maguire on stage with a long and rambling explanation of the need for employees to become more efficient and to concentrate on lowering the company's cost structure. "If you are in that position, then you can keep your prices low, and keep your prices below the prices the competition charges for a similar product," Willmott concluded. Maguire, issued his standard enthusiastic introduction of Smith who, then, in a 37-minute lecture, told the audience Federal Express was at the competitive frontier serving the new technological revolution in America, and it needed to keep innovating if it was to stay out in front. He reiterated in a far less frenetic way what Maguire had told the employees about the competitive battle ahead.

UPS began its new service in September, 1982. Its delivery commitment was by 3:00 p.m. the next day in its initial 24-city market network. It offered no "on-call" pickup service and no tracing service on packages from the point of pickup to delivery. A customer's packages had to be ready to go at the time UPS drivers made their scheduled daily calls to the vicinity of the customer's office, plant, or warehouse. When Fred Smith heard of this he announced publicly, "If you're using UPS and you miss the afternoon pickup, it's too bad. The last stage has left Dodge. There's the 'Get Mad Factor' for UPS to worry about if the shipper has no alternative left to him."

At a meeting of Chicago security analysts held in the Palmer House during October, 1982, Smith was quizzed hard about the competitive threat of UPS. He responded bluntly, "Look, the '21' Club in New York and McDonald's are in the same business, but there is *a great deal of difference*." Federal's counterattack was based on differentiating the quality of service. His public relations staff sent out this message: "UPS is the best in the business at what they do — moving low priority, consumer-oriented parcels where emergency is not a factor. But Federal, in turn, is best at what it does — movement of the most vital and time-sensitive parcels and documents."

Federal's marketing goal for 1983 was to establish clearly in the minds of customers that it offered a superior service. Explained Tom Oliver, head of marketing, "We want to dispel in the minds of the customers the idea that competitors are the equal to us when in fact they are not. We are not going to let competitors equal Federal Express. We will offer 10:30 a.m. delivery, more service options, Saturday pickups, package tracing, and call-backs to shippers informing them that the packages have been delivered."

In the 1980s, the small package market started to get quite crowded. New firms entered and several existing firms like Emery, Airborne, Purolator Courier, and the leading commercial airlines stepped up their marketing efforts. Federal Express had defined the market and established its beachheads and gained control of strategic market areas in the preceding years, and consequently these other firms wanted a part of the action. The competition woke up to the fact that there was a huge market out there for small packages and documents needing some form of priority service.

An all-out media battle commenced among the principal competitors to convince the customer that each company could provide a faster, more reliable service. Federal's original priority commitment had been to deliver before 12:00 noon the next business day. Then, disregarding the enormous initial additional costs of the decision in October, 1982, in response to mounting competition — particularly from UPS — Federal advanced its overnight service commitment to 10:30 a.m. At that time Emery and Airborne offered a "by 12:00 noon at the latest" service. Some of Federal's competitors offered a late afternoon service at a substantially lower price for those customers not caring whether their packages came in the morning or the afternoon. And most companies, including Federal, offered a second-day service at even lower prices.

When the company acquired its fleet of 727s and DC-10s, built its Super Hub in Memphis, installed its state-of-the-arts electronic communication system, and added other support facilities Willmott proudly announced, "We've got the best service; we've got the capacity; we've got the talent; we've got the best team; we're ready and open for business." What Smith and Willmott were telling their competitors in so many words was, "If anyone tries to get Federal Express, we'll get them first."

Clearly, the alligators at Federal Express had lured the Emery and UPS bears into the capital intensive, high-tech swamp and would try to keep them from the high ground.

Chapter 11

Faganomics

In 1973 the company had to tell the world quickly why its service was important. It had to explain to potential customers that the transportation and distribution system it had put in place provided fast, reliable, overnight, air express service. Not only were time and funds unavailable to develop a comprehensive marketing and sales plan, but also the staff was overwhelmed putting out the "small fires" while launching daily service. Art Bass, Mike Fitzgerald and several others assigned to sales and customer service were simply spread too thin.

In these early days of trying to reach the market, stopgap measures were a necessity. Because of the influence of several former United Parcel Service employees, including Mike Fitzgerald, Mike Basch and Ted Sartoian, heavy emphasis was placed on the direct selling techniques used successfully by UPS. But results from these direct calls on potential customers were too slow in coming. The technique of "one-on-one" personal selling was not getting the package count built up or the revenues rising fast enough to meet the targets of the company's business plan. From 1973, through mid-1975, the actual daily package count figures fell far behind the projected daily volumes the marketing staff had promised to the investors.

In the final months of 1974, and the early months of 1975, management shifted the marketing and sales approach. To survive, the company needed volume. Federal Express decided to take a radically different sales approach to marketing its services from the tradi-

"You can . . . never foretell what any man will do, but you can say with precision what an average number will be up to. Individuals vary, but percentages remain constant."
—Sherlock Holmes, *The Sign of Four,* 1890

tional direct mail or "cold call" marketing techniques of UPS. Time was running out. After more than 18 months Federal Express was still struggling to gain public recognition.

To make the American business public aware of its services, Federal decided to use a media approach using the theme, "Give us a try." Television was first choice, but management also realized the importance of advertising in metropolitan dailies, business periodicals such as the *Wall Street Journal* and trade publications such as *Air Cargo Magazine* and *Industry Week* in the effort to get quick exposure. Federal's critics didn't question the use of print media, but in reacting to the unexpected use of television they said in amazement, "Television advertising for a freight company? Why, that's unheard of. Emery has never used it."

The marketing strategy was the special province of newly appointed senior vice president, J. Vincent Fagan. Fred Smith gave Fagan the assignment of developing the corporate marketing plan and supervising the extensive research needed to identify more clearly the characteristics of the market for small packages.

The late Vince Fagan became a crusader in fighting for the dollar and the personnel resources to launch his programs. Company funds were scarce because the monthly deficits were horrendous. Every dollar was needed to keep the company operational. Critics within the company's management staff and several cautious board members often became nervous when Fagan presented bold, untried television ad campaigns which had budgets for far more dollars then they were willing to commit. Art Bass, when he assumed the presidency in February, 1975, fought for Fagan's bold plans and took the brunt of the criticism from the board members when they were skeptical about the potential effectiveness of the television ads. Bass continued to be one of Fagan's chief supporters during Fagan's seven-year association with Federal Express.

Fagan was 39 when Fred Smith convinced him in September, 1974, to leave New York to join Federal Express in Memphis. He came reluctantly, but he liked the idea of joining his long-time friend and former partner, Art Bass. Like Smith, Bass, and the other original senior officers, Fagan was blessed with a strong entrepreneurial spirit. His close associates described Fagan as being a very bright, articulate, and opinionated individual with an enormous ego. They described him as "not just tough, he was 'tough-tough.'" He was always his own man and seldom yielded any ground once he had formulated his marketing plans. "Vince Fagan and Tucker Morse, the company's attorney, were among the few who were not 'yes men' on the staff," said Mike Fitzgerald admiringly. "They weren't afraid at critical times to tell either Fred Smith or the board of directors they were wrong."

One of Fagan's associates remembers one such confrontation between Smith and Fagan. "Take for example the day Vince Fagan, our head marketing and advertising guy, was arguing against one of Fred's marketing suggestions. Fagan kept pointing out the flaws in Smith's idea, but Fred kept coming back as if he hadn't heard Vince's points. What Vince didn't realize was that Fred was using his well-honed 'wear-em-down-technique' on him. Not only was Vince as stubborn as Smith, but also Vince was one of just two or three guys in the company who could get away with telling Fred some of his ideas were dumb. Neither yielded an inch as the argument dragged on. Finally, in desperation, Mike Fitzgerald slipped Fagan a note which read: 'Vince, if Fred orders a chicken to pull a freight train, you go out and hook him up.' Vince was a real prima donna. He would really carry on sometimes when he wasn't getting his way, and he was very rough on some of his subordinates."

The two times I interviewed Vince Fagan I was impressed by this seemingly self confident former advertising executive who inhabited an office, blue with cigarette smoke, and always sat near an overflowing ashtray. Fagan was an imposing figure as he leaned forward with his arms on the desk. He had a shock of silver, curly hair which made him look like an impresario, and as we spoke he looked at me as if he were x-raying me. I was never sure who was interviewing whom. He was the most combative yet cooperative member of this executive team I interviewed, but to be fair, this combativeness, as I learned later, may have been due to his awareness that he was gravely ill with cancer.

Fagan is credited with building the marketing plan which helped the company enjoy increasing consumer success after the struggling and disappointing start-up years of 1973 and 1974. Those who knew him described him as an adept marketer, but often irrascible and sometimes difficult to work with. This, however, did not lessen his colleagues' admiration of him. Reflecting on those difficult years, Bass says of Fagan: "Vince kept his eye on the ball. He was research-oriented and used this tool to back up his recommendations. And he understood how to attract business." Fagan was also an effective salesman for his program. At times Fagan would tell management, "There is an enormous, untapped market in the United States just waiting for a service like that offered by Federal Express. The company shouldn't be timid in going after it." He stressed that the company's marketing needed to address the question of a two-tiered market. One market was the traditional distribution sector. These were the shipping departments and the mail rooms and loading docks of business and industry — what the company called the "back door market." The other market was called the "front door market," since it consisted of executive offices or what are sometimes called the "papermills of America." In this front door market were the ad agencies, architectural firms, banks, consultants, law firms, and similar business and financial services.

In the first tier market, or back door business, Federal Express had to compete head-to-head with Emery, Airborne, United Parcel Service, and the whole gamut of air freight forwarders and commercial airlines. The other tier was a nontraditional market, and a market that few people had precisely identified or understood very well. Within this first tier of potential customers were those in the business and professional service industries. At best, those in the second tier may have shipped by air on rare occasions. But Vince Fagan felt these front office groups might constitute a strong customer base if given a sufficient reason to use air express overnight service. His strategy was to get the attention of the people in the mailroom or the shipping departments as well as the secretaries who daily make decisions about what mode of transportation will be used to ship packages and documents as well as which air express company will be called.

Fagan recognized soon after his arrival in Memphis that the company needed to identify precisely what marketing approach should be taken to build volume quickly. His choice was to use advertising to reach a mass market versus the traditional direct "cold call" approach to reach individual accounts.

In May, 1978, the Sales and Customer Service departments were placed in Vince Fagan's Marketing Department. Management decided it needed to gain more control over direct sales so it could respond to the inquiries of the less frequent shippers who were beginning to call Federal as a result of the company's broad-based advertising. The process of converting potential customers to sales needed improvement. The sales force had been dispersed under the direction of the four divisional general managers while customer service had been handled by the local city stations. As a result, there had been no centralized customer service system. And, in some of the regional areas, it was clear that administrative chaos prevailed.

Fagan had been the company's biggest critic when it came to evaluating the contribution of the sales force. His recommendation had long been, "Let's spend another $1 million on advertising and do away with the salesmen." Consequently, he downplayed the direct "cold call" sales approach in which salesmen call on prospects in person, and one at a time. He considered this costly and nonproductive. This method of selling had been a carry-over at Federal from the days in 1972, when the company was selling exclusively its charter express cargo service. Fagan was negative toward the company's field sales force, since he did not believe it was capable of contributing much business volume. He saw the urgency to build volume.

He had long felt that advertising was the way to stimulate quick growth in package volume. In the years of greatest adversity, 1974 to 1977, Fagan was absolutely right. In 1978, with deregulation safely behind it, Federal Express would be more secure, and it would also have more funds to commit to both advertising and direct sales.

Despite the change, the sales organization continued to be a neglected child. Fagan continued to give it no place of prominence in his annual marketing plans. Not until 1980, when Smith made the decision to transfer the sales function to the Ground Operations Department, did the sales group start receiving serious attention from management.

In Federal's start-up years this sales organization was administered from Memphis. But from 1975 to 1978, control was centered in the field divisions. Following the 1978 reorganization, control reverted back to Memphis. The flip-flopping continued in 1980, when control once again went back to the field. Prior to 1981, the company's direct sales strategy had been so chaotic that it had been impossible to build an effective sales organization. Craig Bell, the veteran head of sales, explained that "key company sales executives were frustrated. Their morale was low." He and his colleagues wanted to set the record straight and prove that the sales organization was contributing far more to the company than it was costing as Fagan believed. With Fagan gone in 1980, they felt they could get top management's "ear." After seven years, Smith finally gave them the resources to emerge from their secondary role following the 1980 companywide reorganization.

The salesgroup was challenged to upgrade its personnel and to prove its effectiveness in attacking the market. One change made was the decision to be more selective in direct sales calls. With each sales call estimated to cost an average of $60, the new approach adopted was to target the sales efforts, and concentrate on accounts shipping at least three packages per day. Previous approaches were often of the "shotgun" variety where salesmen were told to go out and make 20 or 25 calls per day on anybody who would listen to their sales presentations. Sales training was also strengthened as part of the upgrading after the 1980 reorganization.

When the business historian examines Federal Express, the long term contribution of Vince Fagan not only to the company but also to the air freight industry as well will be seen to be substantial. Fagan is responsible for bringing to the industry state-of-the art advertising and marketing concepts. These contributions are basically four in number. He introduced the "Air Express Buying Power Index" which accurately identified the market potential. His market research group contributed mightily to the construction of a rational pricing policy. Fagan seems to have been the first to apply behavioral analysis using "focus group techniques" to the air express customer. But most important were his pioneering efforts in the use of television as an advertising media in the air freight industry where before it had never been tried.

Among the first tasks Fagan's group undertook was organizing an industry monitoring program so the competition and industry trends could be tracked. He felt this would assist in setting prices, uncovering new service opportunities, and measuring Federal's performance or penetration within the major air freight markets. Fagan placed heavy emphasis on developing better package volume prediction models. His "Air Express Buying Power Index" was developed by examining the correlation between certain Standard Industrial Classification (SIC) codes and the actual use of air freight by companies in those industries. His staff measured specific economic characteristics in all cities, including such things as the makeup of the industrial bases, the number of hospital beds, and the specific companies in those cities which might be major prospects for shipping time-sensitive, high priority packages by air express.

Customers were classified by SIC categories and ratios were developed for the number of packages expected to be shipped per employee in each category. This list was then matched against SIC employment figures to develop a Buying Power Index (or as it is known in the industry marketing parlance, BPI) for each metropolitan area. Fagan utilized these figures to identify the top urban markets for potential business. In his first marketing plan in 1975, he selected 23 target markets which, according to his statistical model, had 60 percent of the total air package buying power in the nation. This was the basis for Fagan's initial efforts to allocate on a rational basis, sales and promotion dollars for television and print media advertising, and direct sales calls and special promotions.

In later plans package prediction models were refined. Company researchers examined the evolving characteristics of the expanding Federal Express customer base and noted any features which would appear to call for further adjustments of the model. Thus, if package counts fell below the projected share for a particular city, Fagan's staff would try to find the reasons for the lag. Some of these reasons they found in their investigations were poor station management, local strikes, unemployment, or increasing competition in given metropolitan areas. The package model also served as the basis for the aircraft lift model to determine nightly the type and the number of aircraft to use for the various cities receiving service.

Suggestions on pricing policies and on new types of services were also part of the responsibilities of Fagan's market research group. Competitor's rate structures were carefully watched and questions of price elasticity were considered. The company wanted to know if there was customer resistance to any increases in rates. How high could it raise rates on the Priority 1 or the Courier-Pak products before customers resisted and looked for alternative ways to ship their items? Federal Express had always believed it could prove to customers that it was rendering a valuable service in dealing with time-sensitive shipments, and that customers are willing to pay for the service so long as they felt the value they received from the service exceeds its cost. Yet Federal Express, in preparing its pricing recommendations, had recognized that its rates could not be set too far above any competitor offering comparable types of service.

In the early years, Fred Smith was timid about raising prices for fear of scaring away customers. In order to build market share, the strategy was to opt on the lower side. Fagan, however, argued that prices should be raised. He pointed out that the company's outstanding service was being recognized by customers and that they would pay a higher price for the better product.

The pricing decisions have been worked out jointly between the marketing staff and the corporate financial staff. The trick has been to set prices at a high enough level to protect company profit margins while at the same time making absolutely certain that the company was not pricing itself out of the market. The task in marketing strategy has been to convince customers that Federal Express charges the prices it does because it is rendering a superior type of service. "We're good, that's why!" Federal has consistently bragged to the business press. "We deliver on time all of the time, and we are attentive to the customer's needs."

Behavioral analysis to test consumer reaction to new products or services was another radical technique introduced into the air freight industry by Fagan. He installed the "focus group technique" that has been used so effectively by Procter & Gamble and many other major consumer products companies to elicit consumer reactions to new or existing products as a part of developing marketing plans. In selected test cities a half-dozen or so individuals not employed by Federal Express would be invited to take part in an open, free flowing discussion led by a professional moderator. After a suitable warm-up period in which the discussion leader got the group conversing, the groups are then asked to discuss their opinions or attitudes toward a specific product or a service that Federal Express was considering for introduction. This type of semi-structured market research is designed to identify problems and also to produce new ideas. The responses from such an exercise are ordinarily not quantifiable. "We 'strategize' from what we hear the focus groups talking about," says Alyce Craddock. What she meant by this was that the information is helpful in planning a marketing approach.

An enormous amount of marketing research was undertaken during Fagan's first year with the company. Given the limited funds for marketing in 1974 and 1975, Fagan felt that extensive information was needed to develop the company's marketing plan. When the initial market planning was completed, Fagan strongly recommended that heavy emphasis be given to television advertising with secondary support from print media advertising.

Fagan moved quickly in late 1974 to launch the company's first major advertising campaign. The strategy was to use an advertising technique called "top-of-the-mind awareness." Federal Express needed desperately to make the public aware of its existence, and then convert a large number of people to users of its services.

Advertising budgets given to Vince Fagan to work with in the early years were meager by later standards. This early stringency forced Federal Express to find ways to obtain the highest market penetration within the constraints of thin budgets. The board of directors had to be convinced that the advertising budgets Fagan was promoting would get results. At the June, 1975, board meeting, company president Art Bass was able to tell the cautious and apprehensive board of directors that sales had increased 27 percent in New York and Los Angeles where Federal had targeted its first television campaign, "America, You've Got A New Airline." Bass was convinced there was a causal link between advertising and sales. "These results," he asserted, "showed that to be true." Still, some board members could not help but recall nineteenth-century merchandiser John Wanamaker's statement, "I know half my advertising dollars are wasted, but I don't know which half." The company was operating on very thin budgets in 1975, and Federal's board, which consisted largely of representatives of the venture capital group, was very nervous about spending funds on anything other than operations.

The choice of New York and Los Angeles for the local spot television campaign in the summer, 1975, was based on Fagan's estimate that these two market areas had some 38 percent of the air freight potential. This was the most market coverage the company could get for its paltry $190,000 advertising campaign. In these two metropolitan areas Federal Express faced uphill odds competitively. Emery, plus numerous other freight forwarders, the major all cargo airlines, and the combination passenger-cargo airlines made these two cities, plus Chicago, the most competitive air freight markets in America. The fact that Federal's package volume increased 27 percent after the campaign was a very good omen for the company. In his marketing plan, Fagan decried the fact that Federal's lack of network advertising hindered the development of business across the country.

The plan for 1976, recommended that the sales force concentrate on the top 1,000 shippers in their personal calls, and that a mail campaign be directed to the nation's top 10,000 largest shippers. Heretofore Federal Express had not advertised in the *Yellow Pages*, and it had no "800" number listing in the telephone directories. These shortcomings were singled out for immediate correction.

The overall strategy was aimed at the task of building awareness, particularly in the top ten markets: New York, Los Angeles, Chicago, San Francisco, Philadelphia, Boston, Detroit, Atlanta, Dallas, and Cleveland. The ideal promotion was believed to be a combination of television advertising, newspapers, and popular business magazines, plus direct mail and direct solicitation. Yet once more budget stringencies required hard choices of how to allocate scarce dollars. For media advertising in fiscal 1976, Federal budgeted only $1.2 million.

Emery outspent Federal Express in 1976 in marketing effort and it had twice the number of salesmen in the field making direct calls on customers and prospects. Federal's management girded for what it felt would be a strong marketing counterattack by Emery and Airborne as these major competitors began to recognize the size and character of the market for small packages. Emery started a television advertising campaign, but Airborne continued to sell exclusively by direct customer calls and canvassing by mail. Airborne believed these were the most effective means of landing the accounts of big shippers. And at that time they were correct.

Federal's advertising budget in fiscal 1977 was $2.5 million. The decision was made to use local spot television advertising in the top 17 markets east of Denver. The change of the Federal Aviation Act of 1958, which would have permitted Federal to use larger aircraft, was still an issue before Congress in late 1976 and early 1977. This was the reason management had to downplay the West Coast metropolitan areas in its television advertising campaign. As long as it was limited to flying the company's small Falcons, it was not optimistic about its changes of improving its service to the West Coast.

The new advertising emphasis was placed on building an awareness of Federal Express in "the executive suites" of America. The large metropolitan dailies, plus popular business and weekly news periodicals such as *Business Week* and *U. S. News and World Report*, were used to attract business in smaller regional markets not covered by the spot television campaign. Fagan was anxious to promote greater sales of the Courier-Pak product, and felt that its primary market was in the front offices of business firms, not back in the shipping departments of these same companies.

When air cargo deregulation cleared Congress favorably in late 1977, Federal's growth expectations accelerated. Permission to use larger aircraft meant that theoretically Federal Express could go after every time-sensitive package in America and possibly in a good portion of urbanized Canada.

Reflecting this high optimism, advertising expenditures were increased to nearly $7.8 million in fiscal 1979; $10.6 million in 1980; then to over $25 million in both fiscal 1982 and 1983. The bulk of the 1982 budget was spent on network and spot television advertising. Prime time network programming absorbed the heaviest expenditures. Nightly network news and major weekend sports attractions were popular outlets. Several million potential decision makers who send packages or documents air express were sitting in front of the television sets for these programs. The target audience was both adult male and female. The campaign to introduce the Overnight Letter was budgeted at some $6 million of the $25 million in 1982. About $1 million was allocated for direct mailings, and another $1 million went for listings in the *Yellow Pages*.

In seven years the advertising budget had increased by 25 times.

By any historical standards the recent budgets are exorbitant for an air freight company. But Federal's spending over $25 million is a very modest outlay when compared, for example, with consumer products companies. Procter & Gamble spends almost 21 times as much. McDonald's spends five times as much.

Beginning in the 1980s air express advertising in general has escalated. Most of Federal's major competitors have been forced to spend heavily to try to improve their market shares. They have recognized that Federal Express' aggressiveness in media advertising had helped it maintain its wide competitive lead. Emery came forward first, then it was followed by Purolator Courier, Burlington Northern, Flying Tigers, U. S. Postal Service, and finally, Airborne. All recognized how much success Federal Express had had with Fagan's advertising approach in building awareness and gaining new customers.

Market awareness — the critical focus of Federal's marketing plans in 1974 and 1975 — ceased to be a concern after several years of effective media advertising. Company-sponsored surveys showed a high market awareness. Studies showed that more people were aware of Federal Express than Emery. The statistical difference in Federal's favor was small; but what is significant is that Federal had climbed from obscurity in 1973, to a status of high name recognition in just a very few years.

Federal's marketing strategy, influenced by Fagan's innovations and his persistent defense of these innovations, had carried the company a very long way. Federal found how to use effectively the various media to build volume and customers. It found a vast, untapped market and exploited it while its competitors largely opted to follow along with a "me-too" approach. The use of advertising accelerated from the time Federal entered into the successful marriage with Ally & Gargano, Inc., its innovative advertising agency. Most of Ally & Gargano's campaigns brought results. And the financial outlays to stage them were not particularly burdensome on Federal's annual budgets except in those early crisis years, 1973 through 1975.

Chapter 12

Late to Bed, Early to Rise
Advertise, Advertise, Advertise

When John Moschitta, the slip-tongued executive on Federal's award winning commercial, "Fast Paced World" ends with his "Dick-what's-the-deal-with-the-deal. Are-we-dealing? We're-dealing. Dave-its-a-deal-with-Don, Dork-and-Dick. Dork-it's-a-deal-with-Don, Dave-and-Dick. Dick-it's-a-Dork-with-Don-Deal-and-Dave. Dave-got-ta-go, disconnecting. Dick-gotta-go, disconnecting . . ." the voice-over announcer intones the now famous household phrase, "Federal Express. When It Absolutely, Positively Has To Be There Overnight." Few of us outside the air express industry recognize the revolutionary implications of this kind of ad campaign. The quite simple truth seems to be that Federal Express very largely owes its huge marketing success to the radical implementation of this kind of television advertisement.

Over the years 1974-1983, there have been five basic campaigns devised by Federal's Marketing Department in collaboration with the New York advertising agency of Ally & Gargano. The first of these campaigns began in 1975, and was known around the company as "the establishment stage" since its chief aim was to build a broad public awareness of Federal's existence. This "America You Have A New Airline" campaign was quickly followed by a second stage which focused on competition with Emery. Federal confessed that these memorable "Twice As Good As The Best In The Business" ads were an unabashed attempt to make a name

"Use our cream, And we betcha, Girls won't wait, They'll come, And getcha"
—Burma Shave

for itself at Emery's expense. The third stage in 1976, stressed Federal's efficiency and effectiveness on the theme "Take Away Our Planes And We'd Be Just Like Everybody Else." But it was the fourth campaign in 1977 which really caught the public's purse strings in 1977 with the innovative use of exaggerated humor which attempted to build an empathetic bridge to the customer by focusing on the everyday human foibles of the workaday world. So successful was this introduction of humor that all subsequent advertising campaigns seemed to be blends of earlier themes and this new comic technique.

When Federal put its advertising account up for competitive bidding in 1974, to its great good fortune it selected Ally & Gargano, Inc., a medium-sized New York agency. Management felt that hiring this firm — known best in the industry at the time for its creativity — would insure that the Federal Express account would be taken seriously and that it would get the best efforts of the agency despite the very modest advertising budget Federal was offering. Carl Ally and his partner, Amil Gargano, were veterans in the profession. They had reputations of being less conformist than most of the well-known Madison Avenue agencies. Fagan, when asked why he recommended them answered: "They were 'bomb throwers,' and they could give us the dramatic advertising we needed."

Carl Ally was described by author Robert Glatzer as "an articulate, combative man who talks and acts like a cross between a college English teacher (which he was) and a pool hustler." Prior to his work on the Federal Express account his best advertising campaigns were noted for their pungency. He had earned a considerable reputation within the advertising industry for his work in the 1960s on the Volvo and the Hertz campaigns. Hertz had been under attack for several years by Avis' skillful advertising, and it had lost market share in the rent-a-car industry. The Avis advertising campaign had the well-known theme, "When You're Only No. 2, You Try Harder. Or Else." Hertz had been put on the defensive by this media attack authorized by the then Avis chairman Robert Townsend, author of the caustic, irreverent book attacking corporate management, *Up the Organization*.

Ally was hired by Hertz late in this protracted media war and instructed to help the badly wounded Hertz fight back and regain public confidence. The Ally-directed campaign lasted one year and it contributed to the reversal of Hertz's precipitous slide in rent-a-car market shares.

In order to obtain the largest possible viewing audience in several selected metropolitan markets for the company's advertisements, television was the principal outlet selected for the Federal Express account. Print media was only employed to play a role in those cases where the company wanted to attract the attention of decision makers in special audiences for which these trade and business publications were especially tailored.

The first campaign, the so called "establishment stage," had the paltry budget of $800,000. The first television ad which was aired in only a few major cities had this attention-grabbing message: "America, You've Got A New Airline. But Don't Get Excited Unless You're A Package. No First Class, No Meals, No Movies, In Fact, No Passengers. Just Packages."

In the New York market, this 30-second ad was changed to say, "New York, You've Got A New Airline . . ." and in Los Angeles, it was, "Los Angeles, You've Got A New Airline . . ." The June, 1975, campaign lasted four weeks. Local television 30-second spot announcements were used. Full-page print ads were also run simultaneously in the *Los Angeles Times*, the *New York Times*, the *Wall Street Journal*, and the other leading dailies in the target cities. This ad theme had simplicity. The intention was to build strong recall into the message. Federal hoped that the public's curiosity would be aroused by the tantalizing announcement that this company called Federal Express was operating an airline in which packages would be treated like passengers.

A technique called "comparative advertising" was the foundation of Federal's second campaign. In these ads Federal's aim was to persuade shippers and consignees to use its services rather than those of its competitors by proving their service had a qualitative advantage. Traditionally in the advertising world, it was considered unprofessional or even unethical to publicly insult your competitor in advertising. But that particular ethical standard had been under attack since the 1960s. By the 1970s this tradition had been scuttled and it was fair game to belittle your competitor.

Emery, perhaps the only company with national visibility in the air freight industry at the time, was selected as Federal's prime target. "Let's take on the leader," the Federal Express planning staff wrote in its marketing plan. "If you are No. 1, you don't attack your competitor. But if you aren't No. 1, you attack the leader." It was a technique taken from the handbook of traditional U. S. Naval tactics — "Pick out the biggest one and fire." When John Emery described his company in those days he would say through his public relations staff, "We are the Tiffany, the Rolls-Royce of the air freight business. We are the generic name in air freight." The Emery-Federal Express match-up was staged to be similar to the Hertz-Avis confrontation of the mid-1960s. Its objective was to draw attention to Federal's higher quality of service. Carl Ally, the experienced strategist who led the campaigns of the Hertz-Avis advertising war, knew how to stage a direct attack. Ally had stenciled Emery's name on an arsenal of media bombs and Fred Smith was ready to authorize his media guerrillas to move on Emery.

Federal's second campaign was launched in mid-1975 using the basic theme, "Who's Cheaper? Who's More Reliable?" Vince Fagan explained, "We feel we can take advantage of the Emery image by creating our own image as an aggressive underdog offering a more superior service than the undisputed leader." The decision was really based on management's conclusion, "What do we have to lose by a direct assault on Emery?" Fred Smith, a student of military history, obviously knew that frontal attacks seldom bring a clear cut victory for the attacker. British military historian Basil Liddel-Hart found in his studies that the attacker must have a 3-to-1 advantage in firepower to defeat a well-entrenched enemy. In the staged Federal Express-Emery battle, Emery took some direct hits but refused to retaliate. It grumbled about Federal's research methodology employed to create the data used in the campaign. Emery also was taken back by the brazenness of the comparative advertising campaign, but it did not launch a major counterattack on this brash young upstart company from Memphis.

Federal Express, despite being much smaller and less well-known, did have some special advantages over Emery. First, Federal specialized in small packages and documents rather than in across-the-board, general air freight shipments. And second, it had its own fleet of planes. It could exercise total control over the nightly movement of its packages and documents. Emery had not segmented its market. It was handling all sizes of air cargo. In 1975, Emery was still an air freight forwarder operation utilizing the air lift provided by scheduled passenger carriers to get its shipments to consignees.

As part of this second campaign, Fagan hired Opinion Research Corporation (ORC), a national market research firm located in Princeton, New Jersey, to evaluate the relative performance of five air freight services between 24 city pairs such as Milwaukee to El Paso, Phoenix to Washington, D. C., or Dallas to Kansas City during a two-week period in April, 1975. The services compared were Emery's, Airborne's, REA Air Express', and Federal Express' Priority 1 (overnight service) and Standard Air Service (two-day service). Identical nine-pound packages were shipped to and from a selection of cities — large and small. Logs were kept by both shippers and consignees who were market research correspondents for ORC.

The ORC study found that Federal's Priority 1 service was twice as fast as that of REA Air Express, Airborne, and Emery. It found that Federal's Priority 1 service was cheaper than Federal's competitors. And it found Federal's Standard Air Service to be faster and nearly 40 percent cheaper than any competitors' services. And ORC found that Federal's package tracing capability, while far from ideal in April, 1975, was the best among the competitors.

Using these results Federal prepared an advertising campaign showing graphically two piles of packages — Federal's and Emery's.

Federal's pile was twice as high. Federal used this dramatic display to illustrate its statement that it was twice as good as Emery who was supposed to be the best in the business in getting packages delivered by noon the following day.

John Emery, Jr., yelled, "Foul!" He complained the results were artificial and contrived. "The problem is you can prove anything you want to with such a study," groused Emery. Along with John Emery, the other competitors pointed out that the ORC survey was weighted in favor of off-line areas, that is, those cities and towns not well-served by the scheduled airlines. They claimed that 60 percent of air freight moves exclusively between the top 50 metropolitan cities where commercial airline service was then concentrated.

Federal Express conceded that the ORC study might have been weighted, creating a bias in the results. But this did not dissuade it from capitalizing on this comparison in its advertising copy. It had several thousand brochures prepared to mail to potential customers showing the results of this service comparison. Federal ran ads captioned, "If You're Using Emery, Don't Let Your Boss See These Figures," then it inserted the results of the test study. The advertising theme was "competitive domination" with emphasis on statements like, "Twice As Good As The Best In The Business." Emery's advertising at that same time stressed that it was a dollar less and an hour faster than its competitors. Federal's ad blitz with the ORC results was designed to dispel these Emery claims.

But in 1976, Fagan's arguments about the inefficiency of direct selling had been accepted and because of continued tight budgets, Federal's marketing strategy had to be to spend as efficiently as possible. Instead of sending its sales force out to call on anyone who might conceivably ship a package, Federal decided to concentrate on the top 2,000 industrial and institutional accounts. As a consequence, the strategy of the third campaign was to use television, magazine, and newspaper advertising to capture the attention of these many thousands of occasional shippers who made up the remaining part of the market. The key advertising message of this new campaign launched in 1976, stressed the company's service efficiency because — unlike Emery, Airborne, Purolator Courier, and the others — Federal operated its own planes. The ad caption taunted "Take Away Our Planes and We'd Be Just Like Everybody Else."

Fagan explained the strategy: "We told everybody why we were better than Emery and the rest of them. We demonstrated that the closed loop system — where Federal Express, through the use of its own planes and trucks, maintained control over the package from pickup to delivery — was superior."

Federal's "taking off the gloves" approach to advertising began to pay dividends. In the period from 1975 to 1977, the average daily package count rose from an average of 11,000 to 22,000 per day.

Its customer list tripled to 60,000 accounts.

"Federal Express — When It Absolutely, Positively Has To Be There Overnight" was the theme introduced during the next evolutionary stage of the advertising strategy. This was considered the most forceful and memorable advertising statement to date made by the company. Today it remains the permanent corporate advertising statement, and it is affixed to most advertising copy. "Absolutely, Positively Overnight" identifies Federal Express to the public in much the same manner as "We Try Harder" identifies Avis and as "Breakfast of Champions" has historically identified Wheaties. Dependability of service is what the company most wanted to emphasize in this marketing statement. "We wanted to take the worry out of the mind of the senders of packages," Fagan said at the time.

"Despite the results we were getting from all of these commercials," Fagan felt there was a weakness. "Viewers couldn't remember them. The commercials meant nothing to them. What we finally figured out was that the way to get around this problem was to put everyday people into these ads so they could see themselves and all of the forces aligned against them. We made the decision to introduce comic absurdity into most of our commercials."

Zany humor in commercials was introduced in the early 1960s by comedian-turned-advertising-executive Stan Freberg. "Commercial airlines wouldn't dare use humor," Fagan told me. "They're too conservative. We felt humor helps our advertising break through TV's noise level. Many advertising agencies were afraid of it and felt too much humor might backfire on the advertiser. It could break the so-called 'boredom barrier' and assist Federal Express in gaining rapport with potential customers." The strategy has worked well for the company.

Humor, based on empathy, scored the biggest successes for the company. Ally & Gargano were surprised at the effectiveness of such a contrived effort to achieve empathy. Fagan once remarked about these ads, "People viewing the commercials loved them. They saw themselves. Why, even at Federal Express, we saw ourselves in these predicaments." For example, many viewers could relate to the anxiety of the clerk or the junior executive whose job was on the line if the important package he was responsible for shipping to Birmingham or Peoria did not get there on time. Viewers could relate to the great feeling of relief for these office workers when the package got in the hands of Federal Express. Most of us out there in the audience had somewhat the same crisis at one time or another, and could grasp the great sense of relief when everything finally worked out all right.

The public began to expect most of Federal's commercials to be humorous and regardless of how many times they viewed a particular commercial they still laughed. A typical scene depicts a harried owner of an electric light bulb store phoning Dingbat Air Freight and saying, "If those bulbs aren't here tomorrow morning, I'm out of business; do you hear that?" The fade out on this 30-second commercial shows Dingbat Air Freight's truck pulling up in front of the store which by then had a sign in the window, "Out of Business." This commercial implied that if you don't use Federal Express, the nightmare will come true — and you've gone bankrupt!

Among the most successful television ads have been those using actor John Moschitta playing the role of a fast-talking, decisive chief executive making decisions and barking out orders at a frenetic pace. In a typical ad, this small balding man with unusually deep, penetrating eyes is on the telephone talking at lightning speed with a business contact. Behind him is his harried assistant operating maniacally a duplicating machine at a furious pace. In the space of 30 seconds, Moschitta covers a 182 word script.

The generally successful humor component of Federal's advertising strategy has been retained on a permanent basis. But in a few instances the intended humor backfired. Not everyone thought Federal's commercials were amusing. The television ad titled "Easy To Use," showing the octogenarian chairman of the board trying to call Federal Express, was criticized by the Grey Panthers for poking fun at elderly people. The ad depicted the elderly and presumably senile chairman dialing Federal's phone number and attempting to say, "Hellooooo . . . Federal." But after saying, "Hellooooo," in desperation, snapping his fingers, he cannot remember whom he has dialed. The deep, authoritative voice-over announcer concludes this episode stating: "All you have to do is pick up the phone, and we'll pick up the package. Even the chairman of the board can do that."

The greatest flap, however, came in mid-1982 when the American Postal Workers Union bitterly protested what it considered to be a highly offensive slur upon postal workers. The television sketch showed two postal workers behind the Post Office's Express Mail window either ignoring or being rude to patrons because they were more interested in discussing among themselves the subject of retirement and how many more years they had to work. The Union and the Postmaster General both felt that characterization of postal workers as being lazy, rude, and capable of rendering only poor service was a gross insult. They requested Federal Express and the television networks take the commercial off the air. They were visibly upset, particularly since an opinion poll by the independent Roper organization, commissioned by the Postal Service in August, 1981, found that 85 percent of those persons interviewed were satisfied with their mail service. And in another poll conducted by the Postal Service's own staff, postal workers were rated by the public "above average" in employee courtesy and in efficiency of service. Federal Express, which had attacked the Postal Service previously in their television and print advertising, delayed the cancellation for two or three weeks, thus capturing a great deal more public attention and free publicity. The national news networks all covered the story on their prime time nightly news segments. A CBS-television affiliate in Los Angeles even went to the effort of testing the services of both the Postal Service and Federal Express by sending packages through both systems to see what would happen. The test results showed that Federal's service had lived up to the company's advertised commitment of delivery on-time, while the Postal Service's performance languished far behind its service promise.

In response to the complaints Frank Maguire, then the company spokesman, fired back, "This is a very competitive business we're in. The Post Office . . . chose to enter this competitive market with their overnight business. We play hard ball out there in this competitive market." Federal's attack on the Postal Service had been in planning a year or so before the flap. It was planned in conjunction with the launching of Federal's Overnight Letter product, a private letter service designed to compete head-on with the Postal Service's widely-promoted Express Mail Service. Examples of the stinging captions prepared for print media ads were, "Maybe, Perhaps The Day After Tomorrow Or The Next Day," and the equally abrasive, "Absolutely, Positively Untouched By Civil Servants."

Federal Express definitely wanted combat with the Postal Service.

Some individuals within Federal Express cautioned against this onslaught, but the marketing people viewed it as an opportunity to get the public's attention. Top management decided that the Postal Service was fair game and the American public would not feel much compassion toward it. Financially, much was at stake with Federal's Overnight Letter product, and a number of management careers were on the line. Fred Smith gave this program his blessing and, at the time of the decision to get competitive with the Post Office, said aggressively of the Overnight Letter, "It has the potential to destroy our competitors."

Another pitch used to sell their air express service asserted that Federal Express could eliminate the worry a person might have if he sends a letter through the Post Office. One memorable advertisement, called "Shakes," which won an award from the prestigious *Advertising Age*, shows a man holding a letter shaking violently as he thinks about the consequences of sending a letter through the Post Office. The announcer then says incredulously, "You've got a lot riding on this letter, and you're going to turn it over to the Post Office? Federal Express has an alternative." Federal's president Peter Willmott summed up the company's marketing strategy with classic understatement: "I don't think the Post Office is going to forget we're in the market."

As a counterweight to this comparative attack, at about the same time Federal Express ran an ad playing on the old science fiction horror film, "The Blob." In a commercial directed to the so called "papermills of America" titled "the Paper Blob" the announcer says: "It's coming, it's taking over in offices coast-to-coast. It's the paper blob." Then there is a dramatic scene of a tidal wave of paper coming down a hallway. The announcer continues: "It's packed with important papers that should move out of your office fast but can't get loose. This is a job for the Federal Express Overnight Letter." The episode closes with papers flying off an executive's desk on their way to Federal Express, and the announcer concludes: "You'll never have to worry about the Paper Blob again." It was a comic relief to the company's guerrilla media attack on Federal's competitors, and it seemed a welcome moderation of that effort.

When the Overnight Letter program began in June, 1981, hopes ran high throughout the company that this new product was the profit center Federal needed to propel annual revenues toward the $1 billion sales mark. But the first year's sales of the Overnight Letter fell considerably below target. Internally, the pressure was on the Marketing Department since so much of the company's anticipated future growth hinged on the success of the Overnight Letter. That department's self-assessment of the situation was that the advertising had not been particularly effective, and it had not gotten the job done. Corrective measures were underway. In 1982, Federal's marketing executives had some serious discussions with Ally & Gargano to get better results in 1983. Some wanted to change agencies, but Fred Smith wouldn't hear of it. Since Ally & Gargano had contributed mightily to the success of Federal Express, Smith saw no reason to pin the blame on them.

The advertising campaign objective for 1983 to promote the Overnight Letter was to convince the business public that this was the only way to send an important letter. Emphasis in Federal's media offerings was on instilling in the minds of customers doubts about the quality of service of its competitors. In the 1983 business plan Federal's marketing strategists wrote that the campaign "should demonstrate what goes wrong when someone makes a decision to use an alternative service to save money. We are defining 'value' as the differential between price of the service and end results."

Federal Express is sensitive to the high-price image it has in the marketplace. Every Federal Express customer survey confirms this opinion. The company has attempted to counteract this image by convincing the public that it is offering a substantially higher value in its service and that for such service it is well worth it. Tom Oliver, Fagan's replacement — now senior vice president for marketing — was asked "How effective has Federal's media campaign been in building volume?" Oliver responded: "We have been enormously successful but I guess you could probably over do it, if you relied solely on this strategy. The ability to deliver service is really the main determinant of how well you do." While Oliver may downplay the importance of advertising given the realities of the contribution other departments of the company have made, advertising has made the difference in the battle to maintain momentum.

The company has been flabbergasted by the apparently limitless dimensions of this new front door market. Even though the American business community is changing its operating habits with astonishing speed, it still clings to the antiquated paper medium of an earlier age. We have had for the last 20 years the ability to instantly communicate transcontinentally vast stores of information through the new electronic media, but the business community has refused to endow this electronic transmission of data with the same kind of authority it has invested in paper. Hence the much prophesied electronic "cashless society" has been a technological disappointment. In the same way, the business community remains steadfast in its desire to pass from one hand to another the same piece of paper, even though one hand may be in Maine and the other hand in California. Ironically, Federal Express is the heir to a business created by the lag between the arrival of a new technology and society's inability to replace the 5,000-year-old reliance on the old paper technology. Federal's advertising has perhaps unwittingly amplified and capitalized on the anxiety inherent in this insistance on an immediate exchange of paper. Federal's Priority 1 package service recognizes a more authentic urgency in the back door market. Advertising, especially the comic situational commercials, has created a market where none previously existed, a market whose dimensions have been beyond the wildest dreams of the air transportation industry. Federal knew it had a good product. It knew it had the stamina and the ability to deliver. It knew it had the legal, financial, and entrepreneurial talent, but even so, it was Federal's innovative advertising which propelled the company forward to become the unchallenged market leader.

Chapter 13

Bravo Zulu

Company motivator, Frank Maguire, was the warm-up speaker for Fred Smith at the 1981 First National Sales Meeting held for all of the company's nationwide sales force. Maguire shouted the salutation: "Welcome fellow brothers and sisters from across the country." Then with all the fervor of a crusading evangelist he gave them some of that old time Federal Express religion, and this group of young men and women were spellbound. Backed up by a theatrical set worthy of a Wink Martindale TIC-TAC-DOUGH special, and equipped with a lapel microphone, Maguire paced up and down the aisles stopping now here, now there to single out one wide-eyed salesman after another, saying — as if to that one only: "You have the best job in the world! Nothing we do is trivial! Everything we do has to do with life and death! We have the ability to be open with each other! Openness . . . that's what we have. We tell it like it is! You aren't ordinary people. There is love and respect among you, and for you! Not only are you the best, but you carry with you credibility and openness! The first foundation stone you must deal with is credibility. Don't promise the customer more than you can deliver . . . !"

Although this motivation performance lasted 15 minutes, the youthful sales representatives gave Maguire a standing ovation. A veteran officer standing along side of me said cynically in a side remark: "You don't believe that bull shit and I don't, but these young people believe it because they want to believe it."

Be that as it may, these 150 salespeople were obviously proud to be part of Federal Express. Since none of them were around in 1972 or 1973 when the company started operations, they did not have the camaraderie which those early Federal employees developed through several years of facing adversity and occasionally what seemed to be imminent disaster. Yet, as if by contagion, this apple bright sales force — which in their All-American good looks could just have easily been the cast from "Up With People" — had acquired the same spirit which the company pioneers carried with them.

This company spirit and loyalty is certainly not an exclusive phenomenon with Federal Express. Maguire's audience could just have easily have been employees and managers of IBM, Delta Airlines, Xerox, 3M, Marriott Corporation, Eastman Kodak, Procter & Gamble, Mary Kay Cosmetics, or any one of a dozen other consumer products or service companies. What Federal had done was to copy what it considered to be successful motivational techniques and slogans used by other aggressive companies. But to this Fred Smith has also added his motivational experience as a Marine Corps officer, almost as if he were trying to make them all into first class "Leathernecks." It was obvious the company was communicating its broad corporate philosophy and goals to a pliant and receptive audience.

Federal's communications with its employees all relay much the same message. The company spends considerable staff time and funds to convince them that they are part of a dynamic corporation which cares about each one of them. The theme, "We Are Family," used by James A. Perkins — personnel head and the company's highest ranked black employee — was taken from a song by soul singer Sister Sledge which was widely publicized when Willie Stargell of the Pittsburgh Pirates used it to describe the team's unity in its 1979 pennant drive. The Federal Express employees are told continually that their personal welfare and the company's are inextricably the same.

Keeping morale high on a continual basis is a difficult challenge for any organization. Federal Express, which has now advanced considerably beyond its startup phase of development, has been concerned that employee motivation and morale could slip quickly unless vigilance is maintained at all levels. The "no layoff policy" is one of the decisions Smith made to convince employees that the company will take care of them unless a major financial catastrophe occurs. This is one of several major company commitments Smith has made to keep employees productive and morale high.

Productivity enhancement has become a major priority item. Better training and supervision have been stressed. A major technical unit has been organized with the responsibility for employee training. Management is convinced that if the company is to maintain its competitive lead and keep its profit margins high, it must demand greater employee efficiency and must derive better utilization from its aircraft fleet and its ground support facilities.

Employee relations is an extremely sensitive subject. The overworked company slogan, "Work Smarter, Not Harder," is brief and believable; and it probably describes best management's employee philosophy. To remain the industry leader, the company has to find ways to enhance employee productivity without creating the type of pressure to perform which might create arbitrary and exploitive management styles. There will be a need to fully understand both positive and negative employee reactions to management decisions affecting the mass of employees. As one courier in New York confided to me forcefully: "The way to motivate us is through wages and benefits. If Fred Smith doesn't give us what UPS and Emery pay their drivers, many of us will be gone. That 'We Are Family' crap works as long as we get a good wage."

Smith is adamant on the subject of union organization of Federal Express employees. He does not want unions because he feels they serve no purpose. His labor relations strategy has been a close monitoring of rank-and-file employees to prevent any situations which might precipitate union organizing activity. He has always been concerned, as Perkins once said at a Family Briefing, that "the Teamsters are out there lurking in the woodwork somewhere." A confidant of Smith says, "Go in and tell Fred that while you were waiting in the lobby to see him, you were sitting next to Norman Greene, director of the Airline Division of the Teamsters. Watch Fred come apart!"

Unionization was a threat in some of the company's work groups in the early years. Fred Smith fought the organizational attempts and won. He argued that the flexibility the company needed in order to survive would be seriously impeded if unions got control. Smith told employees he could not pay them more because the company lingered on the border of bankruptcy. This was true, of course, since all Federal needed on more than one occasion was a little nudge, and it would have been out of business.

Smith feared unions would seize control of the work rules, and he would argue: "Drivers at 10:20 a.m. probably would not have the incentive to get those last six packages delivered before the 10:30 a.m. deadline as the company had committed to do. Any strike would be a disaster to us." An aide of Smith says jokingly, "Fred couldn't deal with union officials. This is his company. He's too autocratic. He's the massah of the great Federal Express plantation."

There was really nothing original about Fred Smith's basic objection that a union would dictate the work rules. This has been the fear of many companies trying to fend off unionization.

Federal has never had a work stoppage. No employees in Memphis or in its field operations are represented by unions, though most of the employees of the competition are unionized. The Teamsters represent the majority of employees at United Parcel Service and a portion of both Emery and Airborne, and of course, the Postal Service workers are unionized. Federal stands almost alone as a non-union air express company.

The earliest attempt to organize at Federal was in late 1974, when a group called the United Pilots Association, affiliated with the Air Line Pilots Association (ALPA), tried to organize Federal's pilots. Some of the pilots in the early years were asked to help load and unload planes as well as help out around the various city stations, and many did not like it. Some did not like the unstructured and disorganized system of flight scheduling in the 1973 and 1974 period. The pilots wanted to hear what union representatives had to say, so that a debate was organized between Smith and the union representative. During this debate Smith's main point was economic. He told the pilots: "Look, go ahead and join the union. But if you do, you'll break the company. You won't have a job." When the debate ended, most of the pilots supported Smith. They knew the company was nearly broke, and they also knew how scarce pilots' jobs were in the open market. ALPA has not made any effort to organize Federal since that time, despite record successes in recent years in organizing the pilots of many of the new regional passenger airlines.

Federal's management has always had a somewhat tenuous relationship with its pilots. Although it has always believed that the loyalty of the pilots is just as fervent as that of other company employees, it has considered the pilots "prima donnas" and has often been forced to give in to them on matters it considered either frivolous or unreasonable. Extra special time and energy in the area of human relations has been extended to the pilots. "You're never sure how they are going to react to any change," observes Brian Pecon, a company veteran who has been in charge of flight operations.

In two separate organizational drives in 1975, the Teamsters attempted to organize the field employees and the mechanics. Both efforts failed. One reason was that the Teamsters made a tactical mistake when they personally attacked Fred Smith, an assault resented by most employees. Smith was their friend. As part of the company strategy to defeat the union, Smith invited not only his employees, but also their spouses to come to a local Holiday Inn to hear him state his reasons for opposing the union. By doing this he made their decision about the union a family decision. This strategy of making all members of a family a part of the decision process assured Smith of overwhelming support for his position.

In mid-1978, the Teamsters tried again. Management asked employees to think about unionization carefully before they considered Teamsters membership. The union had obtained a copy of the company's list of employees and their home addresses and had sent out letters in an effort to stir up interest in the union. Federal

Express claimed the list was stolen and threatened the Teamsters with action unless the list was returned.

Despite three attempts, the Teamsters failed to gain a foothold. Employees were reminded by Fred Smith and Art Bass that Federal Express was a people-oriented company and that it operated with a "share the wealth" philosophy through profit-sharing and wages as high and fair as resources would permit. Employees were once again reminded of both the company's "no-furlough policy" and the "promotion-from-within policy." Smith and Bass claimed they were not paranoid about unions. They merely did not want to see a wedge driven between the management and its employees. Smith asserted, "If we do our job with the employees, the Teamsters will fade away." Personnel head Jim Perkins has been given principal responsibility for monitoring any outbreak of interest in unions among company employees through the network of managers and supervisors.

When Smith sought outside consulting assistance to help in employee relations, he retained Charles L. Hughes, formerly an industrial psychologist at Texas Instruments and IBM. "If a company deserves a union, it should get one," is an expression introduced at Federal Express by Hughes. In his book, *Making Unions Unnecessary*, he argues that companies should use preventive maintenance in employee relations rather than after-the-fact fire fighting measures. Hughes' labor relations philosophy is largely a carbon copy of IBM's and Texas Instruments'.

After the 1978 fracas with the Teamsters, Smith began to think about the question, "Where are we vulnerable?" To get some answers in 1979, he retained the University of Michigan's Institute for Social Research to conduct their "Survey of Organizations," a proprietary employee attitude questionnaire of 130 questions to administer to Federal's employees. The results were disappointing, because the company realized afterwards the survey results did not offer much data which had a direct application. The following year it went to Charles Hughes for assistance. He had developed a much shorter survey which Fred Smith felt would be more useful in pinpointing specific problems and in assisting supervisors in reaching solutions. This new survey, which has been administered to all of Federal's employees is designated the "Survey-Feedback-Action Program."

The results of this new survey which have been communicated back to the employees and supervisors indicate that most of the employees are proud to work for Federal Express and that generally they are satisfied with working conditions and company benefits. But management has been quite surprised to find that only 66 percent of the employees have given a favorable response to the item, "I have confidence in the fairness of management." The same survey administered two years in a row indicated no change in this percentage.

In response to the statement, "My job seems to be leading to the kind of future I want," only 64 percent of the employees responded favorably.

The survey results on the "fairness of management" item reinforced a growing feeling that some supervisor-employee relations were harming morale. A concerned Smith prepared his blunt MGMT Memo 11, dated April, 1981, which stated in summary that supervisors must learn to supervise and learn to treat people with respect. A significant number of employee resignations which had occurred shortly before preparation of this memorandum were attributed directly to conflicts with supervisors.

"Managers must grow with the job," cautioned Smith. "Substandard performance in the management ranks cannot, and will not, be tolerated for any sustained period of time." In the tone of a stern father admonishing his unruly children, he added: "The necessity of teamwork in our operating environment prohibits unrealistic and unwarranted egos. To condone either fault would be to begin an inexorable slide toward mediocrity — the fate of most large corporations."

In this same memo, Smith announced the immediate implementation of his "Guarantee of Fair Treatment Policy" — an open door policy between managers and their subordinates to attempt to reconcile differences before it becomes necessary to take these problems "upstairs." This program to handle employee complaints appears to have three origins: the Marriott Corporation's grievance procedure; IBM's "Speak Up" program; and the "open-door" policy of Delta Airlines instituted many years ago by company founder, C. E. Woolman.

Ted Sartoian, whose role is to circulate through the company acting as a part-time ombudsman, had been in contact with Marriott officials about their program. Wall plaques outlining the "Guarantee-of-Fair-Treatment Policy" are hung in every office, every city station, and installation where there are Federal Express employees. In addition, all employees have been issued plastic wallet size cards containing the policy and are asked to carry them in their possession at all times.

Managers and supervisors were put on notice that their actions would be closely monitored and that they would be fired if they were found to be mistreating their subordinates. The results of the annual Survey-Feedback-Action Program for each of the company's numerous work units are now used as one means of measuring a manager's or a supervisor's performance. Employees are shown the results of these performance scores, and supervisors and employees discuss these results as they pertain to their specific company units.

With the rapid growth of Federal Express following deregulation, it needed to fill many new middle management positions. Smith's policy, as he has so often voiced to employees, was to promote from within the company if possible. Advancement was relatively easy as growth escalated. Frequently, however, the newly promoted employees had no prior management experience, and when they assumed their new positions, they received no special managerial training, especially not in the area of human relations. The occurrence of arbitrary actions and mistreatment by supervisors of their employees has been a festering problem, and Smith and his key aides have exerted considerable effort to weed out the miscreants. Federal's management has always prided itself on being able to learn from the mistakes of other corporations, and this particular problem has been one identified with other fast growth companies. Consequently, Federal's management was able to recognize the problem and contain it before morale could be damaged.

Inexperience is natural in a company where the average age of rank and file employees is about 30. For supervisors at Federal it is the early 30s. Many were hired right out of college or high school, and this was their first full time job. Some brought to the company little more than a will to work and a strong back. Others did not know anything about organizational discipline found in mature companies. In some instances, senior officers to whom these supervisors reported had themselves not set very good examples of professional behavior. These problems had to be resolved before they generated the kind of dissatisfaction among employees which could either affect the company's performance or bring back the Teamsters to a more receptive climate.

While women at Federal Express have been given opportunities to move into upper range management positions, none have made it as far as the ranks of senior-level management. The absence of women in top-level positions is not unusual for companies in the broad transportation industry. But at Federal, at least, the company has brought a dozen or so women into the higher middle management level as directors and managers. Two women have made it to the vice-presidency level. One is vice president of marketing; the other, vice president in charge of Midwestern states operations.

Few inside Federal Express believe a woman will ever occupy a senior officer's position under the present management structure. "The executive office in Memphis is a man's world," says a senior officer. "A woman wouldn't be comfortable here. Some of us wouldn't mind a female colleague, but others don't believe a woman could hack it. You know the argument about women getting emotional and their feathers ruffled and all that. I know Fred wouldn't want anybody bringing him any problems. Federal Express is pretty typical of airline companies. It's a macho world up here." Federal, however, does have some women pilots. Among the contingent of 375 active pilots, there are 11 women — four of whom hold the rank of captain.

Management-employee relations were at one time very informal.

In the early years this "we're-in-this-together" atmosphere helped sustain the esprit de corps needed to keep the company alive. Distinctions of rank were not too important. But the company's growth, which escalated rapidly following the deregulation decision in the fall, 1977, changed these relationships. The informality which had existed since 1972, when the company was in Little Rock, began to diminish. Relationships became more formal as more administrative structure was added to accommodate the growth. After 1980, many of the traces of the old informality had completely disappeared. The spirited, boyish-looking Tucker Taylor — a former senior vice president, who with his unruly hair and loosened necktie looks as though he just stepped out of a fraternity house — had left the company by that time and returned for a visit two years later. Taylor said of his visit, "I wouldn't want to work there anymore. It's just like General Motors. It's a real dull place." Apparently, he had with some suddenness realized that the more flamboyant, freewheeling, informal days were over.

The company had changed. Conduct which may have been condoned during the first six or seven years of the company's life was now a cause for either a severe warning or dismissal. Sexual harassment, other employee abuse, misappropriating small amounts of funds, and kickbacks were the most obvious misdeeds. The attainment of managerial effectiveness became a high priority. Emphasis was placed on selecting people who know how to manage. Work rules and regulations were implemented to gain more discipline and productivity among the employees.

Fred Smith inculcated a specific management philosophy to underpin and guide Federal Express. It is not an original creation. It is a synthesis of philosophies taken from such corporate giants as IBM, Delta Airlines, Marriott Corporation and Texas Instruments. Superficially, Federal has absorbed some of the management styles of the Japanese which have been introduced in a number of America's best known corporations. And, of course, Fred Smith has utilized the hard nosed Marine Corps management style to sustain the company since its inception. Federal Express has not had adequate time to do much experimenting with home grown management techniques. It has opted to pick and choose ideas and programs from those corporations it considers well-managed.

Federal's contributions are more apparent in the area of applied technology. A singularly important achievement has been its development of an advanced electronic communications network. Its engineering capability in keeping its fleet of aircraft at peak condition and in designing efficient systems for sorting and handling packages has been first rate.

It has been the IBMs, the Deltas, the Eastman Kodaks, the Marriotts and the Texas Instruments which have served as partial models for the development of a Federal Express corporate management approach. These veteran corporations are still innovative, aggressive, and expansion-minded companies. They have clear strategies and they place heavy emphasis on productivity and service to their customers via aggressive marketing. And, in addition, they all have sophisticated management information systems. In varying degrees they are all paternalistic in dealing with their employees. And in their company discipline, all have military overtones. Esprit de corps, loyalty, sacrifice, and a strong competitive drive are qualities imbued within the work force extending from the top to the bottom ranks of these companies.

As another motivating measure Smith, in early 1983, again dug into his inventory of military techniques. He told his managers that he wanted them to award "Bravo Zulu" stickers to employees when they performed in an "above and beyond" manner. In the U. S. Navy the signal flag for the letter "B" is designated, "Bravo," and that for "Z," "Zulu." When the Navy hoists the Bravo and Zulu flags in that order it signifies a performance "well done." Each manager was given several sheets of these self-adhesive stickers about the size of small postage stamps. Said Smith, "We should never lose sight of our need for incredible levels of cooperation as we put our reputation on the line each time we accept a package or document. I believe a well-deserved Bravo Zulu from time to time will go a long way toward fostering teamwork throughout the organization."

Smith says that when Federal Express hires a new employee it is for life; therefore his personnel department is very selective in the hiring process and sensitive to the employee's needs once he or she has joined the company. The company philosophy is, "If we take care of our employees, they'll take care of our customers and our stockholders." The promise of economic security enhances employee loyalty, reduces heavy turnover, and makes it easier to make internal organizational adjustments as competitive conditions change.

The no furlough policy, the open door policy, and promotions from within the company; anti-unionism; terse, moralistic work slogans and profit sharing plans; family information meetings; company dinners and cash awards for cost-cutting suggestions; as well as slickly produced employee publications have all been skillfully introduced into Federal Express. Management thereby hopes that, with these techniques in dealing with its work force, growth will be facilitated without experiencing the painful wounds which usually arise from internal employee conflict. So far these techniques have worked.

The image Federal Express projects to the public is carefully nurtured. Considerable time and funds have been spent to present itself as a progressive, opportunistic, and efficient company. Smith thinks his company is a prototype of the new generation American companies likely to be spawned in the 1980s and 1990s. One of the first things Smith did in 1972, during Federal's pre-startup days was to select a dramatic color scheme and logo identifying his company visually. He did not want anyone left neutral in their reaction to the brazen purple, orange, and white colors emblazoned on his fleet of planes, delivery trucks, and advertising material. Smith also has stressed personal grooming. He wants customers to have a good impression of company employees. Even the selection of courier uniforms is a major corporate event. The "no beards" rule for uniformed male employees rests on the decision of management that the company must present to the general public a clean-cut, All-American look. Among the senior officers, there are neatly trimmed moustaches, but no beards. Similarly, female employees are urged to avoid extremely trendy hairstyles.

One would be hard pressed to say that Federal Express does not have a distinctive corporate culture. It is apparent to those who are exposed to the company's television advertising. It is apparent to its customers who are exposed to enthusiastic couriers or to the customer service personnel. And it is especially apparent when visiting a Federal Express installation.

The Protestant work ethic prevails in the Bible Belt locale where about half of the company's 13,000 employees reside. Their daily work philosophy coincides perfectly with that expounded by Fred Smith. There is no conflict or frustration in having to express themselves as members of a big corporate family rather than as individuals.

Fred Smith could not have succeeded if Federal Express' headquarters initially had been located in New York, or Cleveland, or Pittsburgh, or Philadelphia, or Los Angeles. Even with his highly skilled powers of persuasion and leadership ability, the forces against him would have been overwhelming. Organized labor would have been much more persistent and probably would have gotten a more sympathetic ear from employees when the unions made their runs at the company. And the type of employees available to be hired would have been more cynical, and less idealistic and preconditioned, than workers raised and educated in Tennessee, Arkansas, and Mississippi.

Chapter 14

Case Butterfly

Fred Smith brought into his new venture in 1972, no corporate administrative or operating experience. Since he had not attended the Harvard Business School or Wharton or any other graduate school of business, and had not read extensively the prolific works of management scholars like Peter Drucker, Douglas McGregor, or George Steiner, he did not realize that what he was doing in those pre-Federal Express years was a pure form of corporate strategic planning. He had the good fortune to be able to look ahead without too much preoccupation with all of the organizational details which had to be considered to build a successful speciality airline and trucking entity. He was not laboring long hours over one-year business plans or budgets, and he did not have to face the clutter of trying to straighten out the infinite details of keeping a company functioning on a day-to-day basis. With formal education in business administration, or with extensive prior corporate management experience, Fred Smith might have been more shackled or restrained in his efforts to think unconventionally about the air freight industry and its potential opportunities.

During 1972 and 1973, there was not much time to develop a long-range plan extending beyond one year. The crisis atmosphere surrounding Federal Express precluded any consideration of time horizons some five or ten years removed. The Business Plan which served that traumatic first year relied heavily on the data included in the General Dynamics feasibility studies prepared in late Spring, 1973, when the General Dynamics board of directors was considering whether to exercise its option to buy Federal Express. There was no operating experience to support the package volume and the revenue projections prepared by that company. Federal Express was literally flying into unknown skies.

Simple survival was the basis of the company's strategic plan. There were no elaborate detailed plans. These were luxuries of the more mature and established companies. Smith had little time to detach himself for any period to work on longer term plans and to commit them to paper. Instead of wondering where the company would be in five or ten years, his main concern was often whether the Falcons would fly that night or whether he was going to be able to pay anyone that week.

With his own employees and often with the curious national business and financial community as well, Smith used a visionary approach in describing his expectations for Federal Express. He told them, "Federal Express has the opportunity to become one of America's great corporations and the dominant force in the small package air express industry. We have found a gap in the transportation industry and we are going to fill it." This rhetoric was about all he could do in the way of a master plan given the pressures.

The only semblance of planning in the company occurred when Art Bass had introduced limited market research in late 1972, just prior to the start of nightly service. Target industrial groups and cities were identified. A much broader concept of market planning was introduced when Vince Fagan joined the company in 1974. Strategic planning on a broader, companywide scale became an absolute necessity after December, 1975, when the Civil Aeronautics Board officially rebuffed the company's proposal to fly the larger DC-9s. This rebuff by the CAB brought strategic planning to the forefront in the company. Operations research and system specialists, Charles Brandon and Ted Weise, were elevated quickly to positions of prominence within the management hierarchy, accordingly. Their skills were needed, and needed quickly. Both understood computer-based modeling techniques and also realized how badly the company needed technical planning direction if it were to survive this CAB setback and keep growing. In 1976, a planning group was assembled to begin work at a furious pace to evaluate alternative sets of assumptions concerning nightly route systems for the Falcons and the locations of regional sorting hubs, aircraft equipment, market to product data, and financial information. With the aid of their computers this group began to provide Smith and his very concerned board of directors with a clearer understanding of what results might be expected if certain decisions were made by the company.

Beginning in 1976, most major decisions were subjected to financial modeling. Problems were examined in infinite statistical detail to measure the degree of risk entailed in different decisions. The arcane world of mathematical models and computers made some of the veteran senior officers nervous. They felt that the flood of numbers produced by the computers would cause decision-makers to stifle creativity, and cause them to lose perspective, and that these methods were an unrealistic substitute for judgment and reasoning. The company might become a slave to its assumptions. Nonetheless, given the company's very limited funds in 1976, and the urgency to find quickly alternative solutions of growth, Smith decided to elevate this type of contemporary management planning technique to a central corporate position. Strategic and tactical decision-making emerging from the chairman's office was assisted by the technical output from the company's sophisticated computer simulation modeling systems.

The Operations Research and Corporate Planning Division began studies to develop the optimal long-term physical and operational system. In what ultimately turned into a three-year planning effort, the company was analyzed as if its life resembled that of a butterfly. The three stages in the metamorphosis process were designated by Fred Smith as: (1) Case Caterpillar; (2) Case Chrysalis; and (3) Case Butterfly. He had remembered from his high school zoology that the butterfly was among the most highly developed insects.

The Caterpillar stage was defined as the company's formative period from 1973 through 1977. The company operated its Falcon 20 fleet backed up with auxiliary support from a separate fleet of smaller, leased aircraft, while it waited optimistically for Congressional relief so it could operate Douglas DC-9s or some other type of aircraft with considerably greater payloads than the Falcons.

While awaiting the decision by Congress, however, Federal's second stage strategy, called Case Chrysalis, was implemented. A chrysalis in the insect world is the pupa of the butterfly. That is to say, it is an inactive organism enclosed in a case awaiting its final development into a butterfly. During this planning stage, Federal began to consider what type of larger aircraft it needed, and what type of a logistical network would be most effective in getting the packages from shippers to consignees. It wanted to be ready to move quickly in the event Congress passed an air cargo deregulation bill in late 1977.

When Congress finally did act favorably in November, 1977, management went immediately to Case Butterfly, its maturation stage. An internal task force was mobilized. It had two major tasks. First, it was to undertake a cost-benefit study investigating the merits of operating with a wholly new network of four to eight regional sorting hubs over the merits of simply expanding the Memphis hub. And second, it was asked to evaluate the mix of aircraft types needed for the fleet and the quantity of each type of plane.

At the time of Fred Smith's 1978 organizational shakeup, management was committed to a regional hub network. This logistical system appeared to be the most cost-effective means to handle the nightly package volume. Later in 1978, Smith decided to scrap this plan. Subsequent studies showed that the introduction of the fleet of 727s changed drastically the company's operating model of its system. A regional hub network, company planners concluded, would create heavy fixed cost commitments in facilities, equipment, and personnel expenses. They concluded that there would not be much savings in variable costs by reducing line haul distance, that is, by requiring all flights to rendezvous at Memphis every night. They also found that the company would have to pay its pilots the same salaries whether they flew in and out of hubs located at Colorado Springs, Colorado, or Newburgh, New York, or any other place, versus flying to and from Memphis every weekday night.

The principal element in Case Butterfly planning was fleet selection. The company faced the question of how to mix the fleet to attain the payload capacity for the projected nightly package volume. The planners considered a variety of aircraft types, the payloads of different types of aircraft, and their operating characteristics. Fuel efficiency became a primary consideration. Federal's staff looked at Boeing 707s and 727s, 737s and 747s, and at Douglas DC-8s, DC-9s, and DC-10s. After exhaustive cost studies, including expenses associated with aircraft crew training, maintenance, Memphis Hub operations and fuel consumption, the conclusion was that Federal's fleet selection had to be a financial compromise between fuel efficiency of particular aircraft on one hand and the capital costs of these aircraft on the other. On these criteria, the 727, 737, and the DC-10 appeared to strike a happy medium for the company.

During the 1978 and 1979 period, used 727-100s in particular were available in quantity. This plane — originally introduced by Boeing in 1964 — was the most widely used jet transport in the world. It was fortunate timing for Federal Express that United, Eastern, and Northwest had only recently discontinued use of their "quick change" combination passenger-cargo 727s, and designated them surplus.

After extensive study, Federal Express designated the 727-100 as the "right" plane for the company. The first 11 used 727-100s came from United Airlines. The next 20 were purchased from Eastern. This was the start of an acquisition program which brought the fleet of 727-100s up to 38 planes in 1983.

In 1978 and 1979, the company purchased four Boeing 737-200 "quick change" aircraft for about $10 million each. It also leased one 737-200. These aircraft with two turbofan jet engines were more fuel efficient than the three-engined 727-100s, but their payload capacity was some 4,000 pounds less. Its "quick change" physical configuration excited the company at the time, because it was seriously considering competing in the daytime commuter airline market.

At the time of the purchase of the new 737s, management believed it had made the correct decision, especially if these aircraft were to be put into daytime scheduled passenger service. But less than two years after acquiring these planes, in a turnabout, management declared the 737s surplus to operations and put them up for sale. Later company studies of the proposed passenger route system pointed to a daytime need for more 737s than could be used economically in the primary business of hauling packages overnight. Fortunately, at the time, some commercial airlines were showing a strong interest in the 737s because of their fuel efficiency. Federal sold them at a profit.

In January, 1980, the company bought four used DC-10-10CF aircraft from Continental Airlines for about $26 million each. These three-engine, wide-bodied aircraft had an approximate gross payload of 120,000 pounds and a net payload of 105,000 pounds. The decision to purchase the DC-10s, like the previous decision to purchase the 727s, was heavily influenced by the results of extensive computer simulations examining all physical and operational characteristics, as well as sales prices.

Continental Airlines declared the four DC-10s surplus to its operations because it was desperate for cash after losing over $13 million in 1979. Continental's plight was Federal's good fortune. It permitted the company to stay committed to its successful strategy of buying quality used aircraft at near bargain prices.

Once Federal's negotiators worked out statistically what the company could afford to pay, they were tenacious in holding firm on an offering price. Fortuitous market timing helped them. There was either a surplus of the appropriate types of aircraft available on the open market, or a particular commercial airline available wanting to sell off part of its fleet.

Temporarily, Smith had been excited at the prospect of adding Boeing 747s to the fleet. This huge, wide-bodied plane would have given the company a payload per aircraft of some 172,000 pounds. The positive feature as far as Smith was concerned was its fuel efficiency. Its liabilities to Federal were its sheer size and cost. The huge 747 made economic sense on the Newark and Los Angeles routes, but volume projections indicated it would be several years before Boston, Chicago, or any other large metropolitan area would have a nightly package market large enough to justify 747 service.

Management wanted to put DC-10s on the Boston, Chicago, Los Angeles and Newark nightly routes. The larger plane was the ideal size. Committing the DC-10s to these major routes permitted the release of several of the 727s to other routes. Planners found that the fuel savings from using the DC-10s were substantial. If, for example, three 727s were used nightly on the Los Angeles-Memphis route, the combined fuel use would be 12,700 gallons. But if a single DC-10 were used to cover the same route, the fuel burned would be 7,400 gallons, a considerable savings just on fuel alone. On March 24, 1980, the first DC-10 began providing new service on the Newark-Memphis route.

But Smith made a major strategy decision in 1982, when he opted to reconstitute a large part of the fleet in the latter 1980s. Federal negotiated with Boeing to buy 15 of the 727-200F series of all-cargo aircraft to phase out its present fleet of smaller and less fuel efficient 727-100s. The first of these 727-200s, each with a payload of about 57,000 pounds, was scheduled to join Federal's fleet in late 1983 or early 1984.

Since the larger planes first came on line at Federal in early 1978, the company has been concerned about the under-utilization of the fleet during the daylight hours. Smith, using the contemporary parlance of the collegiate business schools, announced, "We need to leverage these assets." Smith posed this question: "How can we put these large planes and the ground support equipment to work producing more revenue?" His planners were put to work to answer this question.

One of the most exciting ideas was to launch a daytime commuter airline. The bill deregulating the commercial passenger airlines was approved by Congress in 1978, one year after it passed the Air Cargo Deregulation Bill. New commuter airlines began to emerge to compete in the large and expanding market, hauling business travelers between large urban cities at popularly-priced fares, primarily in the daytime hours.

Chicago's Midway Airport, just 491 air miles north of Memphis, was anxious to attract scheduled passenger service back to this municipal airport that had flourished prior to the mid-1950s opening of O'Hare. Its advantage over O'Hare was that it was less than ten miles from Chicago's downtown Loop area. If Federal Express were to decide to enter the commuter market, it could have its "quick change" aircraft positioned in the early morning to provide passenger service from a hub operation at Midway Airport serving some 25 or 30 metropolitan areas.

If Federal could operate both an overnight package service, plus a largely daylight hour commuter passenger service, it could create the opportunity for two distinct profit centers. Perhaps here was a solution, management surmised, to the vexing problem of how to best leverage its assets — its huge capital investment in a growing fleet of aircraft, maintenance facilities, and other ground support operations.

Federal's initial proposal was to put a fleet of nine 737-200 "quick change" aircraft into commuter service. Initially, management anticipated that its revenues for the first full operating year would be about $149 million, and its profit, $14.5 million. But later, after more detailed study and subjecting the proposed venture to intensive financial analysis, it concluded that the estimated 12 to 13 percent return on invested capital to implement this service was an inadequate reward for the risk entailed. Senior staff debated long and hard this issue before discarding the idea. Vince Fagan was perhaps the most forceful when he warned: "The numbers aren't there. We'd be better off hauling daytime freight than trying to muscle our way into the very competitive passenger business."

Within the company there had developed a growing concern that entry into passenger service might divert the business public's attention away from the company's "bread and butter" small package air express service. Smith and his board members were also concerned that, if passenger service were to be less than first rate, it would endanger the company's credibility as being a totally reliable air carrier to which a customer might entrust his package for on time delivery, "Absolutely, Positively Overnight."

When this disappointment wore off, the next promising idea to surface was passenger charter service. In the latter 1970s there was growing interest of the American public in charter vacation flights. Smith, aware of this, announced enthusiastically, "We will be in this business. We have the planes available in the principal markets where charter business could be heavy."

The aircraft and ground support requirements would have been far less in charter service than in the commuter business. But here again, the results of internal financial planning studies were disappointing. The results of the computer models indicated the projected returns were lower than hoped for and the anticipated risks, greater.

Meanwhile, company planners had been looking for new air express products to offer its customers. It received its opportunity in 1979, when Congress passed legislation amending the Private Express Statutes. These statutes had given the Post Office a monopoly to carry letters since almost the founding days of the Republic. Federal Express had been one of the most vocal advocates for changing the law to permit private companies to carry letters if the Postal Service could not duplicate the service.

The Overnight Letter, Federal's newest product as of 1983, was introduced to take advantage of what appeared to be an enormous unfulfilled demand for reliable overnight service for important letters. Marketing head, Tom Oliver, estimated that this was a potential $1 billion business for the company. Federal's marketing research staff was astounded when it found out the Postal Service was handling over 200 million pieces of certified, registered, special delivery, and Express Mail annually. This volume indicated to Federal that there was an enormous potential in express letters and documents which it felt it was better equipped to handle than the Post Office.

At the time of its introduction, the Overnight Letter was hailed as the new profit center for Federal. The internal forecast was that it would yield at least $100 million in revenues during the first year beginning in 1981; and after a four to five-year period, this product would contribute one-third to one-half of all annual company revenues.

At the end of the first full year the Overnight Letter had contributed only $56 million. One reason for the disappointing yield was the greatly depressed national economy. Another was the failure of Federal's marketing people to draw a clear distinction in the customer's mind between its Overnight Letter product and the Courier-Pak product. This dictated an effort to differentiate the two products. In its 1983 Business Plan, the company resolved to put maximum effort into making the Overnight Letter a success. Federal Express needed a big winner.

There was good reason for concern. The company had only recently experienced its first market failure and it did not want a repetition. The Hotel-Pak service, which had been introduced in September, 1980, was allowed to die quietly in December, 1981. Not only had there been no public announcement of this product's demise, but also, the stockholders were not informed in the 1982 *Annual Report*. The Hotel-Pak had been a marketing and planning gaffe. A hasty decision to proceed was responsible for the failure. In late 1979, when the idea was proposed, it was viewed as an opportunity to create another major profit center. The decision to sign exclusive service contracts with Hilton, Holiday Inns, Hyatt, Marriott and other major chains, and to rush quickly into operation, was based on the concern that Emery, Airborne or some other competitor would beat them to it.

The market analysis supporting the decision was apparently thin. Company estimates were that the first year's volume of items picked up or delivered at the hotels would be about 690,000 pieces. By the end of the third year some 2,700,000 pieces were expected. When service was abandoned after 15 months, it had lost $1.9 million. The company had handled less than 11,000 pieces, not the avalanche predicted by Federal's marketing staff. Apparently, even Federal's marketing staff can occasionally shoot themselves in the foot.

Despite such occasional disappointments, Smith continued to probe for innovative new ventures to help push the company into the ranks of America's corporate giants. At the beginning of the 1980s he turned his attention to the rapidly emerging telecommunications field. Enthusiastically, he told his staff and board of directors, "The revolution in telecommunications will have enormous implications in the way Federal Express does business and we need to be aggressive in this area."

He knew that the company could not stand still and depend solely on its Courier-Pak, Priority 1, Overnight Letter, and Standard Air Service products to carry it into the future. Growth of some of those products was destined to slow down in the latter 1980s. The Courier-

Pak in particular was expected to slow down in its annual percentage rate of growth in volume and in revenues generated. Many of the types of items which customers send in Courier-Paks are considered "communication-type" documents — such as reports, legal briefs, blueprints, and the like. These are the items most likely to become candidates for service via the new electronic facsimile transmission system. Such technology may threaten to eliminate the need to send a large quantity of Federal's ordinary volume of Courier-Paks and Overnight Letters nightly through the Hub in Memphis.

Smith anticipates an enormous market for such an electronic communication service. In 1982 and 1983, he and some of his key associates were totally absorbed in this effort which within the company is called "Project Gemini." The target date for introduction of service is April, 1984. Some financial analysts believe Federal Express is "betting the company" that its facsimile transmission of documents service will elevate it to a new plateau in corporate growth. Management is convinced that this is the really big new profit center it has been looking for since deregulation. Many of the ideas examined since 1978 were found lacking, but the nationwide electronic document delivery network met the criteria established by management to get the green light.

Federal promises a two-hour delivery service to most parts of the Continental United States from the moment a customer calls for a pickup of a document of up to 20 pages until this reproduced document is hand delivered to the consignee. For documents exceeding 20 pages, delivery will be made within two and one-half hours. If the customer brings his documents to a Federal Express location, the items will be immediately transmitted electronically via Federal's satellite to the appropriate company station for delivery by courier within one hour. The consignee will receive an exact duplicate of the original in black and white, only reduced if necessary to standard 8½" by 11" pages.

Competition in the facsimile transmission field is expected to be intense, and this is why Federal Express expedited its planning in 1982 and 1983 to try to establish market position early. It fully expects aggressive competition. Instead of competing just with Emery, Airborne, the Postal Service, Purolator Courier, and UPS in the air express business, it anticipates that several either new or existing technologically-advanced electronics firms will compete. Cash-rich UPS may decide to enter the field. IBM and perhaps entities created by the "new" AT&T organization are also potential rivals. And, of course, the Postal Service has already put its foot in the door with its new E-COM transmission service. Profit margins for Federal will hinge on the ability of the company to attain a quality of service and sustain the degree of competition it is likely to face. Unlike the earlier plodding and relatively unsophisticated air freight industry, Federal Express will encounter firms which are neither plodding nor unsophisticated. The question arises, then, given these hard driving and innovative competitors: Will Federal Express be able to duplicate their earlier successes in this new field? Is the Federal Express alligator crawling out onto the high ground to do battle with the powerful, high-tech bears? The risks of entering this totally different technological field are substantial. Smith has decided that Federal must take these risks if the company is to grow and prosper.

Except during the hectic startup years, most decisions have been fairly cautious ones. Staff research has been handled professionally. And when a decision was made to proceed, management built a safety net in those decisions where substantial capital expenditures were required. For example, millions of dollars were committed to purchasing the fleet of aircraft, which created an enormous debt burden on a young company operating in a highly competitive industry. Yet much of this aircraft equipment was purchased used and at near bargain prices during fortuitous market periods. In most cases, if forced to dispose of some of this equipment to lighten the financial burden, the company could sell it on the open market at reasonably attractive prices.

Smith's decision to emphasize technical research and to elevate it into a premier position in the corporate decision-making process has contributed to keeping the company growing. For the most part, Federal's market research has been reasonably effective. The company's competitors have lagged far behind in their emphasis on both technical and market research. Careful preparation prior to committing to action undoubtedly saved Federal Express from getting involved in the highly competitive and erratic commuter airline business.

Extensive research has also helped the company to exercise patience before jumping into the European small package market. The company's commitment to expand into international air express service remains tentative. At least in the mid-1980s the commitment includes service only to England. Service to Continental Europe may not be inaugurated until the latter 1980s, if then. Smith, who once boasted that Federal would be serving Europe and the Far East, changed his mind and says that he has no desire for the company to become a transglobal operation. When he made that statement, no one close to Smith thought he had closed the door to broad international service. Expediency and flexibility are hallmarks of his management style. With characteristic nonchalance he will more than likely state at some future date that it has always been his intention to operate a worldwide system.

Throughout the company's history Fred Smith has dominated the planning function. He is the idea man. He is the field general implementing those ideas filtering through the evaluation process. Even when he was forced to relinquish temporarily part of his control to the board of directors in the spring and summer of 1975, following his indictment, he exercised strong influence over corporate planning and policy. His senior officers continued to follow his lead, even though major decisions were supposed to be in the hands of the board of directors' executive committee. And during Smith's long hiatus in Washington trying to obtain legislative relief from Congress in 1976 and 1977, he retained tight control over company planning and policy formation. Art Bass, as president, ran the company on a day-to-day basis, but deferred to Smith on all major matters.

As the company has matured, corporate planning has become more structured and formal. Periodically, Smith sets the goals in list form and circulates them within the company. The following list of ten goals he set for Federal Express for the early 1980s is typical: "1) We must continue to expand. 2) We must improve our service and reliability. 3) We must become more productive in handling packages. 4) We must become more productive in handling paperwork and information. 5) We must become more productive in the way we train people. 6) We must become more productive in terms of our management span of control. 7) We must develop a comprehensive long-term fleet and equipment plan. 8) We must protect ourselves against future energy shortages. 9) We must become an increasingly safe and secure operation. 10) We must learn to communicate better to ensure the most important element of our future success — the continuing dedication, professionalism and esprit de corps of our employees."

Smith tells his senior staff that goal setting at Federal Express is a group effort, but few believe him. When asked about this, Frank Maguire said humorously: "Fred's one of a kind. He schedules a staff meeting for a group discussion of corporate goals; then when we get in the Conference Room, he hands us a ring binder with his ideas carefully outlined beforehand. It wouldn't do any good to take too much exception to what he's got down on paper. But it's O.K. He knows what he is doing."

Smith's list of goals is filtered down the line to the various division or unit heads so they may incorporate them into their specific plans, which when reviewed and coordinated, comprise the annual corporate business plans and budgets. The Business Plan document then serves to interlink the commitments of the company's many divisions with the overall company goals.

Integrated within the annual Business Plan document are the Management By Objectives (MBO) and the Management Incentive Compensation (MIC) programs covering all managerial positions. The corporate bonus program was established to stimulate goal achievement. In introducing these programs in 1978 to implement accountability Smith explained, "I consider a smooth-running MBO/MIC program absolutely essential for the long-range success of the company." He created a special group in the 1980 reorganization called the Objectives and Audits Department to report directly to him, and not through the company president's office. James Bailey who heads this unit refers to it as "Fred's CIA." Its mission is largely one of monitoring performance by conducting financial and operational audits throughout the company's divisions. Smith wants to measure the rate of progress the company is making toward the corporate objectives segment by segment.

The changes in management controls to increase efficiency have not been totally accepted by those with management responsibility. There has been some resentment over what some administrators believe has been an excessive tightening of controls over their operations. "We are enmeshed in paper with the ever-mounting administrative procedures and guidelines," stated one veteran officer sarcastically. "This system of checks and balances may be O.K. for all of the inexperienced managers and supervisors we have at Federal Express, but it is really stifling to the initiative and creativity of the experienced people. We're losing those essential things to this growing bureaucracy. Fred thinks the company's internal problems result from rapid growth. That's a lot of horse manure. The real problems arise from dehumanizing the individual." Others, in several different divisions, expressed similar frustration. Several volunteered specific examples to me to illustrate their frustration. "To get a duplicate key made, I had to go through a chain-of-command to get it," explained one. "It went to my boss first, but he said he was not authorized to make the decision, so it was bumped up the line. It took two weeks to get approval."

Preparation of the annual Business Plan has not always run smoothly. Many company managers had only limited previous planning experience. Many literally had to be taught step-by-step how to plan. The installation of the MBO/MIC program also caused the three month Spring ritual of preparing the Business Plan to bog down. The 1982 Plan was the first one ever finished prior to the start of a new fiscal year. By that time most managers were systematic in carrying out their assignments. Over the years a lot of trial-and-error was necessary to smooth out the budget preparation process. "We were always behind the power curve. [The term, "power curve," is one of several overworked cliches at Federal. Its derivation is from the field of aeronautical engineering. At Federal its use covers any critical deadline which must be met.] And the pressures were tremendous in the 100 days preceding May 31 of each year," moans one long time participant. "Then Smith, Willmott, and the senior officers would be tied up for two or three weeks full time going over the numbers before we finally got it together. I think a lot of valuable time was wasted."

Following the 1978 administrative reorganization, Smith became a much more cautious chief executive. He began implementing tighter management controls. He also insisted on more accountability to prevent the company from making foolish decisions which might hurt earnings and cause a loss of investor confidence.

Chapter 15

Kick Ass: Take Names

Five major changes were made in the company's organization chart in the first decade. Fred Smith believes in frequent changes for two reasons. One is that he accepts the modern management principle that structure should follow strategy. The company's leadership — principally Smith assisted by an occasional management consultant — has determined what corporate growth and profit goals it wanted to achieve, then built an organization chart to carry out the plan. Another reason is Smith's fear of complacency or inertia emerging from the success Federal Express started enjoying after 1977, in package volume and profits; and his realization that some of his earliest freewheeling and innovative confidants had outlived their usefulness as the company matured.

Smith has run the company through motivation. "Fred likes to come through the corporate offices periodically and shake things up to spread a little fear," says a colleague. "I think its probably a little trick he learned in the Marine Corps about motivation. It's the 'kick ass, take names' management style." The organizational changes reflect this objective. If someone cannot be motivated or retreaded any more, he is usually gone after a reasonable period of time depending on his past contributions to the company.

Smith claims that Federal Express is philosophically entrepreneurial and non-bureaucratic, and that its management style is simple and flexible. The overworked cliche, "Keep It Simple, Stupid!" — sometimes called the KISS

"Any jackass can kick down a barn, but it takes a good carpenter to build one."
—Sam Rayburn, former Speaker of the U. S. House of Representatives

approach — is one used by Smith to keep reminding himself to rework the organizational chart and the company's operating procedures, if he believes the company is losing its combat readiness. He worries that the company may lose its ability to be flexible enough to react quickly in the marketplace when conditions change. Consequently, in the first decade there have been five organization charts dated July 12, 1973; October, 1973; May, 1975; April 1, 1978; and September 1, 1980.

The first chart was merely an update of the original 1972 chart developed during the Little Rock period. By October, 1973, the company had refined its chart to reflect many new functions which had been added as a result of the organizational needs found after the formal start of service in April, 1973. Several of the original staff Smith had hired in Little Rock had resigned, not because of any friction, but because they preferred the more tranquil working life in Little Rock to that in Memphis. And others were not suited for Federal's style of corporate life. When Fred Juravich, the experienced head of finance, died in 1973, his loss created a gap in financial administration which was not resolved until Peter Willmott reported to Memphis in May, 1974. Roger Frock remained the second in command in the management structure under Smith until Art Bass was elected company president unexpectedly in late February, 1975.

The May 8, 1975, reorganization was a move partially to appease the lenders and partially to get better administrative control over company operations. The lenders wanted to see greater nightly package volume. The decision was made to move three of the most experienced senior officers out of Memphis into the field in an effort to bring Federal's management supervision closer to the field personnel and the customer to improve the upward information flow, and to streamline the overall corporate management structure.

The decentralization made sense in this early stage in the company's life, but in the 12 months prior to Smith's decision in the early spring of 1978 to reorganize, the company had been changing rapidly. The air cargo deregulation victory permitting Federal to acquire larger aircraft was only one example of the changes affecting company operations. The package volume was expanding, new stations were being added to serve more cities, and the company was adding hundreds of new employees to handle the growth. In what seemed like a matter of months Federal Express was a far more complex company. Field decisions were often uncoordinated and fragmented. The four regional divisions were separate corporate fiefdoms headed by highly individualistic, strong-willed personalities. Mike Fitzgerald, Roger Frock, Wes Terry, and Tucker Taylor were enjoying their professional and social lives beyond the day-to-day control of Memphis headquarters. And none of them particularly cared about living in Memphis.

The company was having difficulty managing its growth. When the divisional structure was organized in 1975, nightly volume was 10,000 packages. At the time Smith scuttled the divisions in the spring of 1978, the nightly count had increased to 31,500 packages.

In many cities station salesmen were being used to answer the telephone or to help out in delivering packages. They often did not have time to sell. There were serious customer service bottlenecks because of inadequate telephone lines and inefficient record keeping systems. Records were kept in old-fashioned tub files before the introduction of Federal's customer call centers and the completely computerized Customer Oriented Service Management Operating System — known within the company as "COSMOS."

The problems being created by rapid growth concerned Smith, so early in 1978 he hired management consultants to advise him on the company's organizational structure. In so many words they told him, "The company is out of control; and if it had not been for the rapid growth of package volume, it would have been goodbye for Federal Express." They recommended to Smith that a completely revised organization structure was needed to meet the objectives of the company's new growth strategy, or the company would not be able to respond to the new business opportunities.

Early in February, 1978, Smith, with the advice of one of his consultants, New York-based Paul Lanier, put the final touches on the new company organization plan. On February 14, 1978, Smith released a memorandum titled, "Managing Federal Express or 'Holding On To The Tiger's Tail.'" It is a strongly worded, forceful statement of the company's structural problems and proposals for major changes to help Federal Express adapt to the changing requirements resulting from rapid growth. Art Bass, as president, co-signed the memorandum, although it was exclusively the handiwork of Fred Smith.

Smith attacked the four field divisional arrangement, identifying it as structurally defective. "The divisions are not true profit centers," he explained. "The staff resources available at the division level are about as analogous to the current corporate staff as the Boy Scouts are to the Marine Corps." Smith then explained that the new approach would be to do a few things well rather than many things poorly as he concluded was then the case. To implement this change, Smith emphasized that "this will require greater specialization, more mutual trust, and significantly more professionalism." To further reinforce his resolve to make these organizational changes, he wrote, "There is no place here for those who cannot, or will not, recognize this fact nor for those who cannot, or will not, adjust to this reality."

Smith's decision brought to an end the field division structure. He had concluded that running, in effect, four separate companies was highly inappropriate for the standardized products Federal Express sold, and that the "guerrilla" approach to every problem which seemed to be so essential in the past would bring the company to its knees unless it were changed immediately.

Emphasizing his forceful arguments for change Smith added this list of aphorisms: "What once were attributes can and will become serious detriments in the future. 'Che' was essential to Cuba *until* it was liberated. Trippe built Pan Am and stayed long enough to sow the seeds of its destruction. Patton was marvelous in war, a disaster in peace. Wilson made the world 'safe for democracy' and sowed the seeds of Hitler and Mussolini. The price of not curing the disease will be considerable. Emotion and ego satisfaction are a luxury that Federal Express cannot afford."

Valentine's Day, 1978, Roger Frock, Mike Fitzgerald, Tucker Taylor, and Wes Terry all arrived in Memphis. Fred Smith had planned a meeting for senior officers for 9:00 a.m. the following morning. Frock's notes detailed of this meeting record: "When I checked into my motel in Memphis on the evening of the 14th, I was summoned to meet for dinner at Grisanti's, a popular Italian restaurant not too far from company headquarters."

When Frock got there, he knew it was more than a social gathering for drinking and eating. Behind Fred Smith was a blackboard. Although Paul Lanier had assisted Smith in the reorganization about to take place, he was not present. Instead, seated next to Smith was Frank Maguire whom he had hired in July, 1977, after Maguire had served Art Bass for a period as a management consultant.

After eating, Fred Smith immediately took control of the gathering. Frock records that it was 9:40 p.m. Smith began by presenting a summary of his new reorganization plan and informed them of his decision to implement a centralized telephone answering system — a system which was estimated to cost many millions of dollars. At that point the meeting turned vocal and heated, and it became clear that Smith sought a confrontation.

Roger Frock questioned Smith at length about the reasons for the centralized telephone system. Several others joined in, expressing surprise that they had not been consulted in advance about the changes Smith said he was implementing. Frock's notes stipulate that in exasperation Smith shouts, "A decision has been made, and I am never going to hear another question about the centralized telephone system. Never! Period! I don't want to hear anymore backbiting on this."

Then Smith turned to Frock and added, "It is not a difficult concept and if you're telling me that a man with an MBA from Michigan can't understand what I showed you on that blackboard, one of three things is getting in the way of your understanding: emotions, personality, or compassion. Everyone has got to understand that these three devils stand in the way of constructive solutions to these specific problems." In response to Smith there were comments pointing out that arbitrary decisions, made without their knowledge, were the type of things that would cause Federal Express to die as a company. But Smith, in a testy mood, was ready to fight and responded to what he felt was criticism with this strong counterattack: "You guys sit around and think you're going to contribute a lot of policy formulation in certain areas that you think you have expertise and prerogatives in, but the facts of the matter are, you don't have either the information, nor the energy, nor the time to make the input. And I see it over again and again. You are offended when the policies come out and you don't feel like you were consulted. Most of the input has been verbal, less than cohesive, lacking in quantitative data and it is a symptom of a company three years and $150 million ago."

And Smith didn't let up his attack: "And I am telling you, if we don't get on some more organized basis, all of this esprit de corps and rah, rah, rah, is going to shift like a god-damned counterweight. So many companies have been exactly the same place before, that we have now got to systematize this monster or we've got to get some people in here to systematize it."

The issue of the centralized telephone system had been under study by Tucker Taylor during most of 1976. The exercise was designated Project "Sydney" as a private joke, since Tucker Taylor's first name was "Sydney" and he preferred not to use it socially. When Taylor recommended to Smith in December, 1976, that such a system was feasible and necessary, it apparently set off some disagreements among several of the senior staff.

The next morning at 9:00 a.m., when the senior officers assembled in the company's conference room for the previously scheduled senior staff meeting, Fred Smith announced that it had been cancelled. He told the assembled senior officers that they would receive their new assignments in two weeks. And he left the impression in no uncertain terms that if any of them did not like it, they could leave the company.

Smith, one of these division heads said in the aftermath, had treated them "like dinosaurs awaiting their immortal position in the La Brea tar pits in Los Angeles." Another believed that Smith had been badly misinformed by his consultants as to the effectiveness of the field operations, and was making a colossal mistake in reorganizing the company. Frock did admit that when a small company changes to a large corporation that inevitably it requires frequent organizational changes. "Changes are expected and necessary," he summarized.

While doing research for this book, I asked several who were in that room that night if they thought about quitting after that heated confrontation with Smith. Not one of them said, "Yes." When asked if the plans of Federal Express to go "public" with a sale of stock in April, 1978, had deterred them from quitting, Tucker Taylor, in his typical animated style, thought about the question for a moment, then answered wryly, "We weren't that sophisticated. Only Smith and Pete Willmott understood the company's financial structure. Some of us couldn't read a financial statement. We didn't know the full implications of 'going public.'" Tucker Taylor reminisces: "At many of these senior officer meetings we were on the verge of fist fights. It was the old fighter pilot mentality, I guess. But there weren't any lingering hard feelings afterward."

Through what has since come to be called within the company, "The St. Valentine's Day Massacre," Fred Smith had once again let everyone know he was back full time from Washington and the Congressional deregulation battles and that he was in total control. On March 1, 1978, he issued the details of the reorganization plan in a document labeled, "Action Memorandum." The first page of text was printed on red paper. Typically, Fred Smith, when he wants to get maximum attention with a memorandum, instructs that red sheets be used. This became somewhat of a joke around the company because most of his memos were getting the red page treatment during those days.

The subject was "Organizational Structure." The narrative began with Smith demonstrating that considerable study had been done to develop an optimum organizational structure for managing the company's future growth. "Various approaches were modeled against our present and future tasks," explained Smith. He mentioned that the company's Operations Research staff would be playing a major role in developing the long-term business strategy. The decision-making process would be aided with the results coming out of computer-based simulation models examining numerous "what if"-type questions. One such study had already been completed. It was the plan for the multi-hub system scheduled to be operational about Labor Day, 1979.

In the new reorganization Roger Frock was assigned to be project officer for managing the introduction of the Boeing 727-100s into Federal's fleet. The first 727 had already been brought on-line in January, 1978, to be used on the Los Angeles-Memphis run. There were a myriad of problems to work out; and it was obvious that Frock, with his many years in transportation engineering consulting with A. T. Kearney, Inc., was the best individual to assign to this project.

Mike Fitzgerald who, along with Frock, was probably the most upset about Smith's reorganization, was assigned to manage the company's huge ground vehicle fleet. He had had extensive prior experience in this general area at UPS, so that this assignment appeared to make some sense.

Both Tucker Taylor and Wes Terry were reassigned back into the field as regional vice presidents of completely revised field organizational structures. They were also asked to help organize the regional sorting hubs planned for their regions.

Smith had made the commitment to long-range planning through his operations research group. He saw the need to develop sophisticated data and telecommunications systems. Charles Brandon, who had been the company's computer specialist since 1973, was put in charge of a new department called Datacomm.

Smith also worried about what he felt was a related attitude of his senior officers toward their daily work routines. "Let me give you an example," says one senior officer candidly. "One day Charley Brandon came in late to a staff meeting. By nature Charley is the most inoffensive guy in the world, and when he came in the room, he tried to be inconspicuous as he moved quietly toward his seat. Smith stopped the meeting dead in its tracks to admonish Charley for being late. Fred got pretty worked up. Finally after Fred got through berating him at length, poor Charles slumped down in his seat in total disgrace. Then Smith resumed the meeting. Fred was instituting his brand of discipline."

The effective date of the reorganization was April 1, 1978. In lightning fashion Federal Express, on Fred Smith's personal command, was changed from a heavily decentralized company to a highly centralized one. Decision-making authority and administrative control were now centered in Memphis. The new field managers were given only limited executive authority.

Decentralization as a management tool had been in vogue among many corporations in the 1970s. Heavy emphasis had been placed on establishing the profit center concept within each of a company's major operating divisions. Smith concluded that decentralization was not working for Federal Express and that a 180 degree turn was necessary if the company were to manage the growth it anticipated in the near future.

By his sudden action, Smith violated one of the contemporary trends in the handling of company reorganizations. When making changes, employers are advised to avoid surprises. Such surprises create the potential for ill-will and poor morale. Employees ordinarily resent arbitrary and sudden change. Also, in modern management practice members of the team are supposed to play a part in the corporate decision-making process. Obviously, Smith chose not to play it democratically. A great number of Federal Express employees were affected by Smith's sudden reorganization, not only just the senior officers, Fitzgerald, Frock, Taylor, and Terry, but also many subordinates in the field divisions.

In the immediate aftermath, Fred Smith took much of the heat from internal company critics. In the longer term, Frank Maguire was blamed. They remembered it had been Maguire who had recommended Paul Lanier, the management consultant who helped Smith plan the reorganization. Maguire, a newcomer, was not part of the older senior level "management establishment" in the company. His actions were viewed with suspicion by those veteran officers who had been with Smith since the beginning, or near the beginning, officers who had developed over-the-years into a tight-knit clique.

That anyone would think that Smith did not have a major hand in the reorganization was really surprising. Says one neutral observer, "This is Fred Smith's company. Nothing of that magnitude would be done without Fred calling the shots. Frank Maguire's influence was irrelevant."

This reorganization was a historic turning point in the brief life of Federal Express. It signaled the end of "Phase Two" of the company's life cycle. It marked the beginning of a new period of growth and the consolidation of the company into a more manageable corporate entity.

Months after the reorganization Smith summed up briefly the reason for these changes. He told Federal's employees: "A wrong decision can now mean huge dollar losses. In earlier years many wrong decisions might not have been so costly." He explained he did not want to fall into the trap so many other new venture companies had in the past by not adjusting the organization in time to meet the challenge of new growth and operational complexity.

Federal Express had spent three difficult years of trying to recapitalize to strengthen its financial balance sheet. When the reorganization became effective, it was just twelve days away from its first public sale of stock. The company was preparing to enter "Phase Three" of its growth cycle.

The fifth reorganization plan, implemented September 1, 1980, can best be characterized as "the changing of the guard." New blood was brought up through the ranks into the highest senior level positions. New managers were needed to carry out Smith's changing growth strategy. He was determined to fit the managers to the strategy. Smith and several long-time key senior staff recognized reluctantly that it was time for the company to bring on to the operating line executive personnel with more formal management training and experience. He wanted managers who knew how to manage. Apparently, most of these veterans had admitted that their freewheeling entrepreneurial days at Federal Express were over and that it was time for them to move on to something different. In an interview with *Fortune*, Art Bass, with a good sense of perspective and humor about the reorganization changes, referred to himself and his veteran colleagues as the "undisciplinables." He knew there was not any role for his group to play beyond the near-term future.

Some of the original entrepreneurial group had clearly lost their motivation. For them it was now a long way back to those 16-hour days in 1972 in Little Rock, or to those many nerve-tingling moments in Memphis from 1973 to 1975, when the company neared bankruptcy. Some were obviously uncomfortable working among the bright MBA's hired to fill positions directly under them. Most were now millionaires or close to it. They had purchased large blocks of Federal Express stock at miniscule prices per share, and then watched the stock's price escalate dramatically after the company went public in April, 1978. Unlike Fred Smith few, if any, felt the same urge to "burn the candle at both ends" as they had done so often in the previous seven or eight years. Most of them wanted to enjoy their money and to have some fun.

The major change in the executive ranks was the replacement of Art Bass as president and chief operating officer. Bass was given the title of vice chairman of the company, a unique position created for him by Smith and the board of directors. He was assigned to head a new corporate unit called the Advance Projects and Research Corporation.

Peter Willmott's promotion to the presidency placed administrative management in the hands of a competent financial executive. For over six years he had had a major hand in developing the corporate financial plans and counseling Fred Smith in the tricky waters of the recapitalization effort. Willmott had not been a full-fledged member of the close-knit entrepreneurial group — Bass, Basch, Fagan, Fitzgerald, Frock, and Taylor — which hung closely together over the years. But he was respected by them, despite being much less a free spirit beyond the confines of the corporate offices. Willmott's educational training and corporate experience made him more comfortable in handling detailed administrative tasks than these veteran colleagues.

The company founder, Fred Smith, who was far-and-away the biggest entrepreneur of all of the original senior officers, remained as chairman and chief executive officer. He had worked hard to learn the value of modern quantitative planning techniques and managerial concepts that his new technical people had been introducing to the company. Explains one of the veterans who was unaffected by the 1980 reorganization moves, "Fred fortunately is a blend of entrepreneur and the professional manager. If that weren't the case, I'd leave. He has been flexible. The other guys didn't see any need to adjust."

Unlike the 1978 reorganization, the 1980 changes did not create any outward animosity. Employees speculated about the meaning of the assignment of Art Bass, Roger Frock, Mike Fitzgerald, Tucker Taylor, Wes Terry, and Charles Brandon to the Advance Projects group. Some inside Federal Express referred to the group's new office facilities in East Memphis — some ten miles removed from corporate headquarters — as the "Turkey Farm," implying that Smith had sent all of them into exile. They speculated that Smith was giving them a graceful way out of the company by permitting them adequate time to update their resumes and to look for new opportunities. Veterans Mike Basch, Vince Fagan, Tucker Morse, Brian Pecon, Ted Weise, and a few other senior officers were not part of the reorganization as far as the composition of the Advance

Projects team was concerned.

This new entity was not a dummy operation as some had thought. Art Bass claimed that the mission was to try to take the company into the future — at least to 1990. Publicly, the company announced that if any of these new ventures met the test of economic feasibility, these veteran officers might be the people to head them. This physical separation of their new offices was supposedly to get them away from day-to-day operations which might interfere with their research efforts. Some cynics claim it was Smith's idea to keep them separated from his new cadre of managers.

Establishing a "think tank" operation was highly unusual for a transportation company. Such specialized research centers are generally identified with high-tech industries or specialized industries such as pharmaceuticals and agricultural chemicals. Many felt that Fred Smith had created an expensive toy. And they were correct. The high-paid professional staff and the separate physical facilities put a tremendous burden on corporate overhead. But Smith considered it was a worthwhile gamble. He felt this would provide the backup for the strategic planning necessary to take the company into the future. The projects studied were innovative. And the desire to leverage existing corporate assets had real economic validity. The fleet of aircraft, for instance, was largely idle during the daylight hours. Utilizing this excess capacity offered Federal Express the prospect of a much better financial return on its investment.

Some of the proposed projects studied by Bass' group were not economically feasible; some had technological flaws, like Fred Smith's idea to use dirigibles for less time-sensitive air freight; and some others were premature. Critics within complained about the lack of practical ideas emerging from the studies. The cost was high, but the studies — although most brought negative conclusions — were beneficial and kept Federal from committing huge amounts of capital and staff time to questionable ventures.

But quietly, in early 1982, the Advance Projects group all but ceased to exist. By that time Bass, Brandon, Fitzgerald, Taylor, and Terry had all left the company. Art Bass, whose influence at Federal Express over the years had been second only to Fred Smith's, was one of the last of the Advance Projects group to leave. His formal resignation was dated May, 1982, but he had already been gone several months. In July, 1982, he became chairman and CEO of Midway Airlines based in Chicago. Roger Frock, Smith's initial chief operating officer dating back to Little Rock, stayed on a short time longer, handling some special assignments for Smith. He terminated his relationship in December, 1982, after nearly 11 years.

Several questions must be asked about Smith's strategy. Did the Advance Projects idea serve any useful purpose? Did it merely give Smith the vehicle to get some of his old allies out of the company gracefully, while at the same time giving them one more opportunity to express their entrepreneurial talents before venturing off on their own? There is no doubt that Smith did not think several of them were suited to the new era of corporate life into which Federal Express had moved. Smith had sensed the hostility being expressed by some of the newer senior officers who knew that these "old hands" were drawing higher salaries and contributing far less than they were. Other corporations in similar stages of the development cycle have had to move out much of their original management and replace these people with trained professional corporate managers. Smith apparently did not want to fire his old comrades outright. He owed them a great deal for helping make Federal Express a success and he may have wanted to assure their graceful exits from the company. Moreover, it would have been bad public relations for the company to cut them off quickly.

In making the transition Federal Express was following a familiar trail in the evolution of young, venture capital corporations. Not only did those senior officers Smith had assigned to the Advance Projects group leave the company, but also during 1981 and 1982 long time senior officers Mike Basch, Vince Fagan, and Tucker Morse left, followed by Peter Willmott and Frank Maguire. With few exceptions, there was a complete turnover of senior management in a little over two years.

Fred Smith, as he had been since the start of Federal Express, was the consummate survivor. In the early life-cycle of many rapid growth, venture companies, the founder either has been forced out after the company has gone "public" or has found himself tempermentally and administratively unsuited to continue. Fred Smith was able to make the transition. The original entrepreneur and founder stayed on to take full charge of the subsequent phases of the company's life cycle. Interestingly enough, Smith does not care to look back to recount the past. When I asked him about the company's past history, he told me, "That's of no interest to me. The future is going to be too exciting to be spending time thinking about all that has happened at Federal Express over the past 10 years."

Chapter 16

The King's Two Bodies

In June, 1982, a few weeks after the close of the company's 1982 fiscal year, Fred Smith assembled his Memphis staff and their families in a local auditorium. There was a serious tone to the meeting. Smith had an important message to convey to them and he wanted them to hear it from him *in person*. Characteristically, he looked straight into the eyes of those in the middle of the audience and said: "No company in American business history — no service or industrial company — has grown as fast as Federal Express has for such a sustained period of time — a 50 percent year-to-year compound growth rate for the past nine years." Then he laid down the challenge, "If we hit the billion dollar mark the next fiscal year (at the end of May, 1983), we will be the first corporation in history to hit that mark within ten years of continuing operations." Just a few weeks before the company had reported annual sales of $804 million for the 1982 fiscal year. Federal Express was then within 80 percent of the goal.

That Smith could set a one billion dollar goal for Federal Express in 1983 — a company which just a mere seven years earlier had bordered on bankruptcy — is testimony to Smith's relentless will to succeed despite the obstacles. It was a goal ten times greater than even the most optimistic senior officers had believed possible at the outset in 1973 when service began so inauspiciously. Roger Frock, who prior to joining Smith in Little Rock, 1972, was the project leader of one of the two independent economic feasibility studies commissioned by Smith, told me that he thought, at the time, the top limit for sales was $100 million. But when I asked Fred Smith if he had expected such success when he started Federal, he responded in his typically self-assertive, extravagant manner, "Hell, I thought we would be three times bigger than we are right now." But no one will ever know for certain whether Smith, even in his wildest dreams, truly believed his venture would achieve financial success in so short a time span.

But the goal set by Smith was far more than just seeking a means of ego satisfaction. All indications are that Smith understands the necessity to continue performing well financially so that Federal Express may purchase those expensive additional aircraft and other capital equipment necessary to keep the company growing and vibrant. In 1983 and 1984, it needed to fund between $400 and $450 million in capital expenditures. Smith counts heavily on annual profits to help fund a significant percentage of these costs.

Federal's employees have been told repeatedly, in family briefing and company publications by Smith and Willmott, that profits are the lifeline for the company's future growth, and that to guarantee profits they must become more productive. "The competition," this central management team admonishes employees, "is going to be relentless in the 1980s." "If we concentrate on profits, this will make it tougher for competition to step in to take business from us," Smith lectures them. "If we offer a superior service, we will stay out in front."

Smith asserts: "It is important that we continue to out-perform the industry as we have been doing so far. Excellent margins are required not only to maintain proper investor relations, but also to provide a strong cash flow to fund our high growth rates." To stay on top, he maintains that Federal must continuously improve existing services, plus offer its customers new service benefits not offered by its competitors.

Federal Express has proven in the past that it is an opportunistic company. It carved out for itself a major market niche in just a few, short years in what has been a plodding and relatively unsophisticated industry. The decision to move into telecommunications puts Federal Express into a more sophisticated, faster-paced field where it will find highly talented competition eager for combat. Smith undoubtedly knew when he decided to proceed into telecommunications that Federal was not the only company capable of exploiting this special communications area. However, he seems to expect that a fast start will give Federal a market edge.

The company had been through so many crises in its formative years that perhaps it might have been expected to settle into its special niche of hauling small packages and letters in the 1980s and playing it safe insofar as getting into totally new ventures. As long as Fred Smith is in control this will not happen. The likelihood of

Federal Express becoming sluggish and noncombative with Smith around is next to zero. Even during the height of the recent national recession, Smith kept up the pressure to move the company forward. New products and new services have been introduced. And, as we have already seen, he realigned the organizational structure to keep it wieldy and productive. Smith's concern was that any hesitation to adapt could bring Federal's growth momentum to a halt and cause irreparable damage to Federal's reputation as an industry leader and trend-setter. But more important, it could kill forever the infectious, youthful "rah! rah!" spirit that has permeated the ranks since the first day.

Assuming that Fred Smith continues in a full-time leadership role in the foreseeable future, his pragmatism — which has been one of his key leadership strengths — will be essential to keep Federal Express on the upward growth curve. He has the uncanny knack of concept-ualizing the strategic issues necessary for the company to remain competitive. He also has shown that he has the courage to make the top and middle management personnel changes and the organization structural changes necessary to accommodate these new strategies. His relentless "what-have-you-done-for-me-lately" approach to the question of senior staff retention has helped keep top management lean and hungry.

As we have seen Fred Smith thrives on causes. His initial campaign to raise venture capital and to obtain bank loans to launch Federal Express in 1972 and 1973, was the first major cause. Again he faced countless financial crises as well as family crises to keep the company alive and to maintain his balance. The deregulation fight in Congress was another especially critical point. I am firmly convinced that without a cause Fred Smith will quickly lose interest and undoubted-ly be gone from the company.

Attaining one billion dollars in sales was just one more cause in this long line of causes. As Federal crosses this mark, Smith will probably exhort his staff saying, "Now that we made $1 billion, let's go for $2 billion." If recent growth rates in annual dollar sales volume are sustained, Federal could achieve its $2 billion mark in the latter half of the 1980s.

At the end of fiscal year 1978 (May 31, 1978), the company's revenues were $160.3 million. [See table this chapter.] This was exactly six months after Congress passed the Air Cargo Deregulation Act. Four years later, at the end of fiscal 1982, revenues had reached $803.9 million. During this brief period, the average annual sales growth rate was a spectacular 50 percent. Net income after taxes increased in this same time period from $19.5 million to $78.4 million, an average annual growth rate of over 32 percent.

By any measure, Federal's annual revenue growth rates have been phenomenal. Future rates, however, will be measured from progres-sively larger annual revenue bases. This will result in significantly lower annual percentage growth rates. The company's success in keeping growth rates high will depend on the ability to increase volume and to increase prices, to hold the line on costs, and to raise productivity per employee. Management is confident it can control costs and also can increase productivity. Price increases, on the other hand, will depend on how much Federal's customers are willing to pay for the various services offered. The marketplace is full of competitors offering alternatives.

If Federal, for example, were able to sustain a 20 percent annual growth rate, then potentially the $2 billion goal would be reached in 1987. And by 1990, it would be $3.5 billion. To attain anywhere near these revenues, Federal Express is going to have to replicate the sheer good luck of its first decade. "Luck" may seem an odd word to interject into the Federal Express equation, but besides hard work and effective planning the company has had more than its share of good luck during its first decade. Such services as the Overnight Letter, facsimile transmission, and any new programs Smith might be expected to initiate will have to be market successes. A slip here or a stroke of bad luck there — for whatever reason — will reduce the rate of growth.

Thinking about these dizzying heights may not unnerve most of the company's 13,000 employees. Most were not around those first 27 months when Federal lost $29.3 million. Wall Street analysts and national business writers, as well as Emery's and Airborne's management, had during these previous disappointing months dismissed Federal Express from their concern. These dismal external assessments were made primarily in 1974 and 1975. Three years later, the company reported an after-tax profit margin of 12.2 percent, and then for the following four years ending with fiscal 1982, after-tax margins of 7.9, 9.2, 9.9 and 9.8 percent respectively. These margins equalled or exceeded those of many of America's best known and best managed companies. And they were substantially higher than the after-tax margins of competitors, Emery and Airborne.

Federal's management has been fully aware that a superior financial performance is needed to keep attracting equity capital and funds from institutional lenders. Indeed the company seems obsessive about keeping margins high. Federal Express is relying heavily on its state-of-the-arts technology and a highly productive labor force to keep operations highly efficient and profitable.

Despite substantial profits, Federal, as a matter of corporate policy, has never paid a dividend since the stock began to be traded publicly on April 12, 1978. The stockholders continue to ask the question: "When are we going to start receiving dividends?" Management's answer has been that for the time being profits will be plowed back into the company to help contribute to the capital funds needed to maintain and upgrade the fleet, or for debt retirement and working capital purposes. To the maximum extent possible management's policy has been to commit its cash flow to funding capital expenditures.

Although no dividends have been paid out, some stockholders have realized healthy capital gains from the sale of their Federal Express stock. An original public shareholder, for example, who may have paid $24 a share, when the stock went public in 1978, might have been able to sell on May 6, 1983, that share — which subsequently split to become four shares — for $354.00, when for an instant the stock peaked at a price of 88½ on the New York Stock Exchange. Of course, few stockholders sold exactly at the peak. Many, however, have realized large capital gains during those periods when shares were trading between $60 and $80. Certainly, at some point, stockholders are going to be more militant on receiving dividends. This will be particularly true of those stockholders who purchased their shares at prices near the historic highs. The shares held by present and former senior officers, and by several institutional investors were purchased at minimal prices, prices as low as $2.50 a share. This group of stockholders has achieved huge capital gains on their holdings, and they are less concerned about dividends.

The near-term financing needs of 1983 and 1984 required a strong cash flow to fund the purchase of 15 new 727-200F aircraft from Boeing, and to purchase the facsimile transmission equipment. The aircraft purchase price was $300 million; the near-term capital outlay for the facsimile transmission equipment was about $50 million. And the longer term capital outlay was estimated to be about $150 million if Federal decides to put this facsimile transmission equipment in some customers' offices.

To finance these expenditures Federal's management in the latter half of 1982, when it began to weigh the alternatives, considered its options to be internally generated funds and one or more of the following: bank lines of credit or commercial paper, private debt placements with insurance companies or common equity, convertible preferred stock, and leasing. There was no commitment to any precise financing plan. The staff continued to monitor the national economy closely and to examine Federal's competitive status prior to deciding what recommendation should be made to Fred Smith and the board of directors.

Internally generated funds, that is, profits, depreciation, and deferred taxes, were considered essential by management if they were to raise those additional funds Federal needed to finance its 1983 and 1984 capital outlays. For example, the company's net income of $78.4 million in fiscal 1982, plus $56 in depreciation and $20 million in deferred taxes, was committed to provide over one-half of the funds required for the 727-200F planes.

Borrowing appeared to be the least attractive route. It was an expensive alternative given the prevailing high interest rates. Should Federal Express overextend itself by borrowing, it could be seriously hurt if for some reason its annual cash flow should decline significantly in the mid or late 1980s. A prolonged and deepening business recession — even worse than what had been experienced in the early 1980s — could seriously affect revenues if many customers were to decide to ship by surface transportation, or some cheaper way, in order to cut their own operating expenses. Heavy interest payments could impair or even eliminate profits.

In its earliest years Federal Express was mired in debt. In the contemporary period of the 1980s debt has been manageable so that borrowing part of the funds was still one of the alternatives available to the company if interest rates had moved lower prior to the final deadline for financing the large 727-200 aircraft purchases in 1983 and 1984. In 1982 Federal's revolving credit agreement with a consortium of banks and insurance companies was for a maximum of $150 million, with an interest rate of ½ of one percent above the prime bank rate. Even though the company had no debt outstanding against this line of credit in early 1983, borrowing would ordinarily be only a "worst case" option.

Another option considered in the early fall of 1982 was a return to the equity market. The company had previously gone to the public with stock offerings four times since April, 1978, and it had raised thereby over $135 million. Another $25 million in stock was sold to the public by the original venture capitalists and by Federal's warrantholders, principally the bank lenders when they decided to take their profits.

Of all the options, the company felt it would be best served by having another sale of stock. The success of a new issue depended on catching a receptive market. Federal's stock had fallen to a low of 41¾ in August, 1982, from the low 60s earlier that year. The August price did not offer much incentive to go to the market with an equity issue. But then, as it had happened so often before in recent years, good fortune blessed the company. A dramatic bull market started in late August which, by late October, 1982, pulled the price of Federal Express stock along with the rally. As a result of this opportunity the company saw its chance to proceed with the stock sale. Consequently, on October 25th, the company raised $60 million with a public offering of one million shares priced at $61.50 per share.

Smith's plan to increase the momentum of growth depended on having the fleet of 727-200s for service in the mid-1980s. "These planes will help improve productivity and help us remain the leader in the field. This investment is required to give us a unique level of capacity that our competition in the package business won't match. Our competitors at the end of the 1980s will be stuck with worn out planes," Smith claims. If Smith is wrong, it could be a costly mistake and hurt those profit margins the company considers sacred. But if he is correct, Federal will put an even greater market share distance between its competitors and itself.

Despite what Fred Smith would have us believe, by no means is Federal Express the master of its own destiny. For instance, the question of fuel — its supply and its costs — inevitably changes the way transportation-oriented companies plan their futures. The statement, "As energy goes, so goes society," is sobering. For a company like Federal Express which consumes fuel in large quantities (by recent estimates 75 million gallons per year), the availability of supplies will overshadow most future development strategies. And, of even greater importance, Federal has no control over the nation's or world's economy and politics. For example, Federal should not assume that if it tries to expand into international service beyond just Canada and England that it will be welcomed in all countries.

On the other hand, Federal Express does have some considerable control over its destiny. Fred Smith and his key aides are responsible for sustaining the creativity and vitality which have brought it to the one billion dollar sales level. Yet there are some signs that they may be losing some of their creativity and zest. By gaining tight administrative control over the day-to-day management of the company, Federal has lost its spirited "free-form, guerrilla-style thinking" through which innovative ideas were created by the somewhat irreverent senior staff of earlier years. As of the early 1980s Federal's senior level management was heavily weighted with technical specialists in finance, marketing, management systems analysis, engineering, and law. Their job was to assist Smith in developing corporate plans and objectives. They do not make policy, but they do carry out the mechanics of policy decisions. These management specialists have added a much needed stabilizing foundation to Federal Express. The self-styled iconoclastic and macho Marine and Navy pilots who dominated the upper management structure early on have given way to academically-schooled and decorous MBAs, engineers, and attorneys: the "fly boys" are out and the "number crunchers" are in. Or as Fitzgerald told me recently: "The humanists have been replaced by what Fred and the others call 'professional managers.' "

Despite an escalating bureaucratic structure, Federal still retains its entrepreneurial bloodline through Fred Smith. He establishes the objectives and plans and gives both general and specific direction to his staff of highly trained technical subordinates. And Smith provides the personal leadership to direct the company toward its stated goals, and company image makers have focused the public's attention on him to maintain in the public's eye a corporate rank identity. Smith *is* Federal Express. He is as well known as the company. Most of the rank and file employees believe it; security analysts believe it; the competitors believe it; and certainly Fred Smith appears to believe it.

When I read in *The Commercial Appeal*, a leading Memphis

metropolitan daily, that smith's wife had observed he loves to read books about kings, I realized that Fred Smith is only the most recent incarnation of that ancient tradition of the "King's Two Bodies." Smith is both the man and the company in the same way that the old European kings were both the person and the office, both the man and the land. In fact, defense attorney Lucius Burch had employed just such a legalism to defend Smith in the federal forgery trial of 1975. The "I am Fred Smith Enterprise Company" owes its historic precedent to this ancient tradition, and in some way not quite understood, this has become part of the way Smith conceptualizes his role at Federal Express. The "I am Fred Smith Federal Express" is probably more of a legal and operational reality than "I am Fred Smith Enterprise Company" ever was.

Despite many highly talented subordinates, Fred Smith is a one man show. During Federal's first ten years, employees have willingly, and usually enthusiastically, made the personal sacrifices Smith demanded of them in the name of the company. Not only have they been well paid by Memphis standards and by industry standards, but also they have been united in Fred Smith's cause to build a unique transportation company. And the families have been made an unofficial part of the development of the company as well. Smith expects the wives, or husbands, as the case may be, and the children of his senior officers and managers to be understanding of the company's personality and discipline. The popular Smith has had their blessing. "Fred doesn't have to do too much of a PR job on the families," a company veteran proudly explains. "He's like a god to many of them." To that intriguing question — "Would you want your daughter to marry a Federal Express employee?" — the answer would probably be "Yes!"

Smith is far from being unique as an assertive, hard-driving chief executive officer. He fits very nicely into that special category of skillful, opportunistic, egotistical, strong-willed "one-man shows" heading highly successful ventures in contemporary corporate America. Like most of the Agees, Lings, Perots, Rumsfelds, Turners, and Ylvisakers of the corporate world, he often carries his grand design for the firm around in his head, and dogmatically makes the big company decisions — and often the little ones, too — if it suits him. He meddles in things and manages to stay on top of almost every company matter. "It's maddening; Fred's got his fingers in every pie," a colleague complains. "It's uncanny how he operates. We all wish he would stay away sometimes."

When Peter Willmott resigned as company president in April, 1983, to become president and CEO of Carson Pirie Scott & Co., a diversified Chicago based conglomerate, it may have removed an important element in the daily "give and take" within upper management. Smith had respected Willmott's skills as a financial administrator. "Pete's a financial-type," explains Brian Pecon. "He was a steadying influence on the company and he was a competent numbers guy who made major contributions here ever since the day he arrived back in May, 1974, to straighten out that awful administrative mess we were in." In stark contrast to Smith, however, Willmott was self-effacing, and totally predictable, serious and tacitly reserved. His role often had been as a counterbalance to projects or programs enthusiastically supported by Smith in their initial stages. He marshalled the financial numbers and presented to Smith carefully thought out his assessment of financial risks or rewards entailed in proceeding in one direction or another. On occasion the conservative Willmott would argue vehemently with Smith over a specific course of action but apparently he conceded graciously when Smith announced the decision was final. Charley Lea and some others on the sidelines, when asked the significance of Willmott's resignation, speculated that if Willmott would have stayed, he probably would not have wanted to push as hard in the electronics field that Fred Smith has become so excited about.

Willmott's replacement, James L. Barksdale (B.S., University of Mississippi), had been in charge of directing the company's computer data processing information control and telecommunications operations. The soft-spoken 40-year-old Barksdale, who joined the company in 1979, had been responsible for developing Federal's "same day facsimile delivery service" to be introduced in 1984. Barksdale was brought up from the ranks of the company's "professional managers."

Since the 1980 reorganization, the company has become highly structured and more tightly administered. The new cadre of senior officers who moved into key staff positions are less vocal and far more disciplined than their predecessors. They are less likely to rock the proverbial boat, and more likely to act as though they are loyal soldiers carrying out company programs. The old familiarity, where Tucker Taylor, Roger Frock, or any of the older gang wandered into Smith's office when they felt like it, is gone. The office decorum, though friendly and laced with Southern graciousness, is now formal. "It's also tougher to get an idea into Smith's office," explains an aide. "The only way to succeed is to somehow or other make Fred think it is his idea. Fred also scares a lot of guys off because if they do get in, but don't have all the facts, he jumps all over them. Fred's the guy you hated in school because he always knew the answers. And sometimes he just doesn't listen too well. Most of the guys are less inclined to take a chance, and they opt to play it safe. But it is like that in most mature organizations."

At the middle management level there are signs of uneasiness. Some veteran professionals feel stifled. They worry over the rising level of internal politics, and they are concerned that managers and program directors have become overly protective of their company turfs because of their stake in the employee bonus incentive plan.

For the first time in the company's history there were early signs that some middle management personnel were leaving the company because of frustration. The fact that some of these people had not previously worked in other large organizations compounded the problem. They have had no barometer to measure their frustration level against. They apparently have not understood that most mature organizations over time develop their share of bureaucratic red tape and internal politics. Perhaps they just did not think this would happen under Fred Smith's leadership.

From time-to-time there is speculation that Fred Smith is planning to leave the company to enter politics. One rumor has Smith as a candidate for Howard Baker's Senate seat when Baker steps down at the end of 1984. When I asked Smith if he were interested in a political career, he answered with a neutral, "No." But there is no doubt that if he chose to run for public office, he would be an attractive candidate physically and intellectually. He exudes confidence and he is a prolific idea man. Indeed, when it was suggested to Smith that the company needed an economics unit as a staff function, he felt it was an unnecessary duplication of his role of "the" corporate economist. But Fred Smith is a very private person despite what may appear to be a high visibility in the corporate world since the mid-1970s. He would lose his off-hours privacy if he sought public office.

But what would happen to Federal Express if Smith were to leave? The question which must be asked is: "Would the company continue to grow vigorously in his absence?" And a much more ominous question: "Could it in fact survive?" His presence has been so all-pervasive that it is difficult to conceive of Federal Express without his leadership. There has been no apparent clear-cut survival or succession plan for the company should Smith be totally absent from the scene for whatever reason. The board of directors seems convinced that Federal Express is now such a well-established corporation that is far bigger than any one individual, and that it could go forward without Fred Smith. Yet, when I asked veteran board member, Philip Greer, about a succession plan, he seemed positively shocked that I had asked such a question. After taking a moment to recover, he pointed to his portfolio of performance evaluations of Federal's senior officers and retorted: "There are several good candidates in there. We have some excellent replacements should we need them. We are almost a $1 billion company. It could run without Smith all right. I think you're wrong if you're implying we couldn't make it without Fred."

Despite what Greer and any other board members may think, Fred Smith would be difficult to replace. He has totally dominated the company. His highly personal, inquisitive, and demanding style, and his charismatic public personality reinforced over the years with an avalanche of publicity in the national business press, have made

Federal Express and Fred Smith synonymous. He is as far removed from outliving his effectiveness as it is possible to be. With his intensely loyal employees, Smith has built a major airline and a major trucking company, and in 1984 will launch what may well become a major communications company. He obviously likes to build things and do it with an almost completely free hand. Then there is the matter of how investors would react to Smith's departure for whatever reasons. How much is Smith's leadership a part of the value of a share of Federal's stock? There seems little doubt that his presence at the helm is the principal reason the stock has enjoyed a high price/earnings ratio. He is a large part of "the multiple."

In contemporary business development, Federal's initial survival and its subsequent dramatic growth is almost a fluke. Few companies that were not based initially on high technology have been built as fast. In the late 1960s and the early 1970s the odds were heavily against capital being invested in an air freight operation. Venture capitalists were not ordinarily interested in companies in an industry subject to heavy government regulation. The experience had been that returns on capital invested approached zero in large segments of the transport field. Traditional lenders were even more skeptical. Federal Express was a case of an unproven service business concept being proposed by unproven management operating from an unlikely geographic area, Memphis. Venture capitalists and lenders had turned their attention at that time to the high technology and information-based industries, from semiconductors and computers to the new telecommunications and the biosciences. Why take risks in the capital intensive transportation industry which was at that period enmeshed in the political arena of government economic regulation, and also heavily dominated by organized labor? New high-tech companies in the so-called "Silicon Valley" area in California or along Route 128 ringing suburban Boston looked far more inviting than an airline and trucking operation headquartered in Memphis.

The credit goes to Fred Smith. With his sheer perseverance and his skillful maneuvering and his fortuitous sense of timing Fred Smith cut the Gordian Knot of hide-bound thinking about freight transportation to surmount not only just a few major hurdles, but also a staggering amount of opposition from competitors as well as a few in the finance community who could have snared him and emasculated him many times.

Since Fred Smith is fiercely independent and self-confident, he may decide to stay on indefinitely at Federal Express to see how far he can take it. He appears to be fascinated with the new technological revolution he sees unraveling rapidly and wants Federal Express to be part of it. Smith assembled his management staff in 1982 to tell them enthusiastically: "We are now at the forefront of that revolution, and by the year 2000, this company will be one of the major commercial endeavors of the world." If he stays around to see this through, he will be only 54 years old at that time.

Fred Smith is one of the prominent corporate entrepreneurs being offered to the American business community by the region now popularly called the New South. The southern business leaders are commanding increasing attention as this economic region moves more rapidly into the development of industries other than those related to agriculture, timber, textiles, and other traditional Southern employment bases. What Fred Smith does, and what he says, takes on special meaning transcending just Federal Express. He carries enormous responsibility because national attitudes about change and opportunity in the South may be molded by his actions. He is still under 40 years of age; bright, handsome, and wealthy; and blessed with flair, strong intellectual curiosity, leadership ability, and seemingly boundless energy. He could not have a grander dream than the one he carried away from Yale to Vietnam to Little Rock, then to Memphis. Will he take great risks in the future, and will he be able to surround himself with the same type of creative talent he found in the "undisciplinables" he talked into joining him before the first package was picked up and delivered overnight in April, 1973? It is a good bet that the restless entrepreneur within Fred Smith and his compulsion to build will motivate him to try for greater success. He has the desire for power and achievement found in all great corporate leaders. And he sees himself as a leader in the forefront of exploiting the hot, new high technologies. The price Smith has paid for his corporate success, however, has not been light. Indeed, it is fascinating to realize that it may be said of him, as it was said of his father some 50 years earlier: "The reputation of this man is that of a hard hitting, determined executive, who knows what he wants and is willing to pay the price — no matter how big."

The Company reported in July, 1983, that for the fiscal year ending May 31, 1983, it has achieved revenues of $1,008,087,000 and a net income of $88,933,000. Other financial information for Fiscal 1983 was incomplete at that time. Fred Smith has broken his billion!

Federal Express Corporation and Subsidiary
Selected Consolidated Financial Data*
(In thousands, except per share amounts)

	1982	1981	1980
Operating Results			
Express service revenues	$803,915	$589,493	$415,379
Operating expenses	684,449	489,758	348,378
Operating income (loss)	119,466	99,735	67,001
Other (income) expense	(11,614)	1,691	7,628
Income (loss) before income taxes	131,080	98,044	59,373
Income taxes	52,694	39,908	21,644
Income (loss) before tax benefit			
of loss carryforward	78,385	58,136	37,729
Tax benefit of loss carryforward	-	-	-
Net income (loss)	$ 78,385	$ 58,135	$ 37,729
Earnings Per Share			
Historical—			
Earnings (loss) before tax benefit			
of loss carryforward	$ 3.70	$ 2.83	$ 2.00
Net earnings (loss) per share	3.70	2.83	2.00
Average shares outstanding	20,894	20,111	18,282
Pro forma (See note)—			
Earnings (loss) before tax benefit			
of loss carryforward	$ 3.70	$ 2.83	$ 2.00
Net earnings (loss) per share	3.70	2.83	2.00
Average shares outstanding	20,894	20,111	18,282
Financial Position			
Current assets	$194,265	$166,952	$ 85,454
Property and equipment, net	457,572	373,250	277,702
Total assets	730,291	570,112	395,030
Current liabilities	114,596	113,846	64,351
Long-term debt	223,856	162,705	142,465
Common Stockholders' investment	350,319	270,875	168,745

Note: Pro forma earnings per share have been computed as though the company's recapitalization and stock offerings in April 1978 had occurred at the beginning of fiscal year 1976.

1979	1978	1977	1976	1975	1974	1973
$258,482	$160,301	$109,210	$75,055	$ 43,489	$ 17,292	$ 6,168
218,370	135,064	96,142	65,210	47,613	26,137	9,072
40,112	25,237	13,068	9,845	(4,124)	(8,845)	(2,904)
6,329	5,693	5,390	6,210	7,393	4,521	1,557
33,783	19,544	7,678	3,635	(11,517)	(13,366)	(4,461)
13,400	6,471	3,981	2,032	-	-	-
20,383	13,073	3,697	1,603	(11,517)	(13,366)	(4,461)
-	6,425	4,185	1,982	-	-	-
$ 20,383	$ 19,498	$ 7,882	$ 3,583	$(11,517)	$(13,366)	$ (4,661)
$ 1.17	$ 1.06	$ .27	$ .10	$ (10.86)	$ (81.50)	$ (3.02)
1.17	1.62	.70	.31	(10.86)	(81.50)	(3.02)
16,366	11,512	10,292	10,064	1,060	164	100
$ 1.17	$ .85	$ .24	$ .09			
1.17	1.25	.54	.24			
16,366	15,888	15,580	15,240			
$ 48,975	$ 30,370	$ 20,349	$14,725	$ 9,481	$ 7,981	$ 3,100
123,844	71,813	53,616	55,297	59,276	59,701	51,487
179,823	106,291	75,321	71,229	70,193	70,697	56,771
43,681	24,315	23,275	12,954	11,818	9,136	44,949
45,729	30,825	46,229	56,186	59,892	51,605	11,533
74,946	37,491	(8,488)	(16,561)	(1,517)	(8,694)	289

*Source: Federal Express Corporation

DATE DUE